Going Dirty

Going Dirty

The Art of
Negative Campaigning

DAVID MARK

ROWMAN & LITTLEFIELD PUBLISHERS, INC.
Lanham • Boulder • New York • Toronto • Oxford

ROWMAN & LITTLEFIELD PUBLISHERS, INC.

Published in the United States of America
by Rowman & Littlefield Publishers, Inc.
A wholly owned subsidiary of The Rowman & Littlefield Publishing Group, Inc.
4501 Forbes Boulevard, Suite 200, Lanham, Maryland 20706
www.rowmanlittlefield.com

PO Box 317
Oxford
OX2 9RU, UK

British Library Cataloguing in Publication Information Available

Library of Congress Cataloging-in-Publication Data

Mark, David, 1973–
  Going dirty : the art of negative campaigning / David Mark.
    p. cm.
  Includes bibliographical references and index.
  ISBN-10: 0-7425-4500-8 (cloth : alk. paper)
  ISBN-13: 978-0-7425-4500-7 (cloth : alk. paper)
  1. Political campaigns—United States—History. 2. Advertising, Political—United
States—History. 3. Negativism. I. Title.
  JK2281.M365 2006
  324.70973—dc22   2005028278

Printed in the United States of America

♾™ The paper used in this publication meets the minimum requirements of American
National Standard for Information Sciences—Permanence of Paper for Printed Library
Materials, ANSI/NISO Z39.48-1992.

To my parents, Brian and Madeline Mark

Contents

Acknowledgments

Lawmakers, candidates, and political consultants might not naturally seem eager to describe their experiences engaging in negative campaigning, as I asked them to do for this book. After all, the term has a connotation that is so, well, negative. It would hardly seem in their interest to recount stories about verbally beating up opponents and using underhanded tactics to win elections, including many episodes that have drawn waves of unflattering news stories over the years.

Yet most of the sources I asked for interviews graciously agreed to talk with me, and they were quite open about the effectiveness—and often failure—of negative tactics. I am very appreciative of all those who took time from their busy schedules to share their insights about their campaign histories.

In particular, Garry South provided important resources, ranging from obscure documents to copies of campaign commercials, for chapters 10 and 11. I acknowledge kind permission to reprint quotations from "Anatomy of a Spot," in *Target '82: Politics and the Media—A Working Seminar, for the Democratic National Committee.* Used by permission of Garry South.

And this project received a boost at the beginning from Kyle Longley, professor of history at Arizona State University and author of a groundbreaking biography of Sen. Albert Gore, Sr. In addition to his book serving as an important resource about the 1970 U.S. Senate race in Tennessee, Kyle steered me toward the right people to talk to for my own interviews. In North Carolina, veteran political reporter Rob Christensen of *The* (Raleigh) *News & Observer* walked me through the complexities of Tar Heel State politics. In Delaware, Sam Waltz was exceedingly generous with his time and knowledge of the local political scene and set up a series of visits with candidates and officeholders during my visit to the First State.

On the research side, the good folks at the Julian P. Kanter Political Commercial Archive at the University of Oklahoma Political Communication Center helped me navigate a maze of ancient campaign commercials. The archive, housing thousands of campaign spots stored in a climate-controlled vault, is a treasure trove for serious students of political history and worthy of a visit.

Beyond those I interviewed and consulted, this work would not have been possible without the generous support and friendship of several people. First, thank you to Andrew West for literally giving me the idea for this book. His wise counsel throughout the brainstorming process and editing of my written work—much of it done across the 9,800 miles between Bethesda, Maryland, and Sydney, Australia—were indispensable to the success of this project. Thank you to David Weigel, for his superb research and copyediting. Also, many thanks to Robin Reid, the tireless Baltimore-based writer and editor, and my friend, who helped translate what could have been a bunch of political inside baseball into (hopefully) compelling reading.

Chris Anzalone, Washington editor for Rowman & Littlefield, also deserves kudos for taking a chance on a first-time author and letting me run with the subject matter as I saw fit.

Thank you, finally, to my sister, Rachael, in New York City, for ongoing encouragement. And my parents, Brian and Madeline Mark, in Altadena, California, for all their love and support, in addition to valuable proofreading and editing, on what originally must have seemed like an esoteric book topic.

Eye of the Beholder: Defining Negative Campaigning

Since the 1984 presidential race was a snoozer that would result in Ronald Reagan's 49-state landslide reelection victory, much of the political world turned its gaze to North Carolina. There, a brawl of a Senate race had begun more than a year and a half before Election Day; the incumbent senator, Republican Jesse Helms, was locked in a bitter fight with Governor Jim Hunt, a rising Democratic star.

Helms did not usually like to debate opponents, relying instead on television advertisements that blanketed the Tar Heel State during election season. But the famously conservative senator saw that he faced a formidable challenger who indeed was threatening to end his 12-year career. So Helms engaged in several head-on clashes with the governor, whom he had repeatedly called a flip-flopper lacking core ideological convictions and a "limousine liberal" in his television ads. During their second debate, in Wilmington, Hunt challenged Helms to join him in prohibiting negative ads on television, so they could focus more on what the candidates would do to improve the lives of North Carolinians. Helms's response? "We haven't put on any negative advertising. We just told the truth about you. It's sort of like Harry Truman said one time. He said the Republicans think I'm giving them hell. I'm not giving them hell. I'm telling the truth on you."[1]

Candidates routinely offer similar explanations to defend aggressive campaign tactics, in races from president of the United States to county assessor. Few, if any, of them openly admit to negative campaigning. To office-seekers, criticizing an opponent's voting record is comparative advertising, while spotlighting a rival's marital infidelity or woeful personal finances is perfectly appropriate because it raises character issues for voters. What constitutes negative campaigning is usually a matter of perspective; tactics that to one voter seem misleading, mean-spirited, and immoral can impart to another important and relevant information about how the candidate would perform under the pressures of public office. Negative campaigning, like beauty, is in the eye of the beholder.

Still, general outlines of what constitutes negative campaigning can be defined, whether or not the candidates and their campaign staff members mentioned in this book would agree with those descriptions. This book traces the modern history and evolution of negative campaigning tactics, primarily from the beginning of the television age in politics, in 1952, to the present; for purposes of discussion, the term "negative campaigning" refers to the actions a candidate takes to win an election by attacking an opponent, rather than emphasizing his or her own positive attributes or policies.

First, I want to distinguish negative campaigning—charges and accusations that, while often distorted, contain at least a kernel of truth—from dirty tricks or cheating. Examples abound of campaign dirty tricks, most famously the tactics of Richard M. Nixon's 1972 Committee to Reelect the President (CREEP), which were exposed in the Watergate proceedings of 1973 to 1974. Perhaps the most notorious dirty trick was a letter planted in a New Hampshire newspaper alleging that a leading Democratic presidential candidate, Senator Edmund Muskie of Maine, had approved a slur that referred to Americans of French-Canadian descent as "Canucks." On a snowy New Hampshire day, standing outside the offices of the newspaper, Muskie gave a rambling denial in which tears seemed to drip from his eyes (some contend they were actually melting snowflakes). His emotional conduct, replayed on television, caused him to drop in the New Hampshire polls shortly before the presidential primary. Senator George McGovern of South Dakota, considered a weaker candidate by Nixon political strategists, eventually won the 1972 Democratic nomination and lost the general election to the Republican president in a landslide.

In this book, I'll touch on a few cases of dirty tricks when they directly affected the operations of a campaign. As detailed in chapter 11, "push polling" (more accurately push calling) was used against Senator John McCain in the 2000 Republican presidential primaries when scurrilous smears against his character were advanced over the telephone, along with false rumors in the South Carolina Republican primary that the senator from Arizona had fathered a black baby. (In reality, McCain and his wife had adopted a girl from Bangladesh.) But because dirty tricks are not considered legitimate campaign tactics by most political professionals, and are often illegal,[2] I've largely excluded them.

WHY CANDIDATES MUST GO NEGATIVE

Yet even beyond dirty tricks, many people still recoil at legitimate negative political ads on television, radio, the Internet, and in other forms. Negative campaigning has become a catchall phrase that implies there is something inherently wrong with criticizing an opponent. Negative campaigning is one of the most bemoaned aspects of the American political system, particularly by academics and journalists who say it diminishes the level of political discourse and intensifies the divisions among voters.[3]

These complaints emerge each election cycle, partly because political spots are so different in content, style, and form than ads for commercial products. Anyone peddling breakfast cereal needs to be careful about criticizing competitors too overtly or else run the risk of turning off consumers so much that they'll start their day with another form of breakfast food. Rarely do product advertisements include hard-hitting direct comparisons to competitors. (And when they do, the contrasts are usually mild and fleeting.)

The goal of political marketing is entirely different, whether in a Republican versus Democrat match or a tough party primary. Unlike product campaigns, political campaigns do not mind at all turning off some "consumers," the voters. In fact, political operatives often *prefer* to keep voter participation down among those inclined to vote for the opposition. They are perfectly happy to drive down turnout, as long as those who do show up vote for them.[4] And then there's the timing. The stakes of elections are higher than everyday consumer purchases. Consumers do not have to live with the same cereal or beer for the next few years, but they do have to live with the same president, governor, or member of Congress.

Challengers in particular must, almost by definition, go negative on the lawmaker they are trying to beat. Challengers must demonstrate flaws of the policies put in place by the incumbent and show how they would do things differently. Going negative on the opponent is the best way to draw clear differences and run on the issues the challenger favors. There are exceptions to that rule. During the 2004 presidential race, the majority of President George W. Bush's ads against his Democratic rival, Senator John F. Kerry, were negative. This was a marked departure from Bush's campaign in 2000 when his ads were generally more positive, painting the then Texas governor as a "compassionate conservative."

CANDIDATES' COMPREHENSIVE PLANS FOR NEGATIVE CAMPAIGNING

The most familiar forms of negative campaigning are the hard-hitting television ads that flood the airwaves each election cycle. These often feature grainy black-and-white photos of the opposition, looking as if he or she just rolled out of bed in the morning, tasted a sour pickle, or had a root canal about an hour before.

But television ads by themselves are often only one element in a comprehensive negative campaign strategy. An effective approach revolves around painting an unlikable portrait of the opposition through many different forums, including speeches, candidate debates, press statements, and appearances on talk shows. And, as will be demonstrated in chapter 12, direct mail and more recent technological innovations such as blogs and Web video commercials have become very important tools to use in criticizing opponents.

Often, negative campaigning means telling a damaging story about the opponent over and over again. In 2000, Republicans said repeatedly that Vice President Al Gore, the Democratic presidential nominee, was an exaggerator who would say whatever it took to get elected. Four years later Senator Kerry was portrayed as a flip-flopper lacking the resolve to prosecute the war on terror. Democrats did not come up with equally compelling messages about the potential perils of a Bush presidency, and the party's nominees lost both elections.

Negative campaigning also means honing in on an opponent's gaffes, verbal or physical. Senator Barry Goldwater's politically unconventional statements, many of then joking or before friendly audiences, became fodder for some of the hardest-hitting and funny television ads of his era. The 1964 presidential race, in which President Lyndon Baines Johnson crushed Goldwater 61 percent to 39 percent in the popular vote and took 44 states in the Electoral College, set the standard for using candidates' own words against them. As described in detail in chapter 3, the Republican's words included suggestions that the eastern seaboard be sawed off and that the nuclear bomb was merely another tactical weapon.

Or consider Fred Heineman, a one-term Republican congressman from North Carolina, who rode the national GOP tidal wave in 1994 to a narrow victory over veteran Democratic Representative David E. Price. After losing by a scant 1,215 votes, Price returned to teaching political science at Duke University, but quickly geared up for a 1996 rematch against Heineman, a long-time New York City police officer who moved to Raleigh to become the city's police chief.

During the 1996 campaign, Heineman told a reporter for *The* (Raleigh) *News & Observer* that his congressional salary and police pensions (totaling more than $180,000 annually), made him "middle class," a claim likely to be disputed by many workers who toiled long and hard and earned considerably less. Heineman's comments provided an opening for Price in his comeback bid to label the incumbent as out of touch with regular folks. The campaign aired an "Earth to Fred" ad, featuring a mock conversation between "Mission Control" and the commercial's announcer, with visuals of planets, stars, and space flights. The announcer said, "Heineman claims his $180,000-a-year income makes him, quote, 'middle class.'" Mission Control then responded with "Earth to Fred. Come in!"[5] With the help of the humorous "Earth to Fred" television ad, Price won back his old seat, 54 percent to 44 percent.

Heineman's defeat also illustrates the importance of humor in negative campaigning. In fact, some of the most effective negative ads barely seem negative at all; shrouded by humor or irreverence, the stinging message is delivered in a less-than-harsh manner. The familiar "scorched earth" negative ads, with a scolding voice-over, unflattering pictures of the opponent, and ominous sound effects, have become less effective because viewers are cynical about political ads already. So they just hit the remote.[6] "Humor . . . can be a very effective way to make a point, and connect on an emotional level, which . . . has more impact than sort of a tic-list of failures," said Jim Margolis, a veteran Democratic ad maker, whose work has help elect many U.S. senators and governors.[7]

GOP Senator Mitch McConnell (Ky.) helped set a standard for humorous, effective political ads during his first Senate campaign in 1984 against two-term Democratic incumbent Senator Walter D. Huddleston. McConnell's campaign persistently criticized Huddleston's voting record and attendance at roll-call votes. Most memorably, McConnell's campaign featured a television ad in which bloodhounds tracked the absentee senator (played by an actor), who fled down a city street before being driven up a tree. The bloodhounds also followed the senator to the lawn on the east side of the U.S. Capitol. The spot noted that while Huddleston was missing votes, he was giving speeches for $50,000 a pop. In conclusion, the narrator of the ad said, "We can't find Dee. Maybe we ought to let him make speeches and switch to Mitch for senator."[8] McConnell won by about 5,000 votes out of more than 1.2 million cast.

Tony Schwartz, creator of the 1964 "Daisy Girl" ad for Lyndon Baines Johnson, produced one of the most biting—and memorable—ads of the 1968 presidential campaign. The commercial for Hubert Humphrey, the Democratic presidential nominee, called into question the abilities and qualifications of Republican vice presidential candidate Spiro T. Agnew. The spot simply showed "Agnew for Vice President" on a television set, while an off-screen viewer laughed hysterically. The tag line at the end was, "This would be funny if it weren't so serious."[9]

Campaigns can also go negative by playing the victim. Nancy Reagan played the role to perfection in a commercial for her husband's successful 1980 presidential campaign. In a one-minute commercial, the wife of the former California governor sat in a nondescript office and looked into the camera. "I deeply, deeply resent and am offended by the attacks that President Carter has made on my husband," she began. "The personal attacks that he has made on my husband. His attempt to paint my husband as a man he is not. He is not a warmonger, he is not a man who's going to throw the elderly out on the street and cut off their Social Security. That's a terrible thing to do and to say about anybody. That's campaigning on fear."

Without missing a beat, she then attacked Carter's record, while still seemingly playing the aggrieved spouse, the victim of negative campaigning by her husband's opponent. "There are many issues that are at stake in this campaign. I would like Mr. Carter to explain to me why the inflation is as high as it is, why unemployment is as high as it is. I would like to have him explain the vacillating, weak foreign policy so that our friends overseas don't know what we're going to do, whether we're going to stand up for them or whether we're not going to stand up for them. And the issue of this campaign is his three-and-a-half year record." A narrator then concluded with, "The time is now for strong leadership."[10] In the space of 60 seconds, Mrs. Reagan had offered a strong defense of her husband and then got in the campaign's main line of attack against the opponent.

Campaign attacks that don't seem harsh can come in other forms, such as interspersing optimism about one's own candidate with troubling information about the opponent. President Bill Clinton's 1996 reelection campaign turned the tactic of "positive negative" ads into high art by trumpeting his own accomplishments while at the same time linking the Republican nominee, former Senate Majority Leader Bob Dole, with unpopular House Speaker Newt Gingrich, a development examined in depth in chapter 8. The president's campaign against Dole wasn't the meanest, shrillest, or hardest-hitting White House race in memory. It wasn't particularly competitive either, because Clinton romped to a solid, near-landslide level Electoral College victory. Yet, like other contests mentioned in these pages, the race was instructive because it amplified existing tactics in negative campaigning that later became commonplace in campaigns, including going after opponents early, before they have a chance to define themselves for voters.

Whatever the format, any winning effort needs to convince voters they should vote for one candidate and against the other. It's that simple, said Chris Lehane, spokesman for Al Gore's 2000 presidential campaign and leading practitioner of comparative politics. The Harvard Law School graduate learned his craft working in the Clinton White House during the mid-1990s as part of a rapid response team created to deal with Whitewater and the growing number of other investigations into the administration. He then moved onto the campaign trail for Gore, scoring kudos from members of his party and scorn from Republicans for his hard-charging ways; at one point amid the post-Election Day legal wrangling in 2000, he compared Florida's then secretary of state, Katherine Harris, to "a Soviet commissar."[11]

Unless the race is a sure bet, Lehane said, a negative message about the opponent should be driven home every day. This keeps the opposing campaign off balance and wears down its resources. Even if a campaign's positive ratings are up and things seem to be going well, sometimes it is worthwhile to continue hammering the opponent. It's a method he compares to boxing. Begin with the basic jab, then a series of body shots, to drain the opponent's energy. Next comes a series of "hooks" to the head, which can inflict serious damage, and finally, the knockout punch. "You're either throwing a punch, or being punched," he said.[12]

Late in the 2000 presidential race, Lehane executed a tactically brilliant plan to string out for several days a series of negative news stories about the Bush campaign. The Gore campaign focused on one of Bush's television spots that seemed to subliminally flash the word "rats" across the television screen. The spot's words and standing images criticized the vice president's plan to expand health insurance coverage for prescription drugs as one that would needlessly involve federal "bureaucrats." A retired machinist volunteering for the Gore campaign in Washington State saw the words "rats" flash across the screen for a split second. After further research, Gore's people suspected that subliminal advertising was at work, with the word "rats" appearing for about a 30th of a second. So Lehane and Mark Fabiani, the deputy campaign manager, offered the story as an exclusive to the *New York Times*, along with supporting legal documentation on subliminal advertising and how the Federal Communications Commission (FCC) had declared it deceptive.

The *Times* accepted the pitch from the Gore campaign and on September 12 published a lengthy story that was posted on the paper's website around midnight. Lehane then notified several television correspondents that the story was breaking. Gathered in an Ohio hotel, he allowed the television reporters to watch the tape individually, and each prepared a separate piece, providing further amplification of the negative story about the Bush campaign. The next day, in Orlando, Florida, Bush was bombarded with questions about the "Rats" ad, which gave the story more traction. The day after that, several Democratic senators asked the FCC to investigate, keeping the matter alive even longer.[13]

JUST THE FACTS

Considerable criticism of negative campaign tactics comes from the media, particularly columnists and editorial pages. Yet much of the consternation is misplaced, when editorialists and opinion mavens confuse negative campaigning with healthy debate about contentious and divisive issues. Take the 2004 presidential campaign, the first since the terrorist attacks of September 11. Naturally much of the debate in the White House race centered on which candidate, President Bush or Senator Kerry, could best protect the United States from future attacks. Bush contended his opponent was not up to the task during wartime. Democrats naturally took umbrage with the Republican president's charges. During one campaign stop in Florida, Senator John Edwards (N.C.), the Democratic vice presidential nominee, accused Bush of "exploiting a national tragedy for personal gain." Edwards went on to declare, "George Bush today is making one last stand to con the American people into believing that he is the only one who can fight and win the war on terrorism."[14]

Media outlets echoed the criticism, portraying Bush as the purveyor of unprecedented negative campaign attacks. During early fall 2004, the *New York Times* editorial page scolded Bush and his Republican allies for suggesting that Kerry would be less competent protecting the nation from terrorist attacks. The editorial, "The Un-American Way to Campaign," took issue with comments by Vice President Dick Cheney, House Speaker Dennis Hastert (Ill.) and Senator Orrin Hatch (Utah) that suggested a Kerry presidency would lead to more terrorist attacks, because he would not be as aggressive in confronting the nation's enemies. "This is despicable politics," the *Times* wrote. "It is absolutely not all right for anyone on [Bush's] team to suggest that Mr. Kerry is the favored candidate of the terrorists."[15]

The American people, however, disagreed. To many voters the juxtaposition of facts was not negative campaigning but the telling of a difficult truth. The national audience found the predictions about Kerry to be quite "American," in that they continued the long, important tradition of contrasting candidates' stances and positions—with significant exaggeration to be sure—and letting the voters sort out what was and was not negative campaigning. Bush won the first majority (51 percent) in a presidential race since 1988.

Surveys repeatedly show that voters like to hear about the differences between candidates, as long as they are presented in a factual manner. For instance, one of Reagan's most effective ads in his 1980 presidential run asked starkly, "Can we afford four more years of broken promises? In 1976, Jimmy Carter promised to hold inflation to 4 percent. Today it is 14 percent. He promised to fight unemployment. But today there are 8.5 million Americans out of work." Those were the facts presented in a straightforward way, undoubtedly an important element in Reagan's landslide victory.[16]

While candidates and their campaign consultants usually shy away from focusing on personal problems of an opponent's family, such as a wife's drug
problem or a son's arrest for drug possession, most agree that criticizing an opponent's voting record and policy proposals should be fully open to examina-
tion. "It's completely fair game," said Chris LaCivita, a leading Republican
political consultant based in Richmond, Virginia. "If the candidate is not willing
to define their opponents and their differences, they're wasting their time."[17]

Others contend attacks on voting records are usually distorted, because legislators must often vote on amended bills that contain many provisions they
oppose. "It is one thing to take an even-handed look at one's voting record and
another to twist the facts to make it appear as something that it isn't," said Bob
Garfield, *AdAge* columnist and co-host of National Public Radio's *On the Media*. "It's nominally true, but it's fundamentally a lie."[18]

Some of the nation's most accomplished public servants do not subscribe
to negative campaigning, suggesting voters deserve to hear what candidates
would do for constituents, not how terrible the opponent is. "A campaign
should primarily be about a candidate having ideas about what the state or the
nation or the local district ought to be doing," said Jim Hunt, who narrowly
lost that 1984 Senate race to Helms, before returning as North Carolina governor for two more terms in the 1990s. "A campaign ought to be a time in
which a candidate talks to people, listens to people, discusses ideas with them,
and at the end of the day, when elected, has a mandate about what they want
done."[19] He added, however, that the 1984 Senate race taught him a candidate
should not sit on his hands in the face of campaign attacks, adding there is
nothing wrong with responding in kind, and even turning up the heat higher
on the opponent.

Congressman Jim Leach (R-Iowa) simply declines to criticize opponents,
focusing instead on his own record and accomplishments. A moderate Republican first elected in 1976, Leach has consistently refused to go negative on
opponents on television, radio, the Internet, in person, or in any other way,
even when it has jeopardized his own reelection chances in his Democratic-
leaning district.[20] Leach also does not accept political action committee
money or campaign contributions from people out of state, putting him at a
potential financial disadvantage to challengers. Campaigns should focus on
ideas, he said, not slash-and-burn tactics. "How one runs a campaign is as important as what one stands for. How a game is played does matter."[21]

In 2002, Leach faced one of the most serious threats to his political career, yet did not engage in negative campaigning. The cerebral Princeton-educated former Foreign Service officer faced Dr. Julie Thomas, a pediatrician from Cedar Rapids. She assailed Leach over issues related to health care, Social Security and prescription drugs, and many others. Because of his self-imposed restrictions on negative campaigning and fundraising, the congressman found himself in an unusual position. "We've almost reversed roles," he said at the time. "I'm running the challenger's campaign."[22]

Leach asked the House GOP campaign arm, the National Republican Congressional Committee, to stay out of the race so it could be fought on the local level. But Republican leaders, working frantically to keep their narrow House majority, ran ads anyway knocking Thomas. Leach won the race 52 percent to 46 percent.

Other veterans of the political wars contend deeply negative campaigns are harmful to lawmakers' ability to govern once they are in office. Former GOP Senator Bill Brock (Tenn.) (whose aggressive 1970 campaign against Democrat Albert Gore Sr. is recounted in chapter 5) lamented how much television is now relied upon in political races. He said 30-second spots are not enough to discuss complicated issues. "It has tended to create the impression that solutions are simple," Brock said. "It also leads to polarization in politics."[23]

While tough and harsh political commercials frequently draw criticism, some political professionals and academics extol the virtues of negative campaigning. In a 1996 essay, Northeastern University political science professor William G. Mayer wrote, "No candidate is likely to provide a full and frank discussion of his own shortcomings. Such issues will only get a proper hearing if an opponent is allowed to talk about them by engaging in negative campaigning."[24]

Positive ads, featuring candidates with family members in orchestrated camera shots, listing off their accomplishments, and proclaiming their "family values," do not provide voters enough information to make informed decisions. Many consider *positive* television campaign commercials to be more deceptive than negative ones. Some feel the practice of negative campaigning should be encouraged and expanded, for the good of the electorate. "Campaigns have always been about differences," suggested Carter Wrenn, who, as a leader of Senator Helms's political machine, the Congressional Club, from the 1970s through the early 1990s, helped pioneer many direct mail and polling techniques now familiar on the political landscape. "I think negative campaigning is good. . . . With negative ads you have the virtue of a real debate."[25] Moreover, tough races can sometimes increase turnout. For the vitriolic Helms-Hunt 1984 Senate race in North Carolina, voter turnout reached 68 percent of registered voters.[26]

For better or worse, aggressive campaign tactics have been a vital part of the American political system from the very start. As will be seen in the next chapter, the tenor of modern political campaigns is actually considerably milder than that of old. And, as will become apparent in the following chapters, negative campaign tactics have been constantly reinvented, to adapt to the latest technologies and to fit the prevailing mood of the electorate during different eras of American history.

NOTES

1. William D. Snider, *Helms & Hunt: The North Carolina Senate Race, 1984* (Chapel Hill: The University of North Carolina Press, 1985), 164.

2. Dirty tricks and illegal campaign tactics have been the subject of several worthy books, including, most recently, Andrew Gumbel's *Steal This Vote!* (New York: Nation Books, 2005). Such deceptions can take many forms and range in severity from the outrageous, like breaking into the Democratic National Committee's Watergate building headquarters in Washington, D.C., to more common acts like stealing yard signs in city council and other local races.

Attempts to tamper with voting machinery and voter suppression also fall under the category of dirty tricks and cheating. For instance, a Republican political consultant ended up serving five months in jail for his role jamming phone lines in New Hampshire that Democrats were using for get-out-the-vote operations on Nov. 5, 2002, Election Day. The effort involved making so many calls at the same time that the Democratic phone lines jammed just when voters were expected to call for rides to the polls in Manchester, Nashua, Rochester, and Claremont. The more than 800 computer-generated calls lasted about 90 minutes, as voters decided races for governor, U.S. senator, and hundreds of other offices.

3. Academic research has drawn varying conclusions about the effectiveness of negative campaigning and voters' attitudes toward the practice.

Voters often decry negative campaigning in theory—82 percent of Americans said they believed that "negative, attack-oriented campaigning is undermining and damaging our democracy," and a majority believed that unethical practices in campaigns occur "very" or "fairly" often (58 percent), according to a November 1999 survey conducted by Lake Snell Perry & Associates for the Pew Charitable Trusts and the Institute for Global Ethics, and from a September 2000 survey conducted by Yankelovich Partners, Inc., for the Center for Congressional and Presidential Studies.

Yet other studies have shown voters find negative campaigning helpful in drawing distinctions between candidates. Consider a study by the Pew Research Center for the People and the Press in November 2004, which surveyed voters' attitudes toward the just concluded presidential race between George W. Bush and John F. Kerry, widely considered among the most negative in modern times. More than eight in ten (86 percent) said they learned enough about the candidates and the issues to make an informed choice. That was similar to the results from 2000 (83 percent). At the same time, 72 percent said there was more mud-slinging or negative campaigning in the 2004 election than in previous campaigns.

Other studies have similarly found that despite decrying "negative campaigning" in general, voters still appreciate a full airing of the issues and personalities in campaigns. Data from the 1998 and 2002 California gubernatorial races found that voters generally do not consider all negative advertising unhelpful or uninformative, according to a 2003 study by John Sides of the University of Texas, Austin, and Keena Lipsitz, Matthew Grossman, and Christine Trost of the University of California at Berkeley.

That study of voters' attitudes toward the California gubernatorial races also found that the more voters knew and care about the political process, the more desensitized to negative campaigning they had become. More informed and interested voters tend to be less outraged by campaign practices and generally more sanguine about political attacks.

In an exhaustive study of U.S. Senate races from 1992 to 2002, *Negative Campaigning: An Analysis of U.S. Senate Elections* (Lanham, Maryland: Rowman & Littlefield, 2004), Rutgers University political scientists Richard R. Lau and Gerald M. Pomper found "previous literature on negative campaigning provides no clear evidentiary base for either the unusual effectiveness of the technique or its presumed deleterious effects on the political system." The authors also found that negative campaigning is less prevalent than commonly believed, and varies by campaign situation, party, and gender. In addition, the political science professors concluded, "negative campaigning does not generally reduce turnout; when combined with high levels of spending, it may actually increase turnout" (p. 91).

4. Joshua Green, "Dumb and Dumber: Why Are Campaign Commercials So Bad?" *The Atlantic Monthly*, July/August 2004.

5. David E. Price, *The Congressional Experience*, 3rd ed. (Cambridge, Mass.: Westview Press, 2004), 38–40.

6. Gary Nordlinger, "Negative Ad Survey Results Consistent with Experiences in the Trenches," *Campaigns & Elections*, October/November 1999.

7. Interview with author, Washington, D.C., Feb. 18, 2005.

8. Tape courtesy of the Julian P. Kanter Political Commercial Archive at the University of Oklahoma Political Communication Center.

9. Victor Kamber, *Poison Politics: Are Negative Campaigns Destroying Democracy?* (New York: Insight Books, 1997), 225–26.

10. Ad courtesy of The Living Room Candidate, a collection of campaign commercials sponsored online (http://livingroomcandidate.movingimage .us/index.php) by the American Museum of the Moving Image in Astoria, Queens, New York.

11. Joe Garofoli, "The Spinner: How Chris Lehane, Revered by Some and Reviled by Others, Gets the Campaign Consultant Job Done," *The San Francisco Chronicle*, Oct. 24, 2004.

12. Interview with author, San Francisco, Nov. 29, 2004.

13. Joshua Green, "Playing Dirty," *The Atlantic Monthly*, June 2004. (In March 2001 the FCC concluded that no action was warranted in the matter. In a letter to the two Democratic senators requesting the investigation, Ron Wyden of Oregon and John Breaux of Louisiana, the FCC noted that its Enforcement Bureau had tried to communicate with the licensees of 217 stations specifically alleged to have aired the ad. Of the 179 stations that responded they had aired the advertisement, 162 indicated they were not aware it contained the word RATS! in it. Representatives from the other stations said they realized the word was present on the screen, and therefore it was not subliminal.)

14. Liz Sidoti, "Edwards Accuses Bush of Exploiting 2001 Terrorist Attacks," *The Associated Press*, Oct. 18, 2004.

15. "An Un-American Way to Campaign," *New York Times* editorial, Sept. 27, 2004.

16. Kathleen Hall Jamieson, "Shooting to Win: Do Attack Ads Work? You Bet—and That's Not All Bad," *The Washington Post*, Sept. 26, 2004.

17. Interview with author, Washington, D.C., Jan. 27, 2005.

18. Interview with author, Washington, D.C., Sept. 13, 2004.

19. Interview with author, Raleigh, N.C., Feb. 22, 2005.

20. James Q. Lynch, "Leach Bests Thomas in Hard-Fought Race," *The* (Cedar Rapids) *Gazette*, Nov. 6, 2002.

21. Interview with author, by telephone, Jan. 24, 2005.

22. Robin Toner, "A Tough Race for a Moderate in the GOP," *New York Times*, Sept. 16, 2002.

23. Interview with author, Annapolis, Md., Aug. 5, 2004.

24. William G. Mayer, "In Defense of Negative Campaigning," *Political Science Quarterly*, Fall 1996.

25. Interview with author, Raleigh, N.C., Feb. 22, 2005.

26. Pamela Varley, "The Helms Hunt Senate Race (D): Case-let Sequels, Phase III, and Post Mortem," John F. Kennedy School of Government, Harvard University, 1986.

2

What Good Old Days? Notable Developments in Negative Campaigning from the Late Eighteenth Century through the Dawn of the Cold War

Late in the first presidential debate of 2004, moderator Jim Lehrer offered Senator John F. Kerry (D-MA) an opportunity to harshly criticize President George W. Bush. Lehrer, the respected host of PBS's long-running *The NewsHour*, noted that Kerry had in the past accused Bush "essentially, of lying to the American people about Iraq" and asked the presidential nominee to provide specific examples. Given this opening, Kerry demurred from calling the president an outright liar, responding, "I've never, ever, used the harshest words as you did just then, and I try not to." He then launched into criticism of Bush's postwar planning and lack of diplomatic efforts. Later in that debate, Lehrer questioned Bush on whether there were "underlying character issues" serious enough to deny Kerry the presidency. Rather than emphatically stating yes, Bush praised the Democrat's family and service to his country. The president then ripped Kerry for flip-flopping on issues and sending mixed signals to other governments about U.S. intentions abroad.[1]

The candidates' responses were notable as much for what they did *not* include as what they did. To outright call an opponent a liar or of poor character would have crossed an invisible line of campaign decorum, which many television viewers—and potential voters—would likely have found distasteful. The candidate exchanges pointed to the evolution, and softening, of negative campaign tactics common during the first century or so of the republic, when virtually no label for an opponent was too vile or sinister. Physical violence was not uncommon for much of the period, and campaign rhetoric was considerably shriller, hyperbolic, and downright mean.

Any comparison between the debates of today and those of yore is imperfect, at best, however. During the nineteenth century candidates rarely campaigned for themselves, relying instead on surrogates, such as partisan newspapers, to relay their messages to voters. But even on those unusual occasions when candidates debated each other, attacks were relentless, and rhetorical exaggerations were great.

The vaunted debates in Illinois in 1858 between U.S. Senate candidates Abraham Lincoln and Stephen A. Douglas (an office then appointed by the state legislature), were filled with charges and countercharges of corruption, forgery, and raw appeals to racial fears. Lincoln spent considerable time accusing Douglas of participating in a vast conspiracy to "nationalize" slavery, even though the Democrat favored popular sovereignty to allow newly formed states and territories to decide the issue for themselves. Douglas, meanwhile, called Lincoln "a Black Republican" for insisting that the Declaration of Independence phrase "all men are created equal" included blacks. According to Douglas, Lincoln felt "that the Negro ought to be on a social equality with your wives and daughters." That was a far stretch from the Republican's actual public statements; in fact, only when he was a wartime president would Lincoln adopt a relatively enlightened outlook, for the era, on race relations. Public acceptance of such harsh tactics was reflected in Illinois debate audiences' yells, with each verbal jab: "Hit 'em again!" or "You've got him!"[2]

Other favorite campaign tactics then included portraying opponents as drunks and womanizers. Religion was also a great source of material: In 1856 John Fremont, the first presidential candidate for the new Republican Party, vigorously denied the opposition's charges that he was a Catholic, a denomination often looked down upon by much of the Protestant-dominated populace. Religion-bashing as a political wedge issue continued to be acceptable even long after some other tough-edged attack strategies faded way. In 1928, Democratic presidential candidate Al Smith faced torrents of anti-Catholic

bias from Republicans and a considerable bloc of Southern Democrats; playing on Smith's call to repeal Prohibition, he was derisively referred to as a
"rum-soaked Romanist."[3] Even in 1960, Democratic presidential nominee
John F. Kennedy still had to spend considerable time and energy insisting he
would represent the interests of the American people, not the Vatican.

In a sign of how some standards have improved, by the time Senator Kerry
won the Democratic presidential nomination in 2004, his Catholicism was
largely a nonissue. Similarly, little hostility or bigotry confronted the candidacy of openly religious Senator Joe Lieberman of Connecticut in 2000, when
as the Democratic vice-presidential nominee, he became the first Jewish-
American on a major party ticket.

TOUGH FROM THE START

Since the founding of the United States, compare and contrast has been the
rule for political discourse, starting with the Declaration of Independence. Its
most famous passages include soaring rhetoric about the equality of all men
and governments "deriving their just powers from the consent of the governed." But the document is largely an itemization of "injuries and usurpa-
tions" by the ruling British crown, and an often-stinging explanation about
why King George III of England was "unfit to be the ruler of a free people."
Most historians agree that at the time of the American Revolution, only a sizable minority of Americans supported independence. The rest were divided
among those who opposed it and those who were undecided.[4] The Declaration's drafters provided the fence-sitters with plenty of reasons to break with
the king, among them: "He has plundered our seas, ravaged our coasts, burnt
our towns, and destroyed the lives of our people." The document is, in a sense,
negative, since it includes long lists of grievances but proposes no positive
remedies other than independence.[5]

The nation's earliest political campaigns provided a roadmap for the tough
rhetoric during the following century or so. In 1796, the nation's third presidential election and its first competitive contest (George Washington had won
the first two practically by acclamation) saw the emergence of factions, the
forerunners of political parties. The founders had initially hoped to craft a
government above factions, which they considered evil manifestations of the
corruption of British politics that provoked the colonies to separate from England in 1776.[6] But such idealism quickly fell by the wayside, as roaring

debates emerged about the proper balance of power between the states and the federal government. On one side stood the Federalists, represented by Vice President John Adams and Secretary of the Treasury Alexander Hamilton, who favored a strong federal government, and on the other stood Democratic-Republicans, led by Thomas Jefferson and James Madison, who sought regional autonomy, with the states allied in a loose confederation.[7]

Such starkly different ideologies led the various sides to assail the other's candidates, often in the most personal terms. Federalists claimed Jefferson was, among other things, an "atheist," "anarchist," "demagogue," "coward," and "trickster," and said his followers were "cut-throats who walk in rags and sleep amid filth and vermin." Adams, meanwhile, came in for criticism as being pro-British or pro-French, depending on the accuser. These were particularly sensitive charges in the young republic, at a time when fear of a new monarchy ran strong.[8] Such accusations were, in a sense, the predecessors of later negative campaign tactics that would question candidates' loyalties. Candidates were labeled—often with much validity—"pro-Confederacy" during the Civil War, particularly the northern Democrats who wanted to negotiate peace with the South rather than continue the bloody military conflict. Nearly a century later, during the early stages of the Cold War, candidates on the left end of the spectrum were often labeled "pro-Soviet," depending on their level of opposition to confrontation or support for pacification of the expansionist Russian Communist empire.[9]

President Adams won the 1796 election, but four years later faced a rematch with Jefferson, who had assumed the vice presidency under rules at the time that awarded the second-ranking office to the runner-up. With the country in its infancy and its unique political system still evolving, the election of 1800 was even more negative than the previous one; indeed it endured as the most bitter for nearly a quarter century. The stakes were high, as the first election of the nineteenth century expanded the debate over the proper scope of the federal government's authority. Jefferson believed that if Adams's Federalists prevailed, they would destroy the states and create a national government every bit as oppressive as that which Great Britain had tried to impose on the colonists before 1776.[10]

Adams's foes called the president everything from a fool to a criminal and claimed he wanted to marry off his son to the daughter of George III, creating an American dynasty under British rule. A New York newspaper called him "a person without patriotism, without philosophy, and a mock monarch."[11] Federalist campaigners called Vice President Jefferson a cheat, fraud, coward, and robber. One went so far as to call the man who wrote the Declaration of Independence "a mean-spirited, low-lived fellow, the son of a half-breed Indian squaw, sired by a Virginia mulatto father . . . raised wholly on hoe-cake made of coarse-ground Southern corn, bacon and hominy, with an occasional change of frecassed bullfrog."[12]

When Jefferson emerged the victor of the contested election, after protracted negotiations and deal making in the House of Representatives, the hard feelings were so deep that Adams refused to be part of the swearing-in ceremony, slipping out of town before dawn on Inauguration Day. In modern times it is highly uncommon for a departing officeholder to refuse to attend the swearing-in of their successor. In January 2001, outgoing Democratic Vice President Al Gore, having just lost a bruising contested campaign that was officially decided 36 days after Election Day amid legal wrangling in Florida, stood by stoically as the victor, Republican George W. Bush, took the presidential oath of office. And in November 2003, Gray Davis, a Democrat recently recalled as California governor in a humiliating special election, took the high road and dutifully attended the Sacramento inaugural ceremony of his successor, Republican Arnold Schwarzenegger.

Harsh campaigning reached a high point (or low point, depending on one's perspective) during the 1828 presidential election. Indeed, those who lament the current style of permanent campaigning, which seems to begin the moment a president's hand drops from the Bible after taking his oath of office on inauguration day, should be glad they were not around during the four years before the 1828 presidential race. Back in 1824, Andrew Jackson, military hero from the War of 1812, won the most popular votes; but three other candidates, including John Quincy Adams, siphoned off enough Electoral College votes to deny Jackson victory. The election went to the House of Representatives, where the speaker, Henry Clay, engineered a vote that gave the election to Adams. Coincidentally or not, three days later Adams named Clay his secretary of state. Jackson supporters protested bitterly at the "corrupt bargain" that had been struck.

From the moment John Quincy Adams took the oath of office, Jackson planned his political revenge. He waged what would be a political insurgency against the president for the next four years, constantly carping at Adams's alleged illegitimacy in office. Jackson allies nicknamed Adams "The Pimp," based on a rumor that while he was ambassador to Russia a decade earlier, he had coerced a young woman into having an affair with a czar. Even a White House inventory listing a billiards table and a chess set led to the accusation that Adams had introduced "gambling furniture."[13]

Nor was Adams's camp a pushover when faced with a tough electoral challenge: In 1828 an editorial cartoonist, recalling Andrew Jackson's execution of Seminole Indian sympathizers in his militia days, showed Old Hickory hoisting a man in a noose and declared, "Jackson is to be president and you will be HANGED."[14]

In the end Jackson prevailed, but not before the candidates' wives were dragged into the fray. Jackson forces alleged that Louisa Adams had been an illegitimate child who had indulged in sexual relations with John Quincy Adams before the two were married, a taboo in those days. For Rachel Jackson, rumors and nasty statements had a tragic effect. She had married Andrew Jackson unaware that her first husband had not finalized their divorce. After supporters of Adams brought up the story on the campaign trail, she became increasingly despondent. She died a few days after her husband won the White House. The new president never stopped blaming Adams for his wife's death. The hostile feelings were mutual; like his father before him, John Quincy Adams refused to take part in his successor's inaugural, leaving Washington hours before.

During the following decades, in addition to a candidate's parentage, religious faith, and drinking habits, physical appearance was fair game in campaigns. Running for president in 1860, Republican Abraham Lincoln had to overcome extremely cruel references to his somewhat ungainly appearance, such as "Illinois ape."

Growing sectional differences over the expansion of slavery to new states and territories also exacerbated negativity in campaigns. During the bloody Civil War, from 1861 to 1865, Lincoln, today among the most beloved of American presidents, was reviled by many. The wartime campaign in 1864 between Lincoln and former Union General George McClellan was extremely bitter: Republicans, running under the National Union party banner, accused Democrat McClellan of being a traitor and a coward. The Democratic platform, argued Republicans, "gives a silent approval of the Rebellion itself." Lincoln, meanwhile, was called a tyrant and a dictator for suspending the writ of habeas corpus during the war.[15] Democrats cried that lives were being sacrificed for "degraded negro slaves" instead of the Union. Other campaign epithets hurled at the sixteenth president included "ignoramus," "despot," "fiend," "buffoon," and "butcher."[16]

Sadly, during the Reconstruction period following the war's end and Lincoln's assassination in April 1865, racial issues continued to play a central role in campaign slurs. In 1868, Democrats called Ulysses S. Grant, the Civil War general and Republican presidential nominee, uncouth, tyrannical, and a promoter of black superiority. One campaign song included the lines, "I am Captain Grant of the Black Marines / The stupidest man that was ever seen."[17] Nonetheless, the war hero won the presidency.

The most prominent perpetrators of negative campaign tactics during the nineteenth century were newspapers, which were largely partisan rags. Newspapers reminded voters daily of the reasons why their side should win and, until the 1890s, usually printed the ticket on the editorial page's masthead.[18] During the nation's early days, an editor of a Baltimore paper asserted that it was as unimaginable for a newspaper to be politically neutral as it was for a clergyman to preach "Christianity in the morning and Paganism in the evening."[19] Newspapers didn't hesitate to call political opponents nasty names. In 1876, Democratic presidential nominee Samuel Tilden was often portrayed in opposition papers as a drunken con man suffering from syphilis who had escaped service during the Civil War. Republican Rutherford B. Hayes, the eventual winner that year, was at a certain point described as a sociopath who had pocketed the wages of slain soldiers he commanded during the conflict.

One of the last truly pejorative-laden campaigns, with barbs launched by newspapers on both sides, took place in 1884. Republican nominee James Blaine of Maine, a former speaker of the House and secretary of state, came in for tremendous criticism when he declined to distance himself from a Protestant minister's anti-Catholic slurs, including one late in the campaign that called the Democrats the party of "Rum, Romanism and Rebellion." And Democratic newspapers labeled Blaine a "prostitutor of public trusts" for allegedly using his official position to benefit from stock in railroad companies.

Meanwhile, the Democratic nominee, New York Governor Grover Cleveland, faced repeated written and verbal broadsides for having hired a substitute during the Civil War to fight for him, a common practice at the time for Northern men of means. In addition, charges surfaced that the bachelor had fathered and abandoned a child, leading to the famous campaign slogan, "Ma, ma, where's my pa?" Cleveland responded by admitting he had a lover, Maria Halpin, who claimed he had fathered her son. Her claim was dubious, because she had been known to cohabitate with other men. Nonetheless, Cleveland paid child support until the boy was adopted by wealthy parents. And he won the 1884 election, becoming the first Democratic president since before the Civil War. He eventually married Frances Folsom in the White House in 1886.[20]

Through a confluence of events, campaigns became somewhat more refined, civil, and genteel during the last years of the nineteenth century and the first decades of the twentieth century. For one thing, candidates began stumping for themselves. The campaign trail that we know today began to come about in the late 1800s; before then, most presidential hopefuls remained silent, while newspapers and other outlets acted as henchmen. Or, like Republican Benjamin Harrison in 1888, they conducted "front porch campaigns" from which they made speeches and greeted visitors. William Jennings Bryan, the Democratic presidential nominee in 1896, inaugurated the first whistle-stop campaign, traveling thousands of miles by train on his own behalf (a futile effort, it turned out, as Bryan lost soundly to Republican William McKinley). When candidates became their own advocates, rules of decorum demanded at least a slightly higher level of rhetoric than the unvarnished criticisms that appeared in partisan newspapers—the theory that undergirds the twenty-first-century requirement that federal candidates stand by and endorse their own ads.

Advances in the news business also softened some of the campaign trail's harsh edges. From the late eighteenth to the late nineteenth century, newspapers were the republic's central political institutions, working components of the party system rather than commentators on it. Through a gradual process that built up momentum around 1900 and increased during the following decades, many newspapers evolved into less partisan, more objective publications, and were used less frequently as party organs to advance the fortunes of one candidate and doom another.

The advent of radio broadened the reach of those who participated in the political process. Like candidates' appearances on the campaign trail, their radio voices would be connected to political ads, making them somewhat more hesitant to bitterly attack political opponents—at least directly. Radio also provided an outlet for near-immediate response by the candidate attacked. Radio made its political debut in 1924, when President Calvin Coolidge spoke over a hookup of 26 stations. The medium's effectiveness and reach were clear immediately, and by 1928, both political parties were spending large amounts of money on radio.[21] From about 1920 to 1950 the radio served as a major political information source for most Americans, before television began to take over in 1952.

AN EPIC STRUGGLE FOR THE CALIFORNIA GOVERNOR'S OFFICE

The first modern negative media campaign, including motion pictures, radio, and direct mail, occurred not in a presidential contest, but in the 1934 California governor's race. Novelist Upton Sinclair, a noted socialist, attempted to capture the governorship of California by running as a Democrat. The mood seemed right for such an insurgent social protest movement. With the country mired in depression, Franklin Delano Roosevelt had decisively defeated Republican Herbert Hoover in the 1932 presidential election. FDR's New Deal program, an expansion of government's role in the economy, aimed to restore public confidence in U.S. capitalism. By 1934 the economy largely remained flat, and social unrest was growing; the year witnessed several major strikes in major industrial cities, in some cases under socialist or radical leadership. In California, unemployed migrants from the Midwest, in search of better lives, swelled the state's population. Often, they could only find work in the fields, where pay averaged 10 to 15 cents an hour. These poor wages, combined with tough working conditions there, brought about strikes and in some cases violent clashes. Similarly, in May 1934, longshoremen in San Francisco went on strike. Police and National Guard troops used aggressive tactics there to quell the unrest; several workers were killed and hundreds of others wounded or arrested.

Such strained circumstances allowed a left-leaning candidate like Sinclair to rise in popularity. Born in Baltimore in 1878, he had won notoriety in 1905 with the publication of *The Jungle*. The novel exposed the filthy conditions of the meatpacking industry in Chicago, but served as a broader indictment of the capitalist system. Several left-leaning works of fiction followed, taking on other targets such as the oil industry and organized religion. As a previously active member of the American Socialist Party, he later rejected its more extreme, Communist-leaning elements, and in 1933 decided to enter mainstream party politics. A longtime resident of Southern California, Sinclair announced his candidacy for the 1934 Democratic gubernatorial nomination in the Golden State.

For the campaign, Sinclair wrote a pamphlet, "I, Governor of California, and How I Ended Poverty—a True Story of the Future." He advanced his plan to "End Poverty in California," known as EPIC, which advocated the state taking over idle farms and factories, turning them into cooperatives that would trade among themselves. These cooperatives would compete with privately owned business and corporations, and ultimately prove their superiority. Other less radical planks in the EPIC plan called for a progressive corporate and individual income tax, an inheritance tax, and comprehensive public works program.

Sinclair's campaign gained traction, through the spread of EPIC clubs around the state supporting his program. But California businessmen wanted no part of such proposals, clearly a threat to continued free-market commerce. So the business community responded forcefully to quash his candidacy. Business leaders denounced Sinclair as a Socialist, or Communist threat, depending on the individual or organization leveling the charges. Efforts began in earnest after Sinclair unexpectedly won the Democratic primary over George Creel, a career politician who had served in the administration of President Woodrow Wilson. After that, the business community quickly coalesced behind of candidacy of Republican Governor Frank Merriam, a conservative former lieutenant governor who had moved up to the top spot after Governor James Rolph died in 1934. Merriam aimed to keep as low a profile as possible, leaving the negative campaigning against Sinclair to others, including Louis B. Mayer, head of Metro-Goldwyn-Mayer studios, along with leaders of Southern California Edison, Southern Pacific Railroad, Standard Oil, and Pacific Mutual. The California Real Estate Association announced its backing of the incumbent Republican with the slogan, "It's Merriam or Moscow."[22]

Hired to run the anti-Sinclair campaign were a California husband and wife team, Clem Whitaker and Leone Baxter, who had set up the first political consulting firm, Campaigns, Inc. (later Whitaker & Baxter), in the Bay Area. They offered clients a complete package of campaign services, from developing strategy to writing speeches to catering fundraising dinners. Over the years they helped make campaigns a commodity. Part of the campaign they helped engineer against Sinclair included a flood of negative direct mail pieces, the first time the technique had been used extensively in a political race. The tracts targeted individual audiences and tailored the messages accordingly, with everyone from university professors to the Boy Scouts receiving their own pieces of mail denouncing Sinclair.

Movie studios used their resources to mobilize opposition to Sinclair. Newsreels showed Hollywood actors posing as ordinary voters, denouncing the Democrat. Sinclair supporters, meanwhile, were portrayed as vagrants, often speaking in thick foreign accents; they represented Bolshevik agitators, expressing their support for a Sinclair governorship, with lines like, "His system vorked vell in Russia, so vy can't it vork here?"[23] The press also vilified the Democratic candidate, routinely labeling him a "Communist" and a "Bolshevik." An October 5, 1934, column in the *Los Angeles Times* declared the EPIC movement represented "a threat to sovietize California." It continued, "Gentlemen—and Ladies—This is not politics. It is war."[24]

The establishment Democratic Party did not support Sinclair's efforts either. George Creel, Sinclair's defeated primary opponent, said he was voting for GOP Governor Merriam. And the Franklin Roosevelt's White House kept a concerted distance from the upstart Democratic gubernatorial nominee, not wanting to be associated with so radical a candidate. Despite this wall of opposition, Sinclair still managed a respectable showing in his ultimately unsuccessful race, receiving 37 percent of the vote, to 48 percent for Merriam, and 13 percent for Progressive Party candidate Raymond Haight.

Some of the problems in Sinclair's campaign were of his own making. When Roosevelt announced in June 1934 that he would propose a national social insurance system in the next session of Congress (which would become Social Security), Sinclair declared he would be willing to defer his plan in favor of the president's national solution. That action helped undermine one of Sinclair's strongest campaign issues.[25] But mostly he was undone by the massive negative campaign against him. The race served as the opening salvo for modern campaign media wars, attack ads, smear campaigns, and professional campaign strategists.

Whitaker & Baxter, the political consulting team at the heart of those efforts, became instrumental in helping numerous Republicans win office, until their retirement in 1958. They played an important role on the national scene in 1948 upon being recruited by the American Medical Association

(AMA) to lead the effort against President Harry Truman's proposal for a national health insurance program. (The couple had acted similarly in California in 1945 to thwart a proposal by Governor Earl Warren for compulsory health insurance at the state level.) The AMA spent $3.5 million to successfully fight Truman's plan, including a broad-based public relations effort to sway members of Congress.[26] (The campaign served as a forerunner of the "Harry and Louise" spots that would help doom the Clinton health care proposal in the 1990s.)

ANTI-COMMUNISM AS A CAMPAIGN TOOL

During the 1940s and 1950s, individuals on the left end of the political spectrum were routinely put on the defensive for alleged disloyalties to the United States. With the rise of the Soviet Union and Eastern Bloc after World War II, accusations that individuals were sympathetic to Moscow became commonplace, sometimes with ample justification—Soviet secret documents made public after the collapse of the USSR showed that Communist agents were often active in America, in the federal government, labor unions, and elsewhere. At other times anti-Communism came to be used as a cutting campaign tool in which people, even if fervently anti-Communist, were lumped in with those on the far left end of the political spectrum, and their patriotism was called into question. A consensus developed based on several key assumptions: that all Communists owed their primary loyalty to Moscow; that they unblinkingly followed the party line; and that they would, whenever possible, work to subvert the American system. These assumptions became intertwined with some of the most hard-edged negative campaign tactics of the day.[27]

Upton Sinclair wasn't the first candidate to be assailed for his Socialist associations. The shroud of socialist and Communist sympathies had been raised in campaigns sporadically for decades. Back in 1896, Republicans had applied the same monikers to Democratic candidate William Jennings Bryan for his intense campaign focus on agrarian and labor rights over big business and advocacy for cheaper money in the form of silver, rather than gold. In 1924 Progressive Party presidential candidate Robert M. LaFollette, Sr., too, endured repeated suggestions he was a Communist, when his presidential bid brought together socialists, organized labor, and farm groups. (That was not enough to placate the American Communists, who, running William Z. Foster for president, called the Progressive platform "the most reactionary document of the year.")[28] Fears about the rise of domestic Communism surfaced even before the end of World War II, during FDR's fourth and final White House run, in 1944. New York Governor Thomas Dewey, the Republican nominee, accused the Democratic administration of having ties with the American Communist Party, especially its leader, Earl Browder, who at the time urged his comrades to support Roosevelt (to the dismay of rank-and-file American Communists). Republican campaign literature stated that Dewey and his running mate, Governor John Bricker of Ohio, owed their political platform "to no pressure group, to no Communists and pinks who would discredit the American system."[29] Roosevelt is "indispensable," Dewey argued, "to Earl Browder, the ex-convict and pardoned Communist leader."[30] FDR shrugged off the red-baiting attacks and won another comfortable victory (though with the smallest margin of his four presidential elections, 432 electoral votes to Dewey's 99). With the Soviet Union still an ally against Germany, Communism was less of a black eye than it would become within a few years.

After World War II, President Truman and Congress had initially acted in a relatively bipartisan fashion on foreign policy matters to combat the increasingly expansionist Soviet Union. During the summer of 1945 the Senate ratified the Charter of the United Nations by a vote of 89 to 2. In 1947, the Marshall Plan to fund the reconstruction of Western Europe passed Congress with large majorities on both sides of the aisle. Two years later, Congress overwhelmingly approved U.S. participation in NATO, the charter of which committed its members to view an attack on one as an attack on all.[31]

As the 1950 midterm elections approached, the bipartisan camaraderie in foreign policy began to wane. The 1948 elections had returned Harry Truman to the White House and put Democrats in control of Congress, after a brief interlude of GOP majorities. Republicans were out of power and lacking for coherent domestic issues. So GOP leaders decided the Republicans needed to out "hard-line" the Democrats. Alleged Communist threats on the domestic fronts became a cudgel for candidates to hammer each other. The GOP launched a relentless campaign to portray the Democrats as soft on Communism. Wrote veteran *TIME* magazine journalist Lance Morrow, "The Republican strategy was to make all Democrats seem as pink as possible—dupes, at best, of their own previous liberalism, and, at worst, members of a Fifth Column burrowing away in the woodwork of the American dream."[32] Senator Joseph McCarthy, Republican of Wisconsin, became the most prominent face of this effort. The negative campaign tactics worked effectively in the seething Cold War atmosphere of suspicion and fear.

Many of the familiar tales from the 1950 Senate campaigns exemplify the power of the anti-Communism as a political sledgehammer in the era, during the early stages of the Korean War. For instance, Senator Millard E. Tydings, Democrat of Maryland, lost his bid for a fifth term largely because a photo, of dubious origin and authenticity, showed him with Earl Browder, the American Communist leader. Tydings had headed a subcommittee that in spring 1950 investigated McCarthy's charges that the State Department was riddled with subversives. Tydings found the charges to be unsubstantiated, which brought on accusations of a "whitewash" from the Wisconsin senator. In his reelection bid, Tydings faced Republican John Marshall Butler of Baltimore, a lawyer and first-time candidate. Butler's campaign workers circulated a tabloid with a composite picture that by some descriptions appeared to show Tydings listening intently to Browder. The Republican said he believed the picture was designed to illustrate the "attitude" that Tydings showed when Browder testified in April 1950 about domestic Communist activities. Anything else read into the picture—such as implications that Tydings was a Communist sympathizer—"is a matter of imagination," Butler said.[33] At a time of rampant Communist hysteria, the photo helped sow seeds of doubt in the minds of Free State voters; Butler beat Tydings, 53 percent to 46 percent. Tydings cited the disputed picture in a complaint to the Senate after his defeat. A Democratic-dominated Senate committee later criticized tactics used in the campaign, but no action ever was taken against Senator Butler.

In California, Congressman Richard M. Nixon used the anti-Communist issue to propel himself into the U.S. Senate. Nixon had won his House seat in 1946 by taunting Democratic incumbent Jerry Voorhis over the issue of Communist influence in the labor movement and the five-term incumbent's ties to with national and state labor political action committees. Once in office, Nixon distinguished himself on the House Un-American Activities Committee (HUAC) as a principal assailant of Alger Hiss, who would be sentenced to five years in prison for perjury. Then in 1950, Democratic Senator Sheridan Downey unexpectedly chose to retire, and Nixon, looking to climb the political ladder, jumped into the race, free of Republican primary opposition. In the Democratic primary, Congresswoman Helen Gahagan Douglas, a Broadway and movie actress-turned left-wing political activist, who had served three terms in the House, beat out a more conservative rival for the right to face Nixon.

In Congress, she had enthusiastically supported Truman's Fair Deal, which conservatives denounced as an overreach of government power. Nixon came out swinging from the start: The campaign printed an infamous flier on pink paper that proclaimed: "During five years in Congress, Helen Douglas has voted 353 times exactly as has Vito Marcantonio, the notorious Communist party-line Congressman from New York. How can Helen Douglas, capable actress that she is, take up so strange a role as a foe of Communism? And why does she when she has so deservedly earned the title of 'the pink lady.'"[34] Anyone scrutinizing her votes fairly would have seen that many were minor legislative matters and procedural questions; meanwhile Nixon himself had voted with Marcantonio 111 times. Yet the tactical brilliance of the Nixon campaign rested in its ability to stress Douglas's liberalism in a way that made her seem like a Communist without actually stating that she was one. Nixon instead called Douglas "pink right down to her underwear." He won the race by 680,000 votes, setting him on to the vice-presidency two years later and, ultimately, the White House (and also earning the enduring, unflattering nickname "tricky Dick" from Democrats).

Often the thrust and parry of Communist allegations in campaigns did not reflect divisions between Republicans and Democrats but between Democrats themselves. The red-baiting tactics of the 1950 California Senate race shadowed those employed that same year in Florida during the Democratic Senate primary, when two-term Congressman George Smathers successfully challenged Senator Claude Pepper, a Southern liberal. Smathers later said Harry Truman encouraged him to run against Pepper, who had frequently sparred with the president. (Pepper had encouraged Dwight D. Eisenhower to run as a Democratic candidate for president in 1948). Rapidly shifting world events also helped nudge Smathers into the race: The Soviet Union, an ally during World War II, had cut off Eastern Europe with the infamous Iron Curtain; that part of the world was now ruled by Communists. While Truman expanded the military and fought successfully for the creation of NATO, Pepper urged cooperation with the Soviets, at one point appearing at peace rallies with American Communists and praising Soviet dictator Joseph Stalin.[35]

These actions gave Smathers a political opening to run against "Red Pepper." "The people of our state will no longer tolerate advocates of treason,"

Smathers said in a typical campaign speech. "The outcome can truly determine whether our homes will be destroyed, whether our children will be torn from their mothers, trained as conspirators and turned against their parents, their home and their church."[36] Tough talk it was, but symbolic of Cold War rhetoric on the campaign trial in 1950. When the Communist party paper, *The Daily Worker*, endorsed Pepper and the *Saturday Evening Post* labeled him a "pinko," many former supporters fled, and the senator lost in the Democratic primary. "It was a campaign of vicious distortion," Pepper said three decades later, "calling me 'Red Pepper,' calling me a Communist. That fitted right in, you see, with the McCarthyism that was sweeping the country."[37] After a dozen years out of office, Pepper made an unusual political comeback, winning a Miami-based seat in the U.S. House in 1962, where he established himself as a defender of Social Security and other programs for the elderly, serving until his death in 1989, at age 88.

Some of Smathers's choicer slams against Pepper were probably fiction. The April 17, 1950, issue of *TIME* magazine recounted a report in a "Northern newspaper" of a speech by Smathers in which he asked, "Are you aware that Claude Pepper is known all over Washington as a shameless extrovert? Not only that, but this man is reliably reported to practice nepotism with his sister-in-law, and he has a sister who was once a thespian in wicked New York. Worst of all, it is an established fact that Mr. Pepper, before his marriage, practiced celibacy."[38] No journalist at the speech reported the colorful comments, which seemed designed to mislead ignorant voters with fancy words; Smathers denied ever making the statements, consistently offering $10,000 to anyone who could prove he said them. Even *TIME*, in the same article, described the purported quotation as a "yarn" of doubtful authenticity. An exhaustive 1983 article in the *New York Times* largely debunked the famous quote. Most likely, the statement was part of an arsenal of anti-Pepper humor tossed around at the time by Smathers campaign workers and reporters.[39]

Though less famous in many quarters than the bitter 1950 Senate campaigns in Maryland, Florida, and California, the Senate race in North Carolina that year was equally contentious, fueled not only by charges of Communist sympathies but by bald racist appeals as well. In March 1949 Democratic Senator J. Melville Broughton died after only two months in office. As a replacement, Democratic Governor Kerr Scott appointed to the Senate Frank Porter Graham, president of the University of North Carolina at Chapel Hill. Graham was a liberal by any conventional measure of the term for the South during that era. In addition to supporting civil rights for blacks, he backed labor on many workplace issues, particularly for those who toiled in North Carolina's textile mills. In 1932, he had defended the right of Chapel Hill students to invite Norman Thomas, the Socialist candidate for president, to speak at the university. And he had fought efforts to forbid the teaching of evolution in North Carolina schools. A devout Christian, he neither smoked, drank, nor cursed.[40]

Though Graham described himself as a man who had always opposed "Communism and all totalitarian dictatorships," there were repeated attempts to brand him as a Communist or Communist sympathizer. The attacks were based chiefly on the fact that he had been the first chairman of the Southern Conference on Human Welfare, an organization that was later declared a Communist front by the House Committee on Un-American Activities, although the panel specifically exempted Graham from the Communist charge.[41] When Graham arrived in Washington to serve in the Senate, Ohio's Senator John W. Bricker (Dewey's running mate in 1944) tried unsuccessfully to block him from taking his seat, because the Atomic Energy Commission's security review committee had pointed to his left-wing associations and initially denied him access to nuclear secrets.[42]

As an appointed senator, Graham had to get elected on his own in the 1950 election cycle in order to complete Broughton's full Senate term. It was clear such a left-leaning politician would be challenged. Graham's most prominent opponent was Willis Smith, a well-known lawyer from Raleigh and a conservative Democrat. The former American Bar Association president had served as speaker of the state House of Representatives in the early 1930s. Tall and handsome, the Duke University chairman of the board of trustees stood in striking contrast to the soft-spoken, bookish Graham. Smith set the tone of the race immediately by declaring, "I do not now nor have I ever belonged to any subversive organizations, and as United States senator, I shall never allow myself to be duped into the use of my name for propaganda or any other purposes by those types of organizations."[43]

Two others ran in the May primary, and Graham finished first, 53,000 votes ahead of Smith. But he missed winning the majority he needed to avoid a runoff by one percentage point. At first, Smith wasn't sure if he wanted to request a runoff. Then a group of supporters appeared at his house, including

28-year-old radio reporter Jesse Helms, to persuade him to call for the runoff. A series of Supreme Court decisions issued between the primary and the runoff may have also influenced Smith's decision, including rulings that Pullman railroad dining cars could not segregate blacks and that graduate schools at the universities of Texas and Oklahoma would have to admit blacks.[44] Smith eventually asked for the runoff, and the second campaign produced a set of campaign fireworks rarely equaled in American politics in the twentieth century.

In addition to Graham's alleged softness on Communism, racial issues played an insidious role in the new campaign. That was a somewhat surprising turn of events because in 1950, North Carolina did not outwardly appear to be a hotbed of racial reaction. Two years before, Governor Strom Thurmond of neighboring South Carolina had run for president as a states' rights, anti-integrationist candidate; while he won the Electoral College votes of four Southern states, he received less than ten percent of the vote in North Carolina, as the traditionally Democratic Tar Heel State went for Truman over Republican challenger Dewey. Racial resentments, however, could still be stirred. From the start, the Smith campaign and it allies accused Graham of threatening desegregation in the workplace. Smith benefited from handbills distributed by a shadowy group called Know the Truth Committee that said, "White people, wake up before it is too late! Do you want Negroes working beside you, your wife and your daughters in your mills and factories? Frank Graham favors mingling of the races!"[45] Other printed materials featured photographs of black soldiers dancing and drinking with white women. One pictured a black man dancing with a woman who had the superimposed face of Mrs. Graham.[46] And an ad run by the Smith campaign pictured the South Carolina legislature during Reconstruction when many blacks had been elected to office; the obvious implication was that returning Graham to the Senate would produce a similar result. There were also reports that Graham had appointed a black youngster to West Point (in reality, he had named a black youth as an alternate after competitive exams narrowed his list).[47]

Particularly during the final days before the runoff, North Carolina newspapers were filled with advertisements proclaiming, "The South Under Attack" or "End of Racial Segregation Proposed." Graham got a sense of the electorate's mood on the day before the election, when his entourage stopped at a gas station on the way to a speech before mill workers in High

Point. The men there refused to shake the senator's hand. "We're all Willis Smith men here," muttered one. "We'll have nothing to do with nigger lovers here."[48]

The virulently negative campaign tactics worked, as Smith won by nearly 18,000 votes, and in November 1950 easily won the general election. In the eastern end of the state, 18 counties Graham won in the first primary swung against him in the runoff. How much of the most vicious materials were sanctioned by Smith is a long-running source of debate among North Carolina politicos. Smith partisans claim he distanced himself from the most noxious statements and handbills, while foes contend he provided overt, or at least tacit, approval.

The campaign was Jesse Helms's political launching ground. While officially working as a radio reporter in 1950, Helms became an avid Smith partisan and informal campaign adviser; many consider him instrumental in helping persuade Smith to call for a runoff in the first place. A year after the primary, Helms went to Washington as an administrative assistant for Smith. The campaign also introduced Helms to Thomas F. Ellis, a conservative Raleigh attorney who helped persuade him to run for Senate as a Republican in 1972 and who built the vaunted political machine, the Congressional Club, which was responsible for developing some of the most hard-edged campaign tactics of the 1970s and 1980s.

The vigorous and highly negative Senate races of 1950 were part of the last election cycle before television began to become incorporated into campaigns. As will be shown, this new form of mass communication made it considerably easier for candidates to spread their messages—negative or otherwise—widely and effectively.

NOTES

1. Transcript of the first Bush-Kerry presidential debate, Sept. 30, 2004, University of Miami, Coral Gables, Fla., from the Commission on Presidential Debates (www.debates.org/pages/trans2004a.html).

2. Terry Moran, "When the Gloves Came Off, and Americans Loved It," *The Washington Post*, April 2, 2000.

3. Eileen Shields-West, *The World Almanac of Presidential Campaigns* (New York: World Almanac, 1992), 168.

4. E. J. Dionne Jr., "Thomas Jefferson, Attack Dog," *The Washington Post*, July 4, 2000.

5. William G. Mayer, "In Defense of Negative Campaigning," *Political Science Quarterly*, Fall 1996.

6. H.W. Brands, review of *Too Close to Call*, (book review), *The Washington Post*, Oct. 31, 2004.

7. Victor Kamber, *Poison Politics: Are Negative Campaigns Destroying Democracy?* (New York: Insight Books, 1997), 14.

8. Paul F. Boller Jr., *Presidential Campaigns: From George Washington to George W. Bush* (New York: Oxford University Press, 2004), 8.

9. Bruce L. Felknor, *Dirty Politics* (Lincoln, Neb.: iUniverse.com, Inc. [originally published by Norton], 1966, 2000), 19.

10. John Ferling, "Cliffhanger: The Election of 1800," *Smithsonian*, November 2004.

11. Brands, *The Washington Post.*

12. Boller, *Presidential Campaigns*, 16.

13. Paul Johnson, "Once Upon a Time," *Wall Street Journal*, Oct. 20, 2004.

14. Todd S. Purdum, "The Year of Passion," *The New York Times*, Oct. 31, 2004.

15. Shields-West, *The World Almanac of Presidential Campaigns*, 91.

16. Boller, *Presidential Campaigns*, 116–17.

17. Chris Christoff and Dawson Bell, "Electing a President: Nasty Campaigns," *Detroit Free-Press*, April 26, 2004.

18. Mark Wahlgren Summers, *Party Games: Getting, Keeping, and Using Power in Gilded Age Politics* (Chapel Hill: The University of North Carolina Press, 2004), 35.

19. Brands, *The Washington Post.*

20. Christoff and Bell, *Detroit Free-Press*, April 26, 2004.

21. Elaine Ciulla Kamarck, "Campaigning on the Internet in the Off-Year Elections of 1998," John F. Kennedy School of Government, Harvard University, February 1999, http://siyaset.bilkent.edu.tr/Harvard/kamarck2.htm

22. Greg Mitchell, *The Campaign of the Century: Upton Sinclair's Race for Governor of California and the Birth of Media Politics* (New York: Random House, 1992), 298.

23. Kamber, *Poison Politics*, p. 28.

24. Mitchell, *The Campaign of the Century*, p. 300.

25. California Secretary of State website (www.ssa.gov/history/sinclair.html).

26. Stanley Kelley Jr., *Professional Public Relations and Political Power* (Baltimore: Johns Hopkins University Press, 1956), 72.

27. Lance Morrow, *The Best Year of Their Lives: Kennedy, Johnson, and Nixon in 1948—Learning the Secrets of Power* (New York: Basic Books, 2005), 216.

28. Boller, *Presidential Campaigns*, 220.

29. Lewis L. Gould, *Grand Old Party: A History of the Republicans* (New York: Random House, 2003), 298.

30. Shields-West, *The World Almanac of Presidential Campaigns*, 187.

31. Randall Bennett Woods, "The Cold War," in *The American Congress: The Building of Democracy*, ed. Julian E. Zelizer (New York: Houghton Mifflin Company, 2004), 505.

32. Morrow, *The Best Year of Their Lives*, 40.

33. Martin Weil, "John M. Butler, Senator from Md. in 1950s, Dies," *The Washington Post*, March 17, 1978.

34. Tom Wicker, *One of Us: Richard Nixon and the American Dream* (New York: Random House, 1991), 76.

35. Stephen Nohlgren, "A Born Winner, If Not a Native Floridian: George Smathers Never Lost an Election, but His Legacy Remains Attached to a Campaign Quote He Never Said," *The St. Petersburg Times*, Nov. 29, 2003.

36. Nohlgren, "A Born Winner."

37. Howell Raines, "Legendary Campaign: Pepper vs. Smathers in '50," *The New York Times*, Feb. 24, 1983.

38. "Anything Goes," *TIME*, April 17, 1950.

39. Raines, *The New York Times*, Feb. 24, 1983.

40. Samuel Lubell, *The Future of American Politics* (Garden City, N.Y.: Doubleday & Co., Inc., 1956), 107.

41. "Dr. Frank Porter Graham Dies at 85; Civil Rights Leader in the South," *The New York Times*, Feb. 17, 1972.

42. Ernst B. Furgurson, *Hard Right: The Rise of Jesse Helms* (New York: W.W. Norton & Company, 1986), 48.

43. Furgurson, *Hard Right*, 49.

44. In *Sweatt v. Painter*, 339 U.S. 629, the Supreme Court reversed a decision first made by a Texas trial court that found that a newly established state law school for blacks met the separate but equal provisions of the 1896 *Plessy v. Ferguson* court decision. The trial court decision was affirmed by the Court of Civil Appeals, and the Texas Supreme Court denied *writ of error* on further appeal. The case was then appealed to the U.S. Supreme Court, which reversed the lower-court decision.

In *McLaurin v. Oklahoma State Regents*, 339 U.S. 637, the Supreme Court reversed a lower-court decision upholding the efforts of the state-supported University of Oklahoma to adhere to the state law requiring African-Americans to be provided instruction on a segregated basis. The U.S. Supreme Court ruled that a public institution of higher learning could not provide different treatment to a student solely because of his race and that doing so deprived the student of his or her Fourteenth Amendment right to due process.

In *Henderson v. United States*, 339 U.S. 816, the Supreme Court ruled that segregation of blacks and whites in railroad dining cars violated the Interstate Commerce Act.

45. Rob Christensen, Carol Byrne Hall, and James Rosen, "Jesse Helms: To Mold a Nation (Three Decades of Political Soul)," *The* (Raleigh) *News & Observer*, Aug. 26, 2001.

46. William D. Snider, *Helms & Hunt: The North Carolina Senate Race, 1984* (Chapel Hill: The University of North Carolina Press, 1985), 24.

47. Jack Betts, "Negative Ads Getting to Be a Bad Habit: Bowles and Dole Already Are Twisting Facts—and History Suggests They'll Only Get Worse," *The Charlotte Observer*, Oct. 6, 2002.

48. Lubell, *The Future of American Politics*, 111.

Going Nuclear 1964: The Rise of Television Attack Ads

Few candidates have needed to employ negative campaigning less than President Lyndon Baines Johnson in 1964. The assassination of President John F. Kennedy in November 1963 ensured that the Republicans would face an uphill battle no matter whom they pitted against the Texas Democrat. After all, the new president had ridden a wave of goodwill after the tragic events of Dallas, toward swift passage of much of his predecessor's idling legislative agenda. Most notably, LBJ, the former Senate majority leader, muscled through a recalcitrant Congress the landmark Civil Rights Act of 1964, which guaranteed blacks access to all public facilities and accommodations and banned discrimination because of race, religion, national origin, or sex. The Vietnam War, later to be Johnson's downfall, was escalating. But on Election Day of 1964, it had yet to become a real liability.

The ambitious Johnson did not just want to win his own term as president; he craved a resounding victory that would establish a new White House power base. Then he could push forward his own legislative agenda, which included creation of Medicare and Medicaid, aid to education, regional redevelopment and urban renewal, and scores of other proposals to establish a "Great Society."[1]

President Johnson did not care to take chances on his own reelection; he had a history of tough races that sometimes required aggressive tactics. A gangly 28-year-old Johnson had out-campaigned his nine Democratic primary opponents to win a U.S. House seat from Texas in a 1937 special election. He narrowly lost a 1941 U.S. Senate special election, a contest in which his Democratic primary opponent appeared to have benefited from creative vote-counting procedures and ballot box stuffing in certain Texas counties where his influence ran strong. And in 1948 it looked as if Johnson would lose his second bid for Senate. In what was then a monolithic Democratic state, Johnson had come in second during the primary to Coke Stevenson, though the conservative former governor did not win a majority. In the hard-fought runoff, notable for Johnson's pioneering use of a helicopter as a campaign vehicle, LBJ still came up short. But a series of favorable ballots in Boss George Parr's Duvall County somehow materialized after Election Day, to make Johnson the winner of the crucial Democratic primary, by the infamous margin of 87 votes. The case was challenged all the way to the U.S. Supreme Court. There Justice Hugo Black dissolved a federal injunction nullifying Johnson's runoff victory, ruling that the federal government did not have jurisdiction to interfere in the counting of ballots in a state primary election.[2]

So as he looked toward a victory of historic proportions as president in 1964, Johnson approved his campaign's launch of the first media campaign centered on the rapidly growing medium of television, much of it an assault on the Republican presidential nominee, Senator Barry Goldwater of Arizona. Johnson adviser Bill Moyers said the president "was determined to roll up the biggest damned plurality ever and he felt that anything that could help—and he believed advertising could help—was worth the price."[3]

Goldwater himself became the focus of the election, not foreign policy, taxation, or other issues. According to Johnson's ads, Goldwater would destroy Social Security, end government programs to aid the poor, and potentially launch a nuclear war that could endanger all humanity. While LBJ's victory was never really in doubt, his campaign set the precedent for the television attack ads Americans now take for granted. Many of the spots seem tame and downright quaint compared to the commercials that followed forty years later, but at the time the massive television onslaught of political commercials stunned the Republican opposition.

The 1964 presidential race also offers a vivid illustration of how effectively negative campaigning has worked when it has played into voters' preconceived notions voters about candidates. The Johnson ads did a masterful job of using Goldwater's words against him, which typecast the Republican. The vaunted "Daisy Girl" ad that suggested Goldwater would start a nuclear war (it never mentioned his name) was consistent with many voters' views of the Republican candidate. "The commercial evoked a deep feeling in many people that Goldwater might actually use nuclear weapons," wrote Tony Schwartz, creator of the famous ad. "This distrust was not in the Daisy spot. It was in the people who viewed the commercial."[4]

The strategy of massive negative campaigning on television did the trick, as the president crushed Goldwater by a 16-million-vote margin (43 million to 27 million; 61 percent to 39 percent). Johnson won 486 Electoral College votes to Goldwater's 52; the president fared poorly only in the Deep South, losing Mississippi, Alabama, South Carolina, Georgia, and Louisiana, along with Goldwater's native Arizona.

EARLY POLITICAL TELEVISION COMMERCIALS

In some ways the sitcoms of today bear little resemblance to the early television comedies of the 1950s—in color for one thing, and the language is often cruder and the camera angles always sharper. Yet in some respects the genre of situation comedy has not changed significantly, as the shows center on family situations, with parents using gentle humor to guide their growing children through life's travails. Similarly, while technology used in campaign commercials has evolved exponentially, the themes expressed in candidate spots in the earliest days are also familiar.

Political newsreels began to be played before movie audiences regularly during the 1930s; they served as early prototypes of the hard-hitting campaign ads that would emerge on television decades later. The 1940 Republican National Committee film *The Truth about Taxes*, on behalf of GOP presidential candidate Wendell Wilkie, showed an ironsmith slaving away over a hot furnace. The narrator then explained that all working people had to labor for three months just to pay for what government spent. "Everyone, whether in the factory, shop, farm or office, pays for the cost of government." The narrator continued, "Let us rid ourselves of our New Deal failure, before it's too late. Let us end wasteful spending and return to good, old American sanity in economy. All Americans must unite to stop the New Deal, with its lust for power to perpetuate itself in office for another four years. To save ourselves, we must dismiss incompetents and radicals from high places of government. We must elect Wendell Wilkie president."[5] These same basic themes, minus the overt calls to dismantle the New Deal, would be present in Republican campaigns six decades later, with increasingly sharp language.

Some of the earliest political television advertisements, too, carried arguments that would be present in political television advertising for decades to come. The first batches of campaign commercials made in the early 1950s, included "the general themes of Republicans saying, 'We're strong on the military, and we want to cut your taxes,' and the Democrats saying they are for the common people," noted David Schwartz, curator of the American Museum of the Moving Image in Queens, New York.[6]

The very first political television commercials, made for Democratic Senator William Benton of Connecticut in 1950, were actually positive: They featured the Democratic lawmaker's wife and neighbors lauding him. Those spots played a role in Benton's razor-thin election victory over Republican Prescott Bush, by about 1,000 votes (Benton had been appointed to the seat in 1949 when the incumbent senator, a Republican, died). Benton had come to realize the importance of television through his work in advertising; he cofounded the Benton-Bowles agency in New York and was so successful that he retired at age 36.[7]

It wasn't long before the television commercials featured politicians slinging mud at each other, a reflection of candidates' and consultants' consistent abilities to adapt negative campaign tactics to technological advances in communications. By the 1952 election cycle, about 19 million homes had television sets,[8] and in that presidential race, former General Dwight D. Eisenhower's campaign commercials criticized the Democrats relentlessly without naming his opponent, Governor Adlai Stevenson of Illinois. The spots focused on taxes, high prices, the Korean situation, and alleged government corruption under Democratic President Harry Truman, whose sagging popularity led him to decline a reelection bid. One ad featured two soldiers on the battlefield in Korea, discussing the war's futility. Suddenly, one of the soldiers was killed, while the other charged the enemy. The tag line said simply, "Vote Republican."[9] Stevenson's ads generally featured the erudite governor pontificating on issues of the day in a somewhat academic manner. But he did get in some jabs against Eisenhower by suggesting he would be a puppet of Robert A. Taft, the Ohio senator and anchor of the Republican Party's conservative wing. Eisenhower spent more than $1 million on television commercials on his way to a sound victory, while Stevenson laid out less than $80,000.

During Stevenson's unsuccessful 1956 rematch against President Eisenhower, the challenger's ads got tougher; the arsenal included a television attack against Vice President Richard M. Nixon. The president's heart attack a year before raised the possibility Nixon could be elevated to commander in chief, and Democrats tried to play on voters' fears. The 10-second-long ad showed a picture of the vice president looking shifty and sneering, while the announcer asked, "Nervous about Nixon? *President* Nixon?" Running mates would be the focus of criticism in television spots for decades to come, with increasing degrees of sophistication, Republican vice-presidential candidates Spiro T. Agnew in 1968, Dan Quayle in 1988, and Dick Cheney in 2004 being the most prominent recent examples.

Nixon was on the wrong end of the most memorable negative ad of the 1960 presidential campaign, when he was the Republican presidential nominee. And the person who inflicted the verbal wound was not the sponsor, Democratic Senator John F. Kennedy of Massachusetts. It was Nixon's boss, President Eisenhower. Democrats seized on an offhand comment made by the president in response to a reporter's request to name a "major idea" that Nixon had proposed and the president adopted. Eisenhower replied, "If you give me a week, I might think of one. I don't remember." To capitalize on the remark, the Kennedy campaign built a long, explanatory ad to cause the most damage. An announcer began by saying, "Every Republican politician wants you to believe that Richard Nixon is experienced. They even want you to believe that he has actually been making decisions in the White House. But listen to the man who should know best, the president of the United States. A reporter recently asked President Eisenhower this question about Mr. Nixon's experience." After the president's barb at his understudy, the announcer returned to say, "At the same press conference, President Eisenhower said, 'No one can make a decision except me.'" And as for any major ideas from Nixon, the viewer then saw Eisenhower saying again, "If you give me a week, I might think of one. I don't remember." The commercial concluded, "President Eisenhower could not remember, but the voters will remember. For real leadership in the '60s, help elect Senator John F. Kennedy president."[10] The spot was considered tough for its time, as it focused almost entirely on the opposition, instead of listing any positive attributes of the candidate running the ad. But this style of the slow, almost apologetic attack ad would be antiquated by the end of the 1964 president campaign.

TELEVISION ADS OF 1964: A YEAR OF FIRSTS

During the 1964 campaign, Goldwater's primary opponents stirred up some of the ammunition that Johnson used against him. As the 1964 election cycle began, Republicans were split between a base of activist conservatives and a generally more liberal leadership. Conservatives organized early support for Goldwater, an outspoken libertarian-leaning right-winger. Entering the race with a lower level of grassroots support was New York Governor Nelson Rockefeller, a liberal who had alienated conservatives by inserting moderate planks in the 1960 Republican platform and who had wounded his public image with a highly publicized divorce. Rockefeller, like many Republican donors and voters, was unsure that Johnson could be defeated but was certain that Goldwater would lead the party into an electoral massacre. His political advisor George Hinman said as much to prospective Rockefeller delegates, hinting that "Rockefeller would step aside for another, more electable, moderate at the convention: They were fighting a crusade to save their party from the infidels."[11]

In the primary campaign and at the Republican National Convention, Rockefeller and moderates such as 1960 vice presidential nominee Henry Cabot Lodge Jr. and Pennsylvania Governor William Scranton campaigned to stop Goldwater. They loudly attacked the front-runner's controversial stands on issues, publicized his often-incendiary public statements, and predicted disaster if the party anointed him the nominee. The public and private maneuvering sharply divided the party as it went into the convention at San Francisco's Cow Palace. Cameras picked up NBC anchorman John Chancellor being roughly ejected from the floor,[12] and Rockefeller getting furiously heckled during his speech. According to political scribe Theodore H. White, "As the TV cameras translated their wrath and fury to the national audience, they pressed on the viewers that indelible impression of savagery which no Goldwater leader or wordsmith could later erase."[13] Making his problems worse, Goldwater stoked the crowd by paraphrasing the Roman politician Cicero in his acceptance speech, saying, "I would remind you that extremism in the defense of liberty is no vice! And let me remind you also that moderation in the pursuit of justice is no virtue!" This made Goldwater appear to agree with the most fringe elements of the American right; his campaign bought ads positively defining "extremism" in a vain attempt to blunt the damage.[14]

The Johnson campaign used these events to its advantage. In March, campaign managers had signed with Doyle Dane Bernbach, a New York firm that had risen to prominence with ads for Volkswagen and Avis Rent-a-Car.[15] The agency had never handled a political campaign, and approached the challenge with bracing, aggressive ads that put the Goldwater team on the defensive for most of the race. Part of the Johnson strategy was revealed in the official slogan, repeated in every ad: "Vote for President Johnson on Nov. 3rd. The stakes are too high for you to stay home." That motto underscored the fact that Johnson was already in the Oval Office and had been tested under incredibly trying circumstances; it hinted that replacing LBJ with Goldwater would lead to catastrophe. The rest of the strategy utilized Goldwater's own words against him to paint him as a dangerous extremist, and followed these up with attacks from other Republicans collected from the primary campaign.

One ad that utilized Republican attacks was "Convention," which presented a cluttered floor made up to look like the scene inside the San Francisco Cow Palace after the crowds had emptied out. As the crew picked up placards, a narrator rolled off some of the Republicans' harshest attacks on Goldwater. "Back in July in San Francisco, the Republicans held a convention," said the announcer. "Remember him? He was there, Governor Rockefeller. Before the convention he said Barry Goldwater's positions can 'spell disaster for the party and for the country.' Or him, Governor Scranton. The day before the convention he called Goldwaterism a 'crazy quilt collection of absurd and dangerous positions.' Or this man, Governor [George] Romney [of Michigan]. In June he said Goldwater's nomination would lead to the 'suicidal destruction of the Republican Party.' So even if you're a Republican with serious doubts about Barry Goldwater, you're in good company."[16]

The next group of ads bolstered Goldwater's extremist image by publicizing statements he'd made off the cuff or in front of friendly crowds. In 1961, Goldwater had joked, "Sometimes I think this country would be better off if we could just saw off the eastern seaboard and let it float out to sea." So Doyle Dane Bernbach created an ad showing a cardboard map of the United States getting the East Coast states slowly but steadily sawed off, as a narrator read Goldwater's quote. The senator from Arizona had told an interviewer that the Tennessee River Valley Authority should be sold, and Doyle Dane Bernbach produced an ad portraying an auction on top of a giant dam. The spot opened with the auctioneer in the midst of rapid fire speech, helping bidders raise the price of the commodity he was trying to sell. As the camera panned away from the auctioneer, it was revealed that the bidders were on top of a giant water dam. "In a *Saturday Evening Post* article dated August 31, 1963, Barry Goldwater said, 'You know, I think we ought to sell the TVA.'" The narrator continued, "This is a promise: President Johnson will not sell TVA. Vote for him on Nov. 3rd. The stakes are too high for you to stay home."[17]

Another spot to turn Goldwater's statements against him opened with a Social Security card on a table. As the narrator named media outlets in which Goldwater said he would change the system to make it voluntary "on at least seven different occasions," those newspapers and magazines were thrown on top of the Social Security card. After *The Congressional Record* was named, a pair of hands appeared, tore up another Social Security card, and threw it on the pile. "Even his running mate, William Miller, admits that Barry Goldwater's voluntary plan would wreck your Social Security," the narrator said. President Johnson was then shown, saying, "Too many have worked too long and too hard to see this threatened now by policies which promise to undo all that we have done together over all these years." It was the most repeated ad of the entire campaign, and according to Theodore H. White, "probably had greater penetration than any other paid political use of television except for Richard M. Nixon's 'Checkers' broadcast in 1952."[18] The spot presaged a long line of federal campaigns that would seek to scare voters about opponents' plans for Social Security. Rarely did a candidate make such an explicit statement as Goldwater's suggestion that the system could be made voluntary. But proposals to trim benefits, raise Social Security taxes, and other unpleasant remedies to shore up the social insurance system would be exploited, often quite successfully, in future campaigns.

A couple of ads by the Johnson campaign aired only one time each. The "Daisy Girl" spot, perhaps the most famous campaign ad of all time, ran during NBC's *Monday Night at the Movies* on September 7; it turned Goldwater's outspokenness on military action and nuclear weapons into a story of nuclear apocalypse (he had once joked about tossing a nuclear weapon into the men's room of the Kremlin.)[19] The 30-second ad showed a little girl in a field picking petals from a daisy. As she counted, the camera moved closer, finally freezing on a close-up of her eye. At the same time, an announcer started to intone a countdown. Suddenly, the screen erupted in a nuclear mushroom. The voiceover of Lyndon Johnson then admonished: "These are the stakes; to make a world in which all God's children can live, or to go into the darkness. Either we must love each other or we must die." Then words appeared on the screen: "On November 3rd, vote for President Johnson."[20]

The ad served to remind American voters of Goldwater's propensity for warlike statements, even though the spot never mentioned the Republican or made reference to him. More than forty years after the ad ran, its creator, Tony Schwartz, said it was fair game based on Goldwater's record. "He had made two speeches" on the use of nuclear weapons, Schwartz recalled. "It was a very effective commercial."[21] The Goldwater campaign actually filed a complaint with the Fair Campaign Practices Committee to stop the ad, which didn't go through when the Johnson team made it clear the commercial would only be run once.[22] (Even Senator Hubert Humphrey, the Democratic vice-presidential candidate, publicly disapproved of the spot.) Still, for many Republicans, the Daisy Girl ad eviscerated whatever goodwill existed toward LBJ after he assumed office in place of Kennedy, the martyred president. "That's negative campaigning carried to an unbelievable excess," said Bill Brock, who in 1964 was a freshman Republican House member from Tennessee and later won election to the U.S. Senate.[23]

Though the ad ran only once on commercial television, it earned tremendous airtime through repetition and discussion on news shows. In a sense, the ad served as a precursor of the "free media" effect the Swift Boat Vets would have forty years later, when the group's spots, purchased on an initially small budget, attacked the military record of Senator John F. Kerry, the 2004 Democratic presidential nominee. In 1964 most of the Daisy Girl ad's repetitious playing came from three television networks' nightly news shows. Forty years later, the ability to post such controversial ads on the Internet and send them by e-mail had increased their visibility exponentially.

Ten days after "Daisy Girl" aired, the Johnson campaign ran a similar ad portraying a young girl licking an ice cream cone as a woman off-camera (the first female voiceover ever in a campaign commercial) patiently explained the history of nuclear testing and radioactivity. "Do you know what people used to do?" asked the motherly sounding narrator. She continued:

> They used to explode atomic bombs in the air. Now children should have lots of vitamin A and calcium, but they shouldn't have any strontium 90 or cesium 133. These things come from atomic bombs, and they are radioactive. They can make you die. Do you know what people finally did? They got together and signed a nuclear test ban treaty. And then the radioactive poison started to go away. But now there's a man who wants to be president of the United States, and he doesn't like this treaty. He fought against it. He even voted against it. He wants to go on testing more bombs. His name is Barry Goldwater, and, if he is elected, they might start testing all over again.[24]

This ad, also run just once, played on some of the same emotions as "Daisy Girl," with a slight twist—that if President Goldwater didn't kill your children, he would at least make them sick. Other ads showing mushroom clouds (one based on a comment Goldwater had made about the nuclear bomb being "merely another weapon") or listing other militaristic statements by Goldwater were put into rotation, with the same intent.

The Johnson campaign did run positive ads, mostly in a documentary style that portrayed the president as a careful thinker (a contrast with Goldwater) and a defender of the public programs that helped the poor, sick, and elderly (another contrast). Still, the attack commercials were far more prevalent. Goldwater Campaign Director Denison Kitchel acknowledged that the nuclear ads had been the most devastating to the campaign. "My candidate had been branded a bomb-dropper—and I couldn't figure out how to lick it," Kitchel told political advertising scholar Kathleen Hall Jamieson.[25] The whole Johnson ad campaign was effective because voters had not seen anything like it before on television. "They had not built up the cynicism and skepticism that now condition their response to negative ads," wrote political consultant Dick Morris. "If it was on television, they believed, it was probably true."[26]

For their part, Goldwater's ads were initially dedicated to improving the candidate's image. His campaign bought expensive 30-minute blocks for television specials in which the Arizona senator sat at a desk and answered an interviewer's questions, and another ad that showed Goldwater chatting with former President Eisenhower at his home in Gettysburg, Pennsylvania.

When these spots and films didn't improve Goldwater's poll numbers, his people developed a new tack. Through more polling, the campaign found an increasing number of voters were concerned about President Johnson's "personal honesty," after it was revealed that an old senate staff friend, Bobby Baker, had probably peddled influence to turn a $20,000-a-year job into a $2 million net worth. On October 11, Goldwater adviser Lou Guylay wrote a memo suggesting Goldwater take on a perceived "shocking decline in political morality."[27] Unfortunately, the ads crafted around this theme were clumsy and ineffective. They opened with video of another Johnson ally who was associated with scams, Billie Sol Estes, and a cartoon of Baker, opening the Capitol dome and dipping his arm inside. Another spot matched these images to a hyperbolic announcer, who sounded as if he were selling a B-movie: "Graft! Swindle! Juvenile Delinquency! Crime! Riots!"[28] All of this was accompanied with confusing footage of street violence, before cutting to Goldwater sitting in a quiet den, speaking to the camera. The intention was for Goldwater to seem like a calm presence cutting through the chaos, but the effect was an amateurish-looking campaign commercial.

Still, the campaign kept the "moral leadership" message in the rest of its ads. A final spot featuring then-citizen Ronald Reagan of California saying, "Let's get a real leader and not a power politician in the White House."[29] But that message was overshadowed by Johnson's attack ads, and their focus on fundamental issues of war and social welfare.

Lyndon Johnson's negative campaign commercials would be remembered for the trends they set and themes introduced. "Daisy Girl" was the first in a long series of Cold War–era campaign commercials to focus on a candidate's potential for launching a nuclear conflict. Just four years after that spot aired, the campaign of Vice President Hubert Humphrey, the 1968 Democratic presidential nominee, aired a spot—this time in color—that showed a nuclear bomb exploding. Then, the film of the explosion was reversed to show the mushroom cloud collapsing back into itself. "Do you want Castro to have the bomb?" the announcer asked. "Now? Do you want any country that doesn't have the bomb to be able to get it? Of course you don't. Where does Richard Nixon stand on the UN threat to stop the spread of nuclear weapons? He says he's in no hurry to pass it. Hubert Humphrey wants to stop the spread of nuclear weapons now before it mushrooms. Hubert Humphrey supports the UN treaty now, as do the 80 countries that have already signed it."[30]

The themes of "Daisy Girl" continued to resonate long after the Cold War ended. Many recalled the famous spot when, during the run-up to the 1996 Republican presidential primaries, Senator Richard G. Lugar of Indiana ran a series of spots that warned ominously of nuclear terrorists blowing up an American city. The commercials used actors, dramatic music, and jerky camera shots to depict the terror and chaos of a threatened nuclear attack. The senator, a foreign policy specialist, had warned that the bombings at the World Trade Center in February 1993 and in the federal building in Oklahoma City in April 1995 underscored American vulnerability to terrorism. Lugar, badly trailing his GOP primary foes, said in a letter released along with the ads that "it is not my intent to create unnecessary anxiety."[31] Whatever the intent, Lugar had little support among rank-and-file Republican primary voters, and he quickly dropped from the race.

Over the years, partisans across the political spectrum adopted "Daisy Girl" for their own ideological purposes. Images from the ad made a cameo appearance in an election cycle thirty-two years after its one-time airing, as part of a commercial for 1996 Republican presidential nominee Senator Bob Dole. The issue at hand had nothing to do with nuclear threats. Rather, Dole's television ad, attacking President Bill Clinton, included images of crack pipes and junkies shooting heroin. The spot opened with footage from "Daisy Girl," as the narrator said, "Thirty years ago, the biggest threat to her was nuclear war. Today the threat is drugs," before reeling off a litany of criticisms about the president's inadequate funding for antidrug programs and his first surgeon general, who had raised the specter of legalizing certain drugs (Clinton repudiated the remarks).[32] Dole's advisers thought Clinton could be vulnerable on the drug issue, and the ad became one of the tougher, more memorable spots of a relatively uncompetitive campaign. However, the ad ran in a vastly different context than 1964, doing Dole no good; he lost overwhelmingly to Clinton.

In January 2003, the far-left group MoveOn.org ran an updated version of the "Daisy Girl" spot, as a warning against the pending U.S.-led invasion of Iraq to depose dictator Saddam Hussein. The MoveOn commercial also featured a little girl picking petals from a daisy, unknowingly to the sound of a missile-launch countdown. At countdown's end, the screen filled with the image of a nuclear mushroom cloud, and the ad continued with the warning: "War with Iraq. Maybe it will end quickly. Maybe not. Maybe it will spread. Maybe extremists will take over countries with nuclear weapons. Maybe the unthinkable."[33]

No doubt "Daisy Girl" will continue to be incorporated into future candidacies according to the issues of the moment.

OTHER INNOVATIONS

The 1964 presidential campaign increased the outlets for negative campaigning not just through television advertising, but also with a wide wave of literature critical of the candidates in the form of books. Works such as J. Evetts Haley's *A Texan Looks at Lyndon* painted the political veteran in the worst possible light, as a corrupt power grabber lacking core convictions. Less than a year after the assassination of John F. Kennedy, the air was thick with conspiracy theories. Haley's book included a detailed look at the relationship between Johnson and swindler Billie Sol Estes. Haley pointed out that the three men who could have provided evidence in court against Estes all died of carbon monoxide poisoning from car engines. Other books that year were published with the goal of defeating one of the presidential candidates, early forms of what would become a multimillion-dollar phenomenon forty years later (described in detail in chapter 12). In that cycle, anti-Kerry books such as *Unfit for Command: Swiftboat Veterans Speak Out against John Kerry*, by John E. O'Neill and Jerome R. Corsi, criticized the senator's military conduct in Vietnam and helped cement opposition to his candidacy. And a slew of partisan books, aimed to coincide with the heat of campaign season, emanated from the left.

Other independent attempts at negative campaigning in the 1964 presidential race were almost comical. Perhaps the campaign's lowest moment came in October, when *Fact* magazine published the results of a pseudoscientific "psychiatrists' poll" about Goldwater's mental fitness to be president. The periodical's maverick publisher, Ralph Ginzburg, had rented the American Medical Association's roster of more than 12,000 psychiatrists from a broker of mailing lists. The doctors received a questionnaire asking Goldwater's psychological state of mind. Despite the obvious ethics breached by offering a diagnosis of somebody the professionals had not personally examined, more than one in seven psychiatrists responded. Of those, two-thirds said Goldwater was unfit to serve as president (571 replied that they could not judge the candidate's mental fitness at long range). Republicans suspected Democratic operatives were behind the "scientific" survey; Democrats said they had nothing to do with it.[34] Forty years later, Vic Gold, deputy press secretary for Goldwater's campaign, said the episode was the dirtiest part of the 1964 presidential campaign. "That really crossed the line," he said.[35]

NOTES

1. Robert Alan Goldberg, *Barry Goldwater* (New Haven, Conn.: Yale University Press, 1995), 210.

2. Lance Morrow, introduction to *The Best Year of Their Lives: Kennedy, Johnson, and Nixon in 1948—Learning the Secrets of Power* (New York: Basic Books, 2005), xiv.

3. Kathleen Hall Jamieson, *Packaging the Presidency: A History and Criticism of Presidential Campaign Advertising* (New York: Oxford University Press, 1984), 177.

4. Tony Schwartz, *The Responsive Chord* (Garden City, N.Y.: Anchor Books, 1973), 93.

5. Tape courtesy of the Julian P. Kanter Political Commercial Archive at the University of Oklahoma Political Communication Center. [Known hereafter in this chapter as the Kanter Archive.]

6. Interview with author, Queens, N.Y., Aug. 30, 2004.

7. Victor Kamber, *Poison Politics: Are Negative Campaigns Destroying Democracy?* (New York: Insight Books, 1997), 29.

8. Dick Morris, *Power Plays: Win or Lose—How History's Great Political Leaders Play the Game* (New York: ReganBooks, 2002), 281.

9. Ad courtesy of The American Museum of the Moving Image's "The Living Room Candidate: Presidential Campaign Commercials 1952–2004" (http://livingroomcandidate.movingimage.us/index.php) [Known hereafter in this chapter as The Living Room Candidate.]

10. The Living Room Candidate.

11. Rick Perlstein, *Before the Storm: Barry Goldwater and the Unmaking of the American Consensus* (New York: Hill and Wang, 2001), 264.

12. Perlstein, *Before the Storm*, 382.

13. Theodore H. White, *The Making of the President 1964* (New York: Atheneum, 1965), 201.

14. Jamieson, *Packaging the Presidency*, 183.

15. Jamieson, *Packaging the Presidency*, 172.

16. Tape courtesy of the Kanter Archive.

17. Tape courtesy of the Kanter Archive.

18. White, *The Making of the President 1964*, 352.

19. Jamieson, *Packaging the Presidency*, 186.

20. Ad courtesy of The Living Room Candidate.

21. Interview with author, by telephone, Jan. 25, 2005.

22. Jamieson, *Packaging the Presidency*, 200.

23. Interview with author, Annapolis, Md., Aug. 5, 2004.

24. Tape courtesy of the Kanter Archive.

25. Jamieson, *Packaging the Presidency*, 204.

26. Morris, *Power Plays*, 288.

27. Jamieson, *Packaging the Presidency*, 208.

28. Tape courtesy of the Kanter Archive.

29. Tape courtesy of the Kanter Archive.

30. Jamieson, *Packaging the Presidency*, 252.

31. Howard Kurtz, "Lugar Tries a Dramatic Approach; Ads Focus on Threat of Nuclear Terrorism," *The Washington Post*, Dec. 19, 1995.

32. Howard Kurtz and Spencer Hsu, "Dole Smacks Clinton with Drug-Policy Ads," *The Washington Post*, Aug. 27, 1996.

33. Byron York, *The Vast Left Wing Conspiracy: The Untold Story of How Democratic Operatives, Eccentric Billionaires, Liberal Activists, and Assorted Celebrities Tried to Bring Down a President—and Why They'll Try Even Harder Next Time* (New York: Crown Forum, 2005), 28–29.

34. Bruce L. Felknor, *Dirty Politics* (Lincoln, Neb.: iUniverse.com, Inc. [originally published by Norton], 1966, 2000), 226–29.

35. Interview with author, by telephone, Aug. 9, 2004.

4

Dismissive Politics: The Governor against the Actor

California Governor Edmund G. "Pat" Brown approached a group of well-groomed children in a school library in 1966. On the campaign trail in his quest for a third term, the governor first engaged the integrated classroom in light banter: "I bet you never heard of Governor Brown, did you?" the Democrat asked one shy girl, who shook her head, her lips sealed. "You don't know who's governor, and you don't care." He continued, "Who's president of the United States? Haven't you heard of President Johnson?" to a different school girl, who nodded. "You have. But you've never heard of Governor Brown?" He then jested, "That's terrible," which brought about smiles from his campaign aides and assembled teachers. Brown should have ended the routine photo-op session there; but he could not resist a wisecrack at the expense of his Republican opponent, former movie actor and rookie candidate Ronald Reagan. "And I want to tell you something else," Brown said. "You know I'm running against an actor. Remember this: you know who shot Abraham Lincoln, don't ya?"[1]

The campaign staffers and teachers erupted in laughter at the governor's seemingly lighthearted taunt of his opponent. But the Election Day results showed the joy would be short-lived for Brown. The scene, from the 30-minute Brown campaign film, *A Man against the Actor*, was indicative of the governor's misguided efforts to paint Reagan as a lightweight performer too inexperienced to lead state government. Brown further dismissed Reagan as a right-winger, in the thrall of political extremists out of tune with the California mainstream. For Brown, a self-proclaimed liberal unimpressed with the upstart conservative entertainer, those tactics ultimately backfired, as he lost to Reagan by a million votes.

The 1966 California governor's race did not break records for the highest wattage negativity, in terms of scorching, aggressive attack ads on television or searing campaign-trail rhetoric. But it exemplified an oft-used form of negative campaigning aimed at diminishing the standing of nontraditional candidates and of suggesting opponents were just not smart enough to hold the offices they sought. "They always had the feeling until late in the campaign that he was just another movie actor, and the movie industry is noted for its featherbrained, irresponsible people," said Reagan's campaign consultant Bill Roberts a couple of years after the race.[2]

Whether the candidates have been actors, athletes, or from backgrounds outside the sphere of public office, political opponents have aimed to paint them as inconsequential. The technique should have lost much of its luster in 1966 when the governor of California so badly underestimated his Republican opponent. Yet the attack ads run against the B-movie actor foreshadowed a long list of campaigns in which "serious" officeholders sought to portray their opponents as intellectual lightweights. In many ways, it presaged the tactics opponents used, to varying degrees, against Republican Arnold Schwarzenegger during the 2003 recall election, when he sought to oust a Democratic governor who had been an elected official for twenty years. Reagan's victory helped pave the way for future candidates who weren't politicians. Those who traded acting for politics went on to win after an entertainment career include Fred Grandy—aka Gopher on *The Love Boat*—who served as a Republican congressman from Iowa for four terms, and musician Sonny Bono, Republican of California, who was mayor of Palm Springs and a U.S. representative for three years before he died in a skiing accident in 1998. Well-known athletes who were elected to office include, to name a few: Senator Bill Bradley, D-N.J., previously a professional basketball star; Congressman Jack Kemp, R-N.Y., secretary of Housing and Urban Development and the GOP vice-presidential nominee in 1996, whose first career was as an NFL quarterback; J.C. Watts, a prominent GOP congressman who starred as quarterback at the University of Oklahoma, and Steve Largent, an NFL Hall of Fame wide receiver who served in the U.S. House as a Republican from Oklahoma.

POLAR OPPOSITES

The 1966 California governor's race featured two diametrically opposed candidates in both their political philosophies and their professional backgrounds. Just as Reagan called for less government involvement in people's lives and greater individual responsibility, Brown championed government as a force of good for residents of California, which was in the midst of a post–World War II population boom that made it the fastest growing state in the nation. Governor since 1959, Brown sought a third term as a way of continuing his activist agenda. One of his pet projects was an enormous water-use development program that would shift aquatic resources from lush Northern California to the parched southern portion of the state. He also oversaw the creation of new University of California campuses to meet the higher-education needs of the state's burgeoning population, along with expansion of the state and community college systems. Other tangible results from his administration included laws covering fair employment practices to stamp out racial bias and creating a state economic development commission, along with a consumers' council, to represent the public interest in legislative hearings, regulatory procedures, and court cases.[3]

Brown wanted to go down in history as one of the Golden State's great progressive governors, like Earl Warren, the moderate Republican elected three times before being appointed chief justice of the United States by President Dwight D. Eisenhower, and Hiram Johnson, a two-term GOP governor in the early twentieth century who gave California the recall, initiative, and referendum. A third term would keep alive the political career of the 61-year-old Brown. If he won re-election, he might at some point be appointed attorney general of the United States or Supreme Court justice. Or, just possibly, be in a position to make a credible White House bid.[4] (Brown hoped to be selected as President Lyndon Baines Johnson's running mate on the 1964 Democratic ticket, but the honor went to Senator Hubert Humphrey of Minnesota.)

A third term would also cap a rollercoaster political career in which he lost a few races early and then won the governor's campaigns against prominent

Republican opponents. Unlike Reagan, who at age 55 first won elected office later in life after a success in an entirely different line of work, Brown was a proud career pol. He had attended public schools in working class San Francisco, where local law enforcement regularly turned a blind eye to prostitution and gambling outfits whose payroll they sometimes were on. Brown acquired his nickname during an orating contest (which he won) selling World War I Liberty Bonds; Brown ended his speech with Patrick Henry's revolutionary cry, "Give me liberty or give me death," and the connection stuck.[5] Brown could not afford college; instead he worked in his father's cigar store during the day and studied law at night, receiving a degree from San Francisco College of Law in 1927 (the institution did not require students to have earned an undergraduate degree). He started a law practice in San Francisco and was a Republican at a time when the party had an active presence in the politics in the city later dominated by Democrats. At twenty-three, Brown ran for state Assembly in 1928 on the GOP ticket and lost.

The Depression turned him into a devotee of President Franklin Delano Roosevelt; in 1939 Brown ran for district attorney of San Francisco, this time as a Democrat. He lost that race, but tried for the same position in 1943. He won on that try, beating an incumbent of more than twenty years. A crusading prosecutor, Brown cracked down on prostitution, gambling, and other vices common in the city. In 1946 he lost a bid for state attorney general but won that office four years later. There he continued his crusading ways; he campaigned against slumlords, argued for the repeal of an old law that prohibited the sale of liquor to Indians, and insisted that alcohol licenses be restored to Japanese bar and restaurant owners who had been interned during World War II.[6] By 1958 he was ready to run for governor; he won by more than a million votes over William F. Knowland, the Republican Senate leader who hoped to use the California governorship as a launching pad for a White House bid. Brown enhanced his reputation as a giant slayer in 1962 by soundly beating former Vice President Richard Nixon, who ran for governor of California as a way to resurrect his political career, after his narrow loss to Senator John F. Kennedy in the 1960 presidential election.

PROBLEMS AHEAD

By the time Brown sought a third term, though, the balding, slightly pudgy, bespectacled governor, often referred to in newspaper profiles as "owlish," seemed a spent force. Voters had started to resist some of the progressive legislation he fathered. In 1963, early in his second term, Brown had helped push through the legislature the Rumford Fair Housing Act, which banned discrimination in the sale or rental of housing. Conservative forces objected and placed Proposition 14 on the ballot to nullify the new law. More than 70 percent voted to overturn the housing initiative supported by Brown.

The Free Speech Movement (FSM) at University of California at Berkeley and its protests further put Brown in the political hot seat. In the fall of 1964 students had organized demonstrations to protest for free speech rights on campus and pressing social issues. After the university disciplined several students for trespassing, the FSM held daily rallies and occupied Sproul Hall, the campus administration building. Pressure mounted on Brown to act, and on December 3, the governor ordered the state and local police to restore order at the University of California's flagship campus. More than 700 youths, some students, some not, were arrested, and 578 were found guilty of trespassing, resisting arrest, or both.[7] Brown caught flak from both sides—those who felt the students' civil rights had been violated and those who excoriated the governor for allowing disorder at the campus of the state's top public university.

In the sweltering summer of 1965, the Watts riots erupted in inner-city South Los Angeles. An explosion of long-simmering tension between the local community and law enforcement, and deteriorating social conditions came to a head on August 11, after police arrested a young black man for drunken driving. Rioting broke out and quickly spread, accompanied by looting and arson, and Los Angeles Police Chief William Parker concluded his officers needed help from the state to quell the violence. Governor Brown was on vacation in Greece at the time, and Lt. Governor Glenn Anderson ended up belatedly sending in the California National Guard. Days later law enforcement put down the disturbance, which caused 34 deaths, injured 1,000 people, and damaged more than 600 buildings.[8]

This confluence of events made for an unfavorable environment in which to seek reelection. Not to mention voters' misgivings about granting a governor a third term. "Politicians tend to wear out their welcome, especially in big, diverse states," said Stu Spencer, Reagan's campaign consultant.[9] Some aides urged Brown to retire, but the governor was determined to run again. He asked Fred Dutton, a longtime political adviser and former top aide in the attorney general's office whom the governor later appointed to the University of California Board of Regents, to manage his campaign. A graduate of Berkeley and Stanford Law School, Dutton had moved to Washington to work in the Kennedy administration and stayed in the nation's capital to practice law. Dutton agreed reluctantly to the governor's request, despite the unfavorable political climate. "There was an attitude in the campaign, at state [Democratic] headquarters, that this was really an uphill thing. That Pat was over his best political years," Dutton recalled.[10]

Brown had been in public office for twenty-three years when the 1966 governor's race came along; Reagan had never been an elected as a public official. The contrast made for an inviting target for Governor Brown. He would deride the lack of government experience by Reagan, who portrayed himself as a citizen-politician. After working his way through Eureka College in Illinois, Reagan became a sports radio announcer in Iowa. A screen test in 1937 won him a contract in Hollywood. Although never a major star, during the next two decades he appeared in more than fifty films, including *Knute Rockne— All-American* (1940), *King's Row* (1941), *The Hasty Heart* (1950), and *Bedtime for Bonzo* (1951).

Yet while Reagan had made plenty of campy movies and for a short time in the late 1950s worked the stage circuit in Las Vegas, his career in show business had also been laced with political activism. As president of the Screen Actors Guild, Reagan became embroiled in disputes over Communism in the film industry. Initially an FDR New Deal Democrat, Reagan's views over time shifted dramatically rightward. He toured the country as a corporate television host for General Electric and became a spokesman for conservative causes. He campaigned for Richard Nixon against John F. Kennedy in the 1960 presidential election, giving more than two hundred speeches for the Republican. Reagan gained national fame from his televised speech on behalf of the 1964 Republican presidential nominee, Senator Barry Goldwater of Arizona, a rare bright spot in the landslide GOP loss.

When a group of California businessmen persuaded him to seek the governorship in 1966, the stage was set for a dramatic showdown with Brown. "Reagan was a very well-known person. He was not a stranger to the voters," recalled Lyn Nofziger, the Republican's campaign press secretary in 1966 and later a key White House adviser. Moreover, Reagan had generally played a likable fellow in the movies. Governor Brown "had to change a perception of Ronald Reagan, nice guy."[11]

Those who met Reagan in those days were quickly impressed by his political acumen. That included Stu Spencer, a former parks and recreation director in the suburban Los Angeles city of Alhambra who would became active in local Republican politics and would go on to pioneer modern techniques of political consulting. In 1964, he and partner Bill Roberts worked on New York Governor Nelson Rockefeller's near-miss challenge to Goldwater in the California presidential primary. Their reputations burnished, Reagan wanted to hire the Los Angeles-based firm Spencer-Roberts for advertising and other campaign work. The firm had already been approached by his moderate Republican primary opponent, former San Francisco Mayor George Christopher. The pair signed on with Reagan. "We figured out he was a hell of a communicator," Spencer said. "We just felt he kind of suited the times."[12]

Still, early in 1966 polls showed that Reagan would lose to Brown, while Mayor Christopher could beat the governor if he were the GOP nominee. So the Brown team tried to set up the race they wanted, to get Republican primary voters to choose the seemingly weakest general election opponent for him to run against in the next election. Freelancing for the campaign, Brown's longtime friend Harry Lerner, a former San Francisco newspaperman with a reputation as a street fighter in political campaigns, dug out the records of a 1939 case in which Christopher, then a dairy owner, had been convicted of violating milk-pricing laws.[13] The prosecutor in the case had termed the violations technical ones, and the material had been used and reused without success against Christopher in his San Francisco supervisor and mayoral campaigns.[14] In the gubernatorial primary, however, the episode came to have more resonance with voters: Lerner had leaked the information to Washington columnist Drew Pearson, who wrote about the events from a quarter century earlier. Christopher sank in the polls, and Reagan ended up winning the Republican primary by more than a two-to-one margin.

It was clear the damaging information on Christopher had come from those allied with Brown's campaign. The incident hurt the governor, who had a reputation as a relatively clean campaigner. The negative tactics made him look like just another politician willing to do anything to win. Brown later regretted the episode. "Pat was a very moral man who saw that as an immoral thing to have done," said Fred Jordan, Brown's assistant press secretary.[15]

CAMPAIGN ADS TARGET AN "ACTING" GOVERNOR

After the primaries Brown trailed Reagan in the polls, and it was clear the Republican nominee's candidacy would have to be taken seriously. But Brown refused to take Reagan—The Man—seriously, and this became a central thrust of the governor's campaign to stay in office. With Brown's political problems deepening, his campaign team realized he would have to go negative on Reagan to win. In June, advisers suggested choosing a few issues to hammer Reagan with and raise them repeatedly, starting with his lack of government experience.[16] So the television commercials released by Brown's campaign often focused on Reagan's status as a first-time candidate. Most ended with a variation of the tagline, "Vote for a real governor, not an acting one." The ads, produced by filmmaker Charles Guggenheim, were on the cutting edge technologically. "The photography, the surface lightheartedness that covered a tougher edge underneath," Jordan said. "It would be misleading to say that this was negative advertising. A better word is dismissive."[17]

One Brown ad began with a camera slowly panning the 1966 ballot, showing candidates in races for Congress, state attorney general, and other statewide elected offices, concluding with governor. All candidates had an avocation under their names, except for Reagan; his was left blank. The announcer then said, "If Ronald Regan can't find anything in his background to qualify him for office, how can he expect the rest of us to find it?" Another Brown ad opened with a still shot of the statehouse in Sacramento. The narrator said, "The biggest job in the biggest state is right there." Then Reagan's silky-smooth voice was interspersed, but he sounded flummoxed. He had been asked at a news conference about details of some water project legislation, and he had to admit ignorance about the subject. "Now you've got me on something I don't know about," he said, clearly on the defensive. To make sure the point was not lost on television viewers, the narrator voiced the line, "Vote for a real governor, not an acting one."[18]

Brown's campaign also recruited Reagan's fellow actors to argue the case against him. One ad featured Burt Lancaster, the handsome, vibrant performer, looking straight into the camera in a stand-up shot. Lancaster recalled how he had played many different roles in the movies and onstage, but none readied him to pursue those professions in real life. "I don't think my citizen interest in public affairs qualifies me to run for an office as high as governor," Lancaster told viewers. He continued: "Being a governor requires training and experience of a very special kind. The experience I have as an actor has nothing to do with the experience a man must have to make important decisions affecting the lives and the economy of 19 million Californians."[19] (Reagan had his own entertainment-related ad, featuring a testimonial by Chuck Connors, star of the television show *The Rifleman*; he cited lack of support for Brown by fellow Democrats, including Los Angeles Mayor Sam Yorty, who unsuccessfully challenged the governor in the 1966 primary, and powerful Democratic Assembly Speaker Jesse Unruh, with whom Brown had constantly feuded.)

Brown's ads derided Reagan not only as an actor but as a middling one at that. One Brown spot featured clips from Reagan in some of his less flattering movie and television commercial roles, including as a pitchman for Boraxo waterless hand cleaner. A similar commercial showed Reagan in a scene with a monkey in *Bedtime for Bonzo*," in which he played a young college professor who attempted to raise a chimpanzee like a human child. Each ad ended with the narrator warning, "Over the years Ronald Reagan has played many roles. This year he wants to be governor. Are you willing to pay the price of admission?"[20]

Brown's biographical campaign hammered home this theme of professional-versus-amateur in the 30-minute film *A Man against the Actor*. It ran through Brown's defeats of the Republican political giants Knowland and Nixon; it also noted his California roots, as his Irish and German immigrant ancestors had moved to the state during the mid-nineteenth century. Then the tone of the film changed when the narrator said, "This year he faces a new kind of adversary," imposed over clips from Reagan's movies. On screen, Brown later greeted a child on a bike who was hanging out with his friends in what looked like a typical Southern California suburban neighborhood. The youth was years away from being able to vote, but Brown stopped to talk to him, seeking to show his rapport with all Californians. "I'm running against a motion picture star, Ronald Reagan," Brown said. The boy replied he had not seen Reagan's movies. Brown then waved his hand dismissively and with a wry grin, said, "*Death Valley Days*. Terrible. Don't waste your time," as he walked away, having confused Reagan's films with his television acting roles.[21]

In fact, in the same campaign spot, Brown's interaction with children led to his most famous outburst against Reagan, the crack, "You know who shot Abraham Lincoln, don't ya?." The quip was only a quick clip from the half-hour film; ad producer Charles Guggenheim had included the unscripted moment from the campaign trail to show off the governor's dry sense of humor.[22] As the remark was recounted in news articles, tremendous backlash grew among the press, other politicians, and actors. Jack Palance was particularly upset. He had been participating in a telethon for Brown's reelection but stormed off the set when he heard of the joke. "Attack him if you wish for lack of experience," the movie star said. "But don't go after him just because he's an actor."[23] And actor Dan Blocker, who played Hoss in the television show, *Bonanza*, indignantly resigned from Brown's campaign committee.[24]

Reagan helped himself with a cool reaction to the remark. He first learned of it from Lyn Nofziger, his campaign press secretary, after addressing the Commonwealth Club in San Francisco. Nofziger urged Reagan not to react negatively. So when reporters asked him about the remark, he responded sheepishly, "I just can't believe Pat Brown would say something like that," allowing himself to play the victim of a cheap shot by the incumbent governor.[25] As much as anything else in the campaign, the line made the governor look mean and condescending, and helped convince voters that Brown did not deserve a third term. "It totally backfired on him," Spencer said. "Take that 20 seconds out, and it was absolutely a good documentary."[26]

In hindsight, the effort to demean Reagan as an actor can be seen as fruitless from the start. As Reagan biographer Lou Cannon noted in *Governor Reagan: His Rise to Power*, the San Francisco–bred Brown did not take into account the importance of the film industry in Southern California, where being an actor was not necessarily held against a candidate.[27] By 1966 the population of Southern California had exploded, and being in the movie industry did not carry a stigma. Reagan also deftly shrugged off the insults, even before Brown made the infamous Lincoln remark. No group "should be relegated to second-class citizenship by reasons of their occupation," he said in August 1965 during the exploratory phase of his campaign.[28] And there was already precedent in California for backing a candidate with a show business background to high office: George L. Murphy, a former nightclub dancer and screen actor, who had been elected to the U.S. Senate as a Republican in 1964. Going back further, Democrat Helen Gahagan Douglas, a veteran Broadway and Hollywood actress, won three terms in the U.S. House of Representatives before losing a Senate bid to Richard Nixon in 1950.

Reagan won plaudits in some corners for his handling of the situation. In endorsing the Republican for governor, the *Los Angeles Times* wrote that Reagan's campaign "has been vigorous, clean and positive. Throughout, [he] has steadfastly ignored attacks upon his political integrity and personal motives. He has comported himself with dignity and courage in the face of brutal name-calling and guilt-by-association tactics."[29]

Even Brown seemed to know the actor issue was not playing very well. "I only wish the people down in Southern California would appreciate my greatness as much as you do up here in the north," Brown would tell Northern California audiences late in the campaign, only half-jokingly.[30] Jack Germond, the veteran political journalist, recalled traveling with Brown shortly before the election when the governor admitted he could not understand Reagan's appeal. "I never thought it would end up this way," Brown said aboard his small campaign plane. "I never thought the day would come when I couldn't beat some tap dancer," a reference that suggested the governor was equating his opponent with Senator Murphy.[31]

OTHER LINES OF ATTACK

Reagan's acting roles were not Brown's only source of criticism. The governor's campaign also sought to tie Reagan to the ultraconservative John Birch Society, an anti-Communist group named after an American missionary and U.S. intelligence officer who was killed by the Chinese Communists in 1945. Robert Welch, the society's founder, contended that President Dwight D. Eisenhower and other leading U.S. officials had been communist traitors. A 1961 report by California State Attorney General Stanley Mosk described the society's membership as composed "primarily of wealthy businessmen, retired military leaders, and little old ladies in tennis shows" who were bound together by an "obsessive fear" of Communism.[32] In 1962, Reagan had raised money for a Southern California Republican congressman and John Birch member, John Rousselot.[33] So a Brown campaign ad sought to highlight that and other linkages. "Is it integrity for Mr. Reagan to deny all connection with the John Birch Society, when his state labor chairman and four members of his finance committee are known members of this secret society?"[34]

Like the taunts about Reagan's acting career, these attacks fell flat. By the time Reagan ran for governor, his campaign had gone to considerable effort to distance him from the extremist group, intentionally excluding Birch members. Reagan issued a press release saying he never was a member of the group and disagreed with Welch's "reckless and imprudent statements."[35] Other conservative groups, such as the United Republicans of California, the California Republican Assembly, the Young Republicans, and the Young Americans for Freedom, played only small roles in Reagan's campaign.[36] Reagan also kept his distance from Barry Goldwater, the Republican presidential nominee two years earlier, who was not allowed to campaign on behalf of the GOP gubernatorial candidate. And after he won the GOP nomination, Reagan made a public visit to former President Eisenhower, that symbol of moderation.[37] All this left little fodder for Brown to convince voters that Reagan was an extreme right-winger.

As a challenger trying to oust an incumbent, Reagan employed some negative campaigning himself, but focused largely on public policy issues. He sought to turn Brown's charges of amateurism on their head. In a conventional line of attack for a challenger campaign, a Reagan television ad noted that the state budget had increased dramatically under Brown, by $1.8 billion, which would come out of the pockets of hardworking taxpayers. "That's the price we paid for his eight years of professional experience in Sacramento," the narrator said.[38] The California electorate was receptive to the outsider's message. "The experience thing we dealt with on the basis of being very honest and candid and admitting that he was not a politician; he was a citizen-politician," recalled Reagan campaign consultant Bill Roberts. "This went over great with people, because they could equate themselves with that very nicely and say, 'Yes, by God, this is the way the country was started, with citizens assuming a responsibility in government.'"[39]

Reagan's campaigning took a sharper turn through ads that played upon the public's discomfort with student protestors, urban rioters, and the fissures in society that were being exacerbated by America's growing role in the war in Vietnam. His ads criticized crime rates and lauded private-sector housing and economic development in the vast state. Reagan in particular latched onto "the mess in Berkeley"—the protests associated with the Free Speech Movement. While Governor Brown had sent in police to clear away students who occupied university offices, Reagan said the protests never should have been allowed in the first place, and he promised to get tough on those who stoked unrest on campus. "Will we allow a great university to be brought to its knees by a noisy, dissident minority? Will we meet their neurotic vulgarities with vacillation and weakness?" Reagan asked on January 4, 1966, in his official campaign announcement speech. "Or will we tell those entrusted with administering the university we expect them to enforce a code based on decency, common sense and dedication to the high and noble purpose of the university."[40]

Polls showed California voters thought the behavior of the protestors posed a greater problem for the state than unemployment, pollution, or transportation.[41] The issue gave Reagan an opening to highlight the populist themes of his campaign: morality, law and order, strong leadership, and traditional values.[42] Reagan was particularly skilled in relaying this message in a non-threatening way. While emphasizing support for repeal of the Rumford Act, the open-housing measure, he also stressed his opposition to "anything that smacks of bigotry and discrimination," adding, "We must make those who walk with prejudice walk alone."[43]

The situation played to Reagan's strengths. "He was on the side of public opinion in California at the time," recalled Fred Dutton, campaign manager for Brown. "It was a situation loaded with negatives" for the governor.[44] Here Reagan also laid out an effective populist/outsider style of campaigning that attracted legions of supporters to his side, many of them working-class, high school–educated Democrats, who stayed with him through his 1980 election as president.[45]

Reagan also benefited immensely from entering the political scene at a time when television was becoming increasingly important in advertising and swaying public opinions about candidates. Television fed the alienation many voters felt by bringing into their homes graphic pictures of the problems that most frightened them, such as race riots and student unrest.[46] These images, combined with Reagan's professional delivery and speaking style, hit home for many voters. "He did it with the economy of words that only an actor could bring to it," said Fred Jordan, Brown's assistant press secretary.[47]

On Election Day, California voters were clearly with Reagan. He received 3,742,913 million votes to 2,749,174 for Brown.[48] The landslide victory was clear; Brown won only three counties out of 58: San Francisco, Alameda, and rural Plumas. Republicans across the nation also had a banner year in 1966, picking up ten governorships previously held by Democrats and making massive gains in U.S. Senate and House seats (though not enough to win majorities in either chamber).

Angry populism, a campaign theme that Reagan used heavily in 1966, also became embedded in the campaign culture in future years. Richard Nixon made it a successful plank in his successful 1968 White House bid, which appealed to the "silent majority" of law-abiding citizens sick and tired of societal chaos so often recounted on the evening news. His vice president, Spiro Agnew, took that theme as well, responding to urban riots with calls for law and order, and insisting the disturbances were caused by "this permissive climate and misguided compassion of public opinion."[49] In California in 1969, San Francisco State College professor S.I. Hayakawa earned widespread attention when he pulled an electrical plug on a rowdy group of demonstrators, which deprived them of their public address system.[50] He soon became president of the college and was later elected U.S. senator as a Republican.

Underestimating Reagan was a theme that repeated itself throughout his storied political career. As Reagan geared up for a Republican primary challenge to President Gerald R. Ford in 1976, Stu Spencer, the president's lead strategist, warned of downplaying the threat posed by the insurgent conservative political activist.[51] Spencer knew Reagan's political prowess all too well, having worked for him ten years earlier. Ford, an unelected president unpopular with many conservatives in his own party, narrowly beat back Reagan's challenge that year, but not without having to muster the full powers and patronage of the White House to sway uncommitted delegates to support him. Outside of Spencer, the Ford's campaign team had initially downplayed Reagan's popularity and ability to mount an effective challenge to a sitting president. Reagan shocked the president's team by winning a series of late primaries that year; in fact despite ultimately coming up just short in the delegate count, Reagan actually won more primary votes overall than Ford, 4.61 million to 4.48 million, or 50.7 percent to 49.3 percent.[52] Reagan nearly wrested away the nomination from the incumbent president at the Republican National Convention in Kansas City.

Four years later, Reagan won the Republican nomination. And once again his opponent, President Jimmy Carter, and his advisers dismissed him as a lightweight unprepared to take the reins of the federal government, and a right-winger likely to lead the United States into a nuclear war. Early in the

1980 campaign, Carter's image maker, Gerald Rafshoon, drew up a list of Reagan attributes to be emphasized in TV ads belittling him, including "untested, old, dumb, actor, naïve, inexperienced, Republican, right wing."[53] But as the campaign progressed, the American people, deeply dissatisfied with Carter's performance and encouraged by Reagan's strong debate showing only days before balloting, were quite willing to give the challenger a chance. He won in a landslide, carrying 489 Electoral College votes to Carter's 49.

The Democratic leadership in Congress then underestimated the man who had just scored a crushing win over an incumbent president. Shortly after Reagan's victory, House Speaker Tip O'Neill famously told the president-elect, condescendingly, "You're in the big leagues now." Reagan rose to the challenge, initially running rings around the opposition in Congress and leading the nation in a new direction while O'Neill and other Democratic leaders struggled to pull themselves together from their campaign losses. In his first year in office, Reagan pushed through sharp tax reductions, some cutbacks in federal domestic spending, and a dramatic buildup in defense spending.

That 1966 governor's race is notable for another tactic in negative campaigning that would appear later: meddling with the other party's primary in an attempt to pick the weakest general election candidate. The tactic Brown employed was repeated 36 years later in another California governor's race, again during the Republican primary. The leader going into the March 11, 2002, election was former Los Angeles Mayor Richard Riordan, a moderate whose stands on social issues were well to the left of many Republican primary voters. Riordan had argued that only a centrist could beat Democratic Governor Gray Davis in the November election. So Davis poured $10 million into attack ads against Riordan, emphasizing inconsistencies on abortion and other issues. Riordan ended up losing in the primary to conservative Bill Simon, a businessman and novice candidate, by a wide margin. Simon then fell to Davis in the fall, just as the Democratic governor had envisioned. (Davis's political fortunes were soon to be cut short, as voters recalled him less than two years later, and replaced him with Arnold Schwarzenegger, another actor without a single day of experience in public office.)

Though the 1966 election represented the first of many efforts to dismiss Reagan's intellectual prowess, intellectual snobbery certainly wasn't a new political tactic. When the eloquent and erudite Adlai Stevenson ran for president against Dwight Eisenhower in 1952, a woman supposedly gushed to the

Democratic candidate after a rally, "Every thinking person will be voting for you." Stevenson replied, "Madam, that is not enough. I need a majority."[54] But the California Democratic governor took the "dumb actor/intellectual lightweight" theme to new heights in 1966, thinking that voters would see through a shallow candidate. Instead, those actions helped set Reagan on a political course that would end up in the White House.

NOTES

1. Courtesy of the UCLA Film and Television Archive, "A Man Against the Actor," 1966.

2. Lou Cannon, *Ronnie and Jesse: A Political Odyssey* (Garden City, N.Y.: Doubleday & Company, Inc., 1969), 80.

3. Ethan Rarick, *California Rising: The Life and Times of Pat Brown* (Berkeley: University of California Press, 2005), 342.

4. Rarick, *California Rising*, 99.

5. Judith Michaelson, "Edmund G. 'Pat' Brown, Former Governor, Dies: Democrat Guided California through One of Its Greatest Public and Private Building Booms. He Was 90," *The Los Angeles Times*, Feb. 17, 1996.

6. Jonathan Kirsch, "The California That Pat Built," *Los Angeles Times*, Jan. 16, 2005.

7. Kirsch, "The California That Pat Built."

8. Martin Schiesl, ed., *Responsible Liberalism: Edmund G. "Pat" Brown and Reform Government in California, 1958–1967* (Los Angeles: Edmund G. "Pat" Brown Institute of Public Affairs, 2003), 10.

9. Interview with author, Palm Desert, Calif., Nov. 27, 2004.

10. Interview with author, Washington, D.C., Feb. 16, 2005.

11. Interview with author, Washington, D.C., Feb. 14, 2005.

12. Interview with author, Palm Desert, Calif., Nov. 27, 2004.

13. Rarick, *California Rising*, 354.

14. Cannon, *Ronnie and Jesse*, 70.

15. Interview with author, by telephone, Jan. 26, 2005.

16. Matthew Dallek, *The Right Moment: Ronald Reagan's First Victory and the Decisive Turning Point in American Politics* (New York: Free Press, 2000), 229.

17. Interview with author, by telephone, Jan. 26, 2005.

18. Courtesy of the UCLA Film and Television Archive, "Reagan vs. Brown (Political Spots)."

19. UCLA Archive, "Reagan vs. Brown (Political Spots)."

20. UCLA Archive, "Reagan vs. Brown (Political Spots)."

21. UCLA Archive, "Reagan vs. Brown (Political Spots)."

22. Dallek, *The Right Moment*, 235.

23. Dallek, *The Right Moment*, 235.

24. Lyn Nofziger, "Ronald Reagan: 1911–2004—How He Always Left His Detractors Bewildered," *The Sacramento Bee*, June 13, 2004.

25. Interview with author, Washington, D.C., Feb. 14, 2005.

26. Interview with author, Palm Desert, Calif., Nov. 27, 2004.

27. Lou Cannon, *Governor Reagan: His Rise to Power* (New York: PublicAffairs, 2003), 151–152.

28. *The Sacramento Bee*, Aug. 3, 1965, as quoted in Rarick, *California Rising*, 343.

29. *The Los Angeles Times*, as quoted in Gerard J. De Groot, "'A Goddamned Electable Person': The 1966 California Gubernatorial Campaign of Ronald Reagan," *History* 82.267 (1997): 440.

30. Cannon, *Ronnie and Jesse*, 86.

31. Jack W. Germond, *Fat Man in a Middle Seat: Forty Years of Covering Politics* (New York: Random House, 1999), 154.

32. Cannon, *Governor Reagan*, 152.

33. Seth Rosenfeld, "The Campus Files: The Governor's Race," *The San Francisco Chronicle*, June 9, 2002.

34. Courtesy of the UCLA Film and Television Archive, "Reagan vs. Brown (Political Spots)."

35. Rosenfeld, *The San Francisco Chronicle*, June 9, 2002.

36. Dallek, *The Right Moment*, 231.

37. De Groot, *History*, 436.

38. Courtesy of the UCLA Film and Television Archive, "Reagan vs. Brown (Political Spots)."

39. Cannon, *Ronnie and Jesse*, 82.

40. Rosenfeld, *The San Francisco Chronicle*, June 9, 2002.

41. California Poll, June 24, 1966, as quoted in Rarick, 362.

42. Gerard De Groot, "Reagan's Rise: Ronald Reagan in California during the 1960s," *History Today*, September 1995.

43. Cannon, *Ronnie and Jesse*, 86.

44. Interview with author, Washington, D.C., Feb. 16, 2005.

45. De Groot, *History Today*, September 1995.

46. De Groot, *History*, 430–31.

47. Interview with author, by telephone, Jan. 26, 2005.

48. Cannon, *Governor Reagan*, 160.

49. Francis X. Clines, "Spiro T. Agnew, Point Man for Nixon Who Resigned Vice Presidency, Dies at 77," *New York Times*, Sept. 16, 1996.

50. De Groot, *History Today*, September 1995.

51. Interview with author, Palm Desert, Calif., Nov. 27, 2004.

52. Craig Shirley, preface to *Reagan's Revolution: The Untold Story of the Campaign That Started It All* (Nashville: Nelson Current, 2005), xix.

53. Walter Shapiro, "Underestimating Intelligence Isn't Very Smart," *USA Today*, June 8, 2004.

54. Shapiro, "Underestimating Intelligence Isn't Very Smart."

5

"The Truth Shall Rise Again": Brock versus Gore for U.S. Senate, 1970

When Al Gore ran for president in 2000, news profiles of the vice president often gave only passing mention of the defeat of his father and namesake, a U.S. senator, three decades earlier. And while Albert Gore Sr. is not as famous as his son, the stately populist Democrat was on the losing end of a long, divisive, and hard-edged campaign that stands out as being among the most negative of its era.

In the 1970 U.S. Senate race in Tennessee, Gore and Republican Congressman William E. Brock of Chattanooga sparred over the war in Vietnam, prayer in school, gun control, school busing, confirmation of Southern Supreme Court nominees, and many other searing issues of the day. The contest offered a blueprint to scores of campaigns in the following decades in which Republican candidates assailed their Democratic opponents as liberals who were out of touch with the constituents they sought to represent.

The Senate campaign was also the linchpin of President Richard Nixon's "Southern Strategy," which was designed to turn the region from a reliably Democratic voting bloc to a solidly Republican one; critics charged the tactic depending on using race as a wedge to split the Democratic base. And the

1970 race made modern, television-age campaign techniques a mainstay in Tennessee and other parts of the South. Brock's television spots proved particularly effective because they put much of the negativity in the mouths of ordinary citizens, not the candidate himself.

The campaign produced wounds that for Gore's supporters have never quite healed. They contend there were less-than-subtle racial overtones to Brock's message. Republicans argue that Gore's alienation from his own constituents and his aloofness brought about his defeat, a reflection of Vice President Spiro Agnew's characterization of him at the time as the "Southern regional chairman of the eastern establishment."[1]

TWO SONS OF TENNESSEE

Both Gore and Brock were native sons of the Volunteer State, though from different social strata. Born in 1907, Gore boosted himself up from humble origins to a successful political career. After attending a one-room school in Possum Hollow, Tenn., he worked his way through college, attending classes as his finances allowed. He studied law at night at Nashville's YMCA Law School and married a fellow law student, Pauline LaFon. Gore was eventually elected local superintendent of schools in Smith County, and in 1938 he won election to the U.S. House of Representatives. In Congress he was among the first lawmakers to warn of looming threats from Nazi Germany and Imperial Japan, at a time when many of his colleagues, like broad swaths of the nation, were isolationist.[2] He also was a strong proponent of free trade.

Gore advanced to the Senate in 1952 when he successfully challenged Senator Kenneth McKellar, age 83, in the Democratic primary, thereby knocking off the chairman of the powerful Senate Appropriations Committee. McKellar's campaign signs read, "Thinkin' Feller, Vote McKellar." Gore's campaign posted signs next to them that read, "Think Some More, and Vote for Gore"; in the Democratic-leaning state, the primary win was tantamount to victory, and Gore cruised to election in November.

In the Senate, Gore's notable accomplishments included authorship of legislation that led to the construction of the national interstate highway system. He also supported the federal minimum wage and opposed across-the-board tax cuts; he favored those that aimed to help the middle class and poor.

Compared with most Southern senators, Gore was progressive on civil rights legislation: He was among the few legislators from his region to reject the Southern Manifesto, a document opposing the Supreme Court's *Brown vs. Board of Education* decision, which mandated desegregation, over a period of time.[3] The issue came to a head in 1956 when he squared off on the floor of the Senate against Strom Thurmond of South Carolina, then a Democrat. Thurmond wanted Gore to sign the manifesto, and Gore responded simply, "Hell no."[4] (Gore did vote against the Civil Rights Act of 1964, calling it a "sledgehammer" approach to solving racial problems.[5] He later said this vote was among his worst mistakes as a legislator.) Gore supported the 1965 Voting Rights Act, a move not popular with many Tennessee residents during a time of massive racial strife across the South.

Gore's only run at national office came during the 1956 Democratic convention, when he sought to be added to Adlai Stevenson's ticket as the vice-presidential nominee. One rival was Massachusetts Senator John Kennedy; both ultimately came in behind Tennessee's other senator, Estes Kefauver.

As Gore became more of a national political figure who used his Senate perch to focus increasingly on international affairs, his popularity in Tennessee began to wane. He received a minor scare at the polls in 1964, an election that provided the first indication of his vulnerability. Republican Dan Kuykendall of Memphis challenged Gore, and in a year that President Lyndon B. Johnson beat Republican nominee Barry Goldwater in the state 558,000 to 413,000, Gore beat Kuykendall by a narrower margin, 471,000 to 420,000.[6]

After that reelection victory, under Johnson's leadership the United States became further mired in the Vietnam conflict, and Gore became increasingly critical of American policy regarding Southeast Asia. He clashed with LBJ over the war, and his criticism did not win many plaudits from his constituents, who largely supported the military effort. Four years later, after Johnson's withdrawal from the race and Vice President Hubert Humphrey's defeat at the hands of Republican Richard Nixon, the liberal wing of the Democratic Party found itself reeling and leaderless. So Gore expanded his criticism over Vietnam policy to focus on President Nixon, who during his first year in office had failed to bring about a swift end to the war. The issue later became personal when his only son Al, a recent Harvard graduate, enlisted in the U.S. Army.

The senator also clashed with the new president over a proposal to create an antiballistic missile (ABM) system; he argued the Soviets would be hesitant to negotiate if the weapons system were adopted, making it more difficult to achieve broader arms limitations. The administration would do better to focus on stopping the nuclear arms race, he said.[7] Then, to further alienate himself from the White House (and his constituents), Gore became one of the most prominent voices in the ultimately successful battle to deny Senate confirmation of two Nixon Supreme Court nominations, Clement F. Haynsworth and G. Harrold Carswell.

Gore found himself on the liberal side of many national issues, not a comfortable side to take in Tennessee at the time. This was a state where in the 1968 presidential race Democrat Hubert Humphrey received only 28 percent of the vote to Richard Nixon's 38 percent and American Independent George Wallace's 34 percent. In the 1970 Democratic primary, Gore faced a challenge from the right from Hudley Crockett, a former television newscaster who quit his job as press secretary to Governor Buford Ellington to run. Crockett differed from the incumbent over Vietnam, approaches to crime, civil rights, handling of college campus disturbances, and other issues. He accused the senator of "failing to represent" Tennessee voters properly.[8]

Gore overcame the challenge with 51 percent of the vote to Crockett's 45.2 percent. But his Democratic primary opponent had brought up many of the themes that would be used by the Republicans in the fall. "Hudley Crockett roughed him up pretty badly, and Buford Ellington and the Democrats under Buford didn't lift a finger to help Albert in the general election," recalled John Seigenthaler, who in 1970 was in the midst of his storied career as editor of the (Nashville) *Tennessean*, which endorsed Gore in 1970. "Many of the things that were said in Brock's campaign repeated themes that emerged in Hudley's campaign." [9]

As Gore faced growing opposition in his effort to continue representing Tennessee in Congress after 32 years, William E. Brock was a politician on the rise. Born in 1930, his parents were heirs to a prosperous candy manufacturing company in the Chattanooga area, and his grandfather, a Democrat, served in the U.S. Senate from 1929 to 1932. After graduating from Washington and Lee University, Brock served in the Navy; he then returned home and worked as vice president of the Brock Candy Company. He won election to the U.S. House in 1962, becoming the first Republican elected from his district in 42 years. He compiled a conservative voting record, establishing himself as a dependable vote against Johnson's Great Society initiatives. Like Gore, he opposed the Civil Rights Act of 1964.

The Tennessee Senate race occurred during an era when Democrats dominated Southern politics, as voters associated Republicans with the carpetbaggers who occupied the South a century earlier. But Tennessee had been more hospitable to Republican candidates than had other Southern states. Much of east Tennessee had remained loyal to the Union during the Civil War, and Republicans had been winning office there for decades. From 1900 to 1950, Republicans won only 80 of 2,565 House races across the entire South; 50 of those came from two east Tennessee districts.[10]

By 1970, Republicans were also making inroads in the state's growing middle-class suburbs of Memphis and Nashville, along with the affluent neighborhoods in smaller cities, towns, and hamlets.[11] With Brock's victory in 1970, Tennessee became the first Southern state with two Republican senators—Brock and Howard Baker, who served together from 1971 to 1977.

And Nixon's presidential victory in 1968 showed Democrats could no longer assume they would win Southern states. Except for Texas, Democrats had been shut out of the South in the Electoral College in 1968 by Nixon or George Wallace, the former Democratic governor of Alabama.

So as the 1970 election cycle approached, it was clear Gore would have a serious fight on his hands.

"GONE WASHINGTON"

Gore's left-leaning stands on public policy issues were not his only vulnerabilities in 1970. Though he was a Tennessean through and through, Gore had taken an affinity to the Washington society scene during his three decades–plus in Congress. Many people back in the Volunteer State suspected he had caught "Potomac fever" and lost touch with where he had come from. Gore's personal style sometimes fed this perception. Critics would label him imperious, arrogant, and aloof, but more sympathetic voices said he reflected the dignity and traditions of the Senate. "Albert is an old-style Senator, a Roman Senator really," wrote journalist David Halberstam in his seminal piece about the 1970 Tennessee Senate race, in *Harper's* magazine. "One can almost imagine him seated with Webster, Calhoun, and Clay." Gore was proud of his service in Washington, and it showed. "It is not so much his ego which is on display," Halberstam wrote, "It is the U.S. Senate's ego and dignity which is on display, which is why he seems at times aloof and untouchable."[12]

Thus his opponent's strategy aimed to make Gore look foreign to voters in his home state. "People viewed him as very arrogant," Brock recalled more than three decades later. "It sounded like he was talking down to people."[13] So Brock's campaign put up billboards around the state proclaiming "Bill Brock believes," which later became "Bill Brock believes the way you believe." For many, this seemingly bland political boilerplate slogan carried deeper meanings at a time the country was torn apart by the war in Vietnam and racial tensions at home. Democrats viewed this as wordplay to tap into white Tennesseans' racial fears and animosities.

Brock used the Gore-as-outsider theme to highlight his own record of service. One campaign commercial offered testimonials from ordinary folk on the street in Tennessee about the Republican's constituent service, whether for Social Security payments, veterans' disability benefits, or gaining passports. "He listens, and he responds. That's why so many of us are for Bill Brock for United States senator," said a young man in one commercial.[14] "The whole thing was meant to define Gore as being alien to the common culture," recalled James Sasser, at the time a young lawyer and the senator's campaign manager for the Nashville area, who would go on to serve three terms in the U.S. Senate and as U.S. ambassador to China.[15]

The Brock campaign tied Gore to the national liberal Democratic leadership, a campaign tactic Republicans successfully used for decades to come. One billboard, on U.S. Highway 11, announced, "Birds of a Feather Flock Together" and listed Gore's name with Democratic Senators Edward M. Kennedy (Mass.), George McGovern (S.D.), and William Fulbright (Ark.), a leading critic of the Vietnam policies.[16]

Brock hammered these themes home further in a series of television ads in which Tennessee residents raised questions about Gore. In "Seniority," a constituent asked Brock how the state would be hurt by losing Gore's 18 years of service in the Democratic-dominated chamber. "The longer a man stays, the more damage he can do," Brock replied. "And I think that's the problem with Albert Gore." He added, "His seniority is now hurting Tennessee more than it did 10 years ago, because he's in a position to do greater damage." In another television ad Brock told constituents, "I think Al Gore has misrepresented the people of Tennessee. I'm going to come home and listen to you. Not talk down to you, but listen to you."[17]

The idea that Gore had lost touch with Tennessee stemmed from the senator's focus on foreign affairs, said John Seigenthaler, the *Tennessean* editor and longtime chronicler of Volunteer State politics. Gore was in the mold of Cordell Hull, the former congressman, senator, secretary of state under President Franklin Roosevelt, who was instrumental in the founding of the United Nations, according to Seigenthaler. "It was definitely not my impression that he had lost touch," Seigenthaler said.[18]

The racial aspect of the advertising, meanwhile, was complex. Compared to neighboring states, Tennessee had a relatively moderate record on racial issues. In fact, pro–civil rights candidates had success in Tennessee at a time when their cohorts in other Southern states were losing. Senator Estes Kefauver, a supporter of civil rights legislation, won reelection in 1960 after overcoming the active opposition of a staunch segregationist, Andrew T. Taylor, in the Democratic primary. On the campaign trail in 1970, Gore aimed to defuse racial questions, trying to appeal to black voters and low-income whites. "If you scratch a Wallace voter, you find a populist," he told an interviewer. "We disagree on civil rights bills, I tell them, but I represent their economic interests."[19]

VIETNAM AND OTHER DIVISIVE ISSUES

The ongoing military action in Southeast Asia created a backdrop to the campaign that put Gore on the defensive. At that time, James Sasser said, "It was considered patriotic to support the war."[20] Gore urged an end to the fighting, while Brock supported Nixon's policy of "peace with honor," although it included no specific plan to decrease the number of troops in Southeast Asia and end American involvement. "The central core of the campaign was wrapped around Vietnam," Brock said. "Albert Gore and I really disagreed on Vietnam."[21]

Brock pointed to his "90/10" rule: Because Gore represented a small minority of viewpoints about Vietnam, it was completely fair to point out that he disagreed with most people in his own state. For defenders of Gore's legacy, his stance on Vietnam is a reflection of how he was often ahead of his constituents, many of whom did not want to hear the bad news about what was occurring in the battlefields, jungles, and enemy waters of Southeast Asia. Still, after the election Gore noted he was out of step with the electorate on this key matter. "The popular support of the Vietnam War was perhaps as strong in Tennessee as in any state in the union," he said later. "And yet I was at least one of the leaders in opposition to it. This created a reservoir of antagonism toward me on this issue."[22] Still, he tried to turn the issue to his advantage. His son, Al, appeared in uniform in campaign commercials, one of which ended with the senator advising, "Son, always love your country."[23]

Republicans also knocked Gore off stride by publicizing his opposition to voluntary school prayer, which Brock supported. In late October, Senator Howard Baker submitted a rider to the Equal Rights Amendment, under consideration in the Senate, to allow voluntary prayer in public buildings, including schools. Gore voted against it, as he had twice before.[24] This didn't endear Gore to many conservative Tennessee voters. "The undercurrent of an image of a United States senator who turned his back on religion was there," Seigenthaler said.[25]

Sasser recalled the first time he realized his candidate was in real trouble was while working phone banks for Gore; people he called repeatedly expressed anger about the senator's opposition to school prayer.[26] This marked one of the first times the prayer in school issue had been raised in a political campaign. While the measure had little chance of passing in the Senate, it put lawmakers on record. Their votes could then be used in 30-second campaign ads, a foreshadowing in many ways of politicking-by-legislation that appeared decades later on divisive issues, such as gay marriage.

WHITE HOUSE INVOLVEMENT

Early in the campaign cycle for the 1970 midterm elections the Nixon White House painted a bull's-eye on Gore. In December 1969, Special Counsel to the President Harry Dent sent Richard Nixon a memo in which he called the Tennessee Senate race "one of our most winnable."[27] Sasser recalled other Democratic Senate targets by the White House targets included Vance Hartke of Indiana and Ralph Yarborough of Texas. (Hartke won, while the liberal Yarborough was defeated in the Democratic primary by the more conservative Lloyd Bentsen, who then beat Republican Congressman George H. W. Bush in the general election.)

The Nixon White House sent help to Brock's campaign. Harry Treleaven and Kenneth Reitz, GOP political consultants who had worked on Nixon's 1968 campaign, went to Tennessee for the Senate race, bringing with them sophisticated polling and research techniques to aid the Republican candidate. And White House Chief of Staff H. R. Haldeman wrote a memo urging the Brock campaign to go through the society pages of the *Washington Post* to find the menus of dinners Senator Gore attended, suggesting "the Frenchier the better,"[28] (a derogatory reference that would be resurrected more than 30 years later when Republicans whispered that Senator John Kerry, the 2004 Democratic presidential nominee, "looks French"[29]).

Much of the venom against Gore was personal, particularly for Vice President Spiro Agnew. Gore had taken great offense at some of Agnew's more impolitic remarks, such as his response to a question about why he did not campaign more in poor areas—"When you've seen one slum, you've seen them all"—or a reference to an Asian American reporter as a "fat Jap." Gore remarked in October 1969 that Agnew was becoming "our greatest disaster next to Vietnam." The vice president then called for the senator "to be removed to some sinecure where he can simply affect those within the sound of his voice and not the whole state of Tennessee."[30]

Agnew was a hot orator on the circuit, launching verbal attacks on Democrats as "radic-libs" and "ideological eunuchs" for encouraging protests against the war. Yet when Agnew visited Tennessee on Brock's behalf, Gore blunted some of his political punch by showing up, uninvited, in the receiving line at the Memphis airport, thus dramatizing his chosen role as the lone battler against the assembled power of the Nixon administration.[31]

Despite the strong White House support, Nixon himself suggested that Brock would have to present some sort of positive vision about what he would do for Tennessee upon election. The president noted the negativity of Brock's approach and expressed some concern about its effectiveness. "Brock has voted against everything—Social Security, Appalachia, everything," Nixon said. "While Family Assistance is not a good issue generally, it could be good for Brock. Let him be for something. On the economic issue, he has got to prove he isn't an encrusted old type."[32]

Despite the president's mild doubts, the White House was foursquare behind Brock. Nixon visited Tennessee himself on October 20, along with former General William Westmoreland, then the Army chief of staff and former head of military operations in Vietnam. Speaking about the Republican challenger at East Tennessee State University in Johnson City, Nixon told the crowd of more than 30,000 people, "the president that Tennessee voted for should have a man in the United State Senate who voted with him on the big issues." Regarding Vietnam, Nixon said, "We are working for peace . . . My program, the program Bill Brock supports, says, 'End the war in a way that will win the peace.'"[33]

Decades later, Brock said that the Nixon political operation played a more limited role in his race than is often portrayed. The Nixon team helped him raise money, but Brock sought to run his own independent campaign. Much of the criticism he leveled at Gore in the general election had already been used by Hudley Crockett in the Democratic primary challenge. It was Crockett who was the first to charge that Gore was an out-of-towner who had lost touch with Tennessee, Brock said; he just echoed that theme.[34]

THE ROLE OF TELEVISION

By 1970 television was the favorite form of political communication across the country, and Tennessee was no exception. Senator Baker had used television effectively in his successful 1966 race. And back in the 1950s, Senator Estes Kefauver became an early television celebrity of sorts, as chairman of the Special Committee on Organized Crime in Interstate Commerce. But in many corners of the state, politics was still conducted in local venues, like rural courthouse steps. Candidates went from one county seat to another, sometimes making six to eight appearances a day. They would also attend barbecues and turkey shoots. Even in 1964, when LBJ was blanketing the airwaves with political commercials, Gore had done relatively little television advertising. "Tennessee is a small state, and it is a mark of the old-breed politicians that they were known by their first names—not Kefauver, Gore, and [former Governor] Clement, but Estes, Albert, and Frank," David Halberstam wrote in his *Harper's* article.[35]

The 1970 Senate campaign helped push Tennessee and other states in the region with a more cozy form of politics into the mass-media age. Brock ran a series of spots showing him talking to constituents on the street, listening intently with his suit jacket slung over his shoulder. The constituents raised questions about Gore on public policy issues such as busing, Vietnam, and gun control. They were the critics, not Brock. This was a tactic that would be picked up, amplified, and used repeatedly in political television commercials for decades to come. Each one ended with a slogan similar to that used on his billboards: "Bill Brock believes in the things we believe in. Bill Brock for

United States senator." Using ordinary citizens to make the charges against Gore was extremely effective, John Seigenthaler said. Many of the slogans were Republican standards, and over time they created a very negative impression of Gore. The conventional wisdom of the ads was, "You're looking at your next-door neighbor and listening to him or her tell you what a bastard Albert Gore is," Seigenthaler recalled wryly. The television campaign was "Not like anything anybody in that state or I daresay any other state, had seen before . . . And it was well executed. It was sort of *vox populi*. It was extremely well produced."[36]

The contest also set a precedent for the outsized role of political consultants would later play in running campaigns. Kenneth Reitz, the Republican consultant who had worked for Nixon's 1968 presidential campaign, arrived in Tennessee in spring 1969 to begin planning details of campaign strategy, organization, and ads. Charles Guggenheim, a leading filmmaker who often worked for Democratic candidates, created Gore's television commercials. In the Democratic primary Hudley Crockett blasted Gore for hiring an out-of-state consultant, saying it showed he had lost touch with Tennessee. The *Washington Post* noted presciently, shortly after Election Day, "The senatorial race this year was between incumbent Democrat Albert Gore and Republican William Brock. But it was also a race between rival image-makers, media coordinators, and advertising agencies, all working for big money in by far the costliest senatorial race in the state's history."[37] These trends grew exponentially across the American political landscape in the following decades.

FAITH IN THE VOTERS

Senator Albert Gore was hardly the first candidate to believe voters would see through campaign attacks that he ignored; like many before and after, he did so at his own peril. James Sasser said Gore had a somewhat naïve view about the power of negative campaigning. The senator's campaign advisers warned of negative tactics, which had also been employed by Lloyd Bentsen in his successful Texas Senate Democratic primary race against Ralph Yarborough earlier that year. Bentsen had played on voters' fears of societal breakdown and urban riots, and made an issue of Yarborough's opposition to the Vietnam War; he had run ads criticizing Yarborough's apparent sympathy for student demonstrators at the 1968 Democratic convention in Chicago.[38] When it appeared Brock was making headway in the campaign, Gore stepped up efforts to defend himself against the charges. At a town-hall-style meeting shown in a television commercial, Gore said Nixon's two rejected Supreme Court nominees were mediocre, and he suggested the South could produce higher quality judges. "What I owe the people most is the best judgment of which I am capable," he said.[39]

Gore's most effective ad was one showing him playing checkers with two seniors, in Smith County, Tenn. "If you beat me two straight games, I'll cut you off Medicare," Gore joked. The commercial aimed to show his populist streak and his trademark sense of humor, John Seigenthaler recalled. Unfortunately for Gore, too many charges had already been leveled against him. "I thought it was a powerful answer, but it came very late," Seigenthaler said.[40]

Gore's most famous campaign commercial was also positive. It showed the senator, his cheeks pink with good health, riding horses with his son across the family's land in Carthage. The commercial's broadcaster then intoned, "The pace and direction a man sets for his life can tell you a lot about his inner spirit. . . . The people of Tennessee have learned to take the measure of Albert Gore by the battles he's fought for them along the way, for TVA, tax reform, Medicare, interstate highways, Social Security, and education. . . . 'I may have run ahead of the pack sometimes,' he says, 'but I'm usually headed in the right direction.'"[41]

Yet the effectiveness of Gore's commercials was not always clear. The horse spot in particular, snippets of which got replayed repeatedly during his son's 2000 presidential bid, for some television viewers reinforced the idea that the senator was distant and arrogant. One constituent even wrote, "I saw your television ad. It confirmed my feeling that Albert is on a high horse."[42]

Gore took verbal shots at his opponent at the end of the campaign. Standing before 500 people at a rally in Memphis two days before the election, Gore said: "The people have examined the records—mine and that of my opponent, William E. Brock III—and they have seen that it is I who has represented Tennessee and it is Congressman Brock who has misrepresented our state throughout his eight years in the House."[43] Gore's campaign also took the offensive by papering the state with hundreds of thousands of copies of a *Congressional Record* reprint, comparing his votes with Brock's on 50 federal aid programs carrying benefits for Tennessee. On all of them Gore and the majority of the state's delegation had voted yes; Brock had voted no.[44]

A LASTING LEGACY

The aggressive Republican tactics and shifting attitudes among Tennesseans were too much for Gore to overcome; Brock received about 559,000 votes (52.1 percent) to 513,000 (47.9 percent) for Gore.[45] Due to what Gore felt was the campaign's highly negative tone he refused to make the customary concession call to the victor. When the results came in, Gore spoke to supporters gathered at the Hermitage Hotel in Nashville, quoting the poet Edwin Markham: "Defeat may serve as well as victory to shake the soul and let the glory out." He continued. "I told the truth as I saw it. The causes for which we fought are not dead." He then added, "The truth shall rise again."[46]

Brock went on to become a well-known Republican senator. Seen as a rising star in the GOP, he was considered for the vice presidency when Gerald Ford vacated the job to become president after Nixon's resignation in August 1974. Ford considered Brock against two years later, when the president was looking for a running mate to replace liberal Republican Vice President Nelson Rockefeller. Former California Governor Ronald Reagan, Ford's primary opponent, who nearly wrested the GOP nomination from the sitting president, also considered Brock for his running mate.[47]

Neither Gore nor his supporters got over the senator's loss easily. At the time participants felt the campaign set trends in its negativity, as Gore had been portrayed as antiprayer, anti-South, soft on communism, and unduly sympathetic to school busing for racial integration.[48] "We thought we'd been through a rough effort that was kind of a harbinger of things to come in politics," said Congressman David E. Price,[49] who in 1970 was a newly minted Ph.D. from Yale University in political science who organized campus groups and get-out-the-vote operations for Gore. (After a long teaching career at Yale and Duke universities, Price was elected to Congress from North Carolina in 1986.)

Supporters could not just dismiss what they considered to be a racially charged campaign that slandered a dedicated public servant who had given 32 years of his life for the people of Tennessee. "I thought he'd been terribly wronged," James Sasser said. "It was his campaign really that got me into politics."[50] When Brock came up for reelection in 1976, Sasser and the Democrats sought to take revenge, a job made easier by Brock's political vulnerability that year. The Watergate investigation showed that Nixon operatives had poured illegal funds into the 1970 Senate race, although no one from Brock's campaign was implicated. That campaign spent about $1.25 million, a tiny amount by modern standards but at the time accounting for one of the costliest Senate races in history. Significant portions of the money, by some reports as much as $200,000, were funneled into Tennessee through Operation Townhouse, run by Nixon operatives.[51] After the election, the victor's finance chairman said the campaign's financial records had been "flushed," and Brock himself said, "I don't want to know" where the money came from.[52]

In 1976 several Democrats sought their party's nomination for the right to face Brock in his first reelection bid; Sasser, elected chairman of the state Democratic Party in the early 1970s, won the nod. Sasser ran an aggressive campaign, emphasizing how the affluent Republican senator, through his accountants' apparent skillful use of the tax code, had been able to pay only $2,026 of income tax on $51,670 of adjusted gross income for 1975.[53] Sasser won with 52 percent of the vote. Jimmy Carter's Southern sweep certainly helped Sasser's fortunes, but Brock was unable to hold onto many of the same voters he attracted in 1970. These turned out to be more anti-Gore than pro-Brock.[54]

While Al Gore, the vice president and 2000 Democratic presidential nominee, has gone on to greater fame than his father, the 1970 Senate race is remembered in the annals of negative campaigning as a landmark matchup. Brock later said the negative tactics used in his Senate race were mild compared to those employed now. "That was almost a milquetoast exercise," he recalled of the 1970 contest. "I don't think either one of us thought it was anything other than trying to delineate differences. We were just trying to say 'these are two radically different positions.'"[55]

NOTES

1. Bill Turque, *Inventing Al Gore: A Biography* (New York: Houghton Mifflin Company, 2000), 2.

2. Kyle Longley, *Senator Albert Gore, Sr.: Tennessee Maverick* (Baton Rouge: Louisiana State University Press, 2004), 51.

3. 347 U.S. 483 (1954).

4. Longley, *Senator Albert Gore, Sr.*, 124.

5. James H. Neal, "Albert Arnold Gore, Sr., 1907–1998," *The Tennessee Encyclopedia of History and Culture* (http://tennesseeencyclopedia.net/).

6. David Halberstam, "The End of a Populist," *Harper's*, January 1971.

7. Longley, *Senator Albert Gore, Sr.*, 217.

8. David S. Broder, "Gore Rides Hard Race Astride a White Horse," *The Washington Post*, Aug. 2, 1970.

9. Interview with author, Rosslyn, Va., Feb. 1, 2005.

10. Clay Risen, "Southern Man: Bredesen in 2008?" *The New Republic*, Jan. 31, 2005.

11. Earl Black and Merle Black, *The Rise of Southern Republicans* (Cambridge, Mass.: The Belknap Press of Harvard University, 2002), 95.

12. Halberstam, *Harper's*, January 1971.

13. Interview with author, Annapolis, Md., Aug. 5, 2004.

14. Tape courtesy of the Julian P. Kanter Political Commercial Archive at the University of Oklahoma Political Communication Center. [Known hereafter in this chapter as the Kanter Archive.]

15. Interview with author, Washington, D.C., Oct. 13, 2004.

16. Longley, *Senator Albert Gore, Sr.*, 230.

17. Tape courtesy of the Kanter Archive.

18. Interview with author, by telephone, Jan. 24, 2005.

19. Turque, *Inventing Al Gore*, 78.

20. Interview with author, Washington, D.C., Oct. 13, 2004.

21. Interview with author, Annapolis, Md., Aug. 5, 2004.

22. David Maraniss and Ellen Nakashima, *The Prince of Tennessee: The Rise of Al Gore* (New York: Simon & Schuster, 2000), 120.

23. Tape courtesy of the Kanter Archive.

24. Longley, *Senator Albert Gore, Sr.*, 238.

25. Interview with author, Rosslyn, Va., Feb. 1, 2005.

26. Interview with author, Washington, D.C., Oct. 13, 2004.

27. Longley, *Senator Albert Gore, Sr.*, 223.

28. Turque, *Inventing Al Gore*, 76.

29. Adam Nagourney and Richard W. Stevenson, "Bush's Aides Plan Late Campaign Sprint in '04," *The New York Times*, April 22, 2003.

30. Longley, *Senator Albert Gore, Sr.*, 222.

31. David S. Broder, "Gore Battles Back," *The Washington Post*, Oct. 28, 1970.

32. Longley, *Senator Albert Gore, Sr.*, 229.

33. Longley, *Senator Albert Gore, Sr.*, 237.

34. Interview with author, by telephone, Aug. 9, 2004.

35. Halberstam, *Harper's*, January 1971.

36. Interview with author, Rosslyn, Va., Feb. 1, 2005.

37. Don Oberdorfer, "Rival Image Makers Clash in Tennessee," *The Washington Post*, Nov. 22, 1970.

38. Turque, *Inventing Al Gore*, 74.

39. Tape courtesy of the Kanter Archive.

40. Interview with author, by telephone, Jan. 24, 2005.

41. Broder, *The Washington Post*, Aug. 2, 1970.

42. Longley, *Senator Albert Gore, Sr.*, 231.

43. David M. Shribman, "Casting a Long Shadow: George W. Bush and Al Gore Both Had Fathers Who Lost Elections in 1970. Those Losses Changed Their Lives Forever," *The Boston Globe*, Jan. 9, 2000.

44. Broder, *The Washington Post*, Oct. 28, 1970.

45. Longley, *Senator Albert Gore, Sr.*, 238.

46. Longley, *Senator Albert Gore, Sr.*, 238–39.

47. Craig Shirley, *Reagan's Revolution: The Untold Story of the Campaign That Started It All* (Nashville, Tenn.: Nelson Current, 2005), 26, 223, 234.

48. Charles Babington, "Attacks on Brock in Md. Senate Race Evoke 1970 Battle Against Gore Sr.," *The Washington Post*, Aug. 16, 1994.

49. Interview with author, Washington, D.C., Feb. 9, 2005.

50. Interview with author, Washington, D.C., Oct. 13, 2004.

51. Maraniss and Nakashima, *The Prince of Tennessee*, 123.

52. Don Oberdorfer, "The Purchase of Power," *The Washington Post*, Nov. 14, 1971.

53. Rowland Evans and Robert Novak, "Post-Watergate Politics in Tennessee," *The Washington Post*, Oct. 25, 1976.

54. Black and Black, *The Rise of Southern Republicans*, 95.

55. Interview with author, Annapolis, Md., Aug. 5, 2004.

6

Confrontation, Bluster, and No Compromise: The Campaigns of Jesse Helms

During Senator Jesse Helms's thirty years in Congress, critics had no shortage of nasty names for the North Carolina Republican. But even his most severe detractors could not honestly tag him with the frequent politician's labels of inconsistent, flip-flopper, or wishy-washy. Helms knew exactly where he stood on issues—strongly anti-Communist, antigovernment on economic matters, and staunchly socially conservative—and North Carolina voters could judge him on that basis. His campaigns were filled with confrontation, bluster, and no compromise on conservative issues. Helms's margins of victory reflected this strategy, as he was never a wildly popular figure with voters in North Carolina. From his first election in 1972 through his retirement thirty years later, Helms never won more than 54.5 percent of the vote.

Critics considered him a pioneer in slash-and-burn politics, employing questionable tactics to exploit weaknesses in opponents and bringing underlying social issues such as race into campaigns. "What is unique about Helms is his willingness to pick at the scab of the great wound of American history, the legacy of slavery and segregation, and to inflame racial resentment against African Americans," wrote venerable *Washington Post* reporter David Broder in response to Senator Helms's retirement announcement in 2001.[1]

One thing that is indisputable is that Helms and his political team knew how to win. Two of his reelection victories, against Governor Jim Hunt in 1984 and architect Harvey Gantt in 1990, introduced new strategies in negative campaigning that became popular in the campaign industry in the following years, or refined and built upon existing tactics. During those races the Democratic candidates got in their share of licks against Helms, making North Carolina ground zero for some of the toughest campaigns in recent decades.

A RICH POLITICAL HISTORY

The Tar Heel State has long been home to a spicy blend of politics and personalities, and its races have often been at the forefront of negative tactics. "Our candidates don't use fists," wrote veteran (Raleigh) *News & Observer* political reporter Rob Christensen in 2002. "They use switchblades, brass knuckles, and Saturday night specials. You turn on your television during election years at your own risk."[2]

Modern traditions of tough campaigning go back even before television became mainstream, to at least the 1950 Democratic Senate primary runoff (see chapter 2) between Senator Frank Porter Graham, an appointed officeholder, and Willis Smith. North Carolina was largely a one-party state at the time, and securing the Democratic nomination was tantamount to victory. While the liberal-leaning Graham, a former president of the University of North Carolina, had beaten Smith, a Raleigh attorney and traditionally conservative Southern Democrat, in a tough primary, he had failed to garner the 50 percent of the vote needed to avoid a runoff election. Smith initially hesitated before calling for a runoff; he received encouragement from a 28-year-old radio Raleigh reporter ostensibly covering the race named Jesse Helms. The small town police chief's son organized a rally in Raleigh to demonstrate the city's support for Smith, and the event helped persuade the challenger candidate to call for the runoff. The campaign that followed was among the ugliest in North Carolina's history. Smith and his allies attacked Graham as a member of Communist societies and played upon the racial fears of white voters. Smith won the election, and Helms, one year later, joined him in Washington as an administrative assistant.

When Senator Smith died in office in 1953, Helms returned to North Carolina. He headed the state's Banker's Association and later served on the Raleigh City Council. Helms further built his public profile as a commentator on Raleigh television from 1960 to 1972. During the broadcasts he often inveighed against big government, the fledgling civil rights movement, and what he deemed the liberal media.

Thomas F. Ellis, a conservative Raleigh lawyer and early Republican activist in a state long dominated by Democrats, helped persuade Helms to run for the U.S. Senate on the GOP ticket in 1972. In that first Senate campaign Helms used tactics many considered unseemly. Billboards throughout eastern North Carolina read "Vote for Jesse; He's One of Us"—a less-than-subtle reference to the ethnic roots of his Democratic opponent, Congressman Nick Galifianakis, son of Greek immigrants.[3] Helms won but incurred a large campaign debt in doing so. To help pay the debt off, Ellis created the Congressional Club, a Republican fundraising organization and political machine that was later to aid not only Helms's campaign but also those of conservative candidates in North Carolina and around the country.

Helms's political influence grew during the 1976 presidential primary campaign when former California Governor Ronald Reagan was on the verge of dropping out, after losing a string of early primaries to President Gerald Ford. Helms and his campaign operatives devised the issue of opposing turnover of the Panama Canal as a way of mobilizing conservatives to support the challenger. Reagan won the North Carolina primary, putting him on a path in which he nearly succeeded at denying the incumbent president renomination —and led him to the White House four years later.

CLASH OF THE TITANS

After twelve years as the Senate's leading conservative, Helms in 1984 faced a daunting reelection challenge when he squared off against Jim Hunt, a moderate Southern Democratic governor thought by many pundits to be White House material. The contest had a full menu of negative campaign tactics— personal attacks, large sums of money raised and spent by both candidates, below-the-radar smears by allies, and a series of combative debates. During a year in which President Ronald Reagan cruised to reelection in North Carolina and 48 other states, this Senate contest took on national importance for both parties. As the highest-profile congressional race it also drew significant international attention. It has remained one of the most bitter and negative Senate campaigns of recent decades, during an era in which each election cycle has pushed the boundaries of acceptability in campaign tactics.

The race is often remembered for its sheer meanness, which is no doubt fair. But it also involved a series of negative campaign techniques that would be picked up on and amplified in subsequent decades, including going after an opponent early to define that person, the potency of labeling a political rival a flip-flopper without core beliefs, and linking an opponent to unsavory foreign characters—in this case Salvadoran death squads.

The costs were also eye-popping for the time and for years after. Even as the expenses of campaigns rose through the late 1980s and into the next decade, the $27-million race in 1984 between Helms and Hunt for years held the record as the most expensive Senate campaign in history. Helms spent $16.9 million, while Hunt pulled in and spent a respectable $9.5 million—between the two, the *Washington Post* noted wryly at the time, "enough to pay the salaries of all 100 senators for nearly three years."[4]

Many of Helms's contributions came from out-of-state supporters, while Hunt received sizable chunks of campaign cash from Democrats across the land eager to contribute to the defeat of an enduring bogeyman. (Author Gore Vidal and former Secretary of State Dean Rusk contributed to Hunt, while actors Charlton Heston and Bob Hope supported Helms.)[5] After the Republican National Convention in Dallas in August 1984, Helms made a long swing through other Texas cities, picking up campaign cash from like-minded conservatives. Hunt, meanwhile, took five days to return to Raleigh from the Democratic National Convention in San Francisco, stopping for fundraisers in Portland, Denver, St. Louis, and Chicago.

In 1984 Hunt was not as widely known as Helms nationally, but he was a titan of North Carolina politics. They two shared initials, JH, but the similarities ended there. James Baxter Hunt Jr. grew up in Wilson, N.C., in a strong Baptist household, which led him to a career in public service. Hunt went to North Carolina State University and earned a law degree at the University of North Carolina; he and his wife also spent time in the Himalayas of Nepal while he was an agricultural advisor for the Ford Foundation. After returning to North Carolina he practiced law and got involved in Democratic politics, and in 1972 was elected lieutenant governor, at age 35. Hunt swept into the governor's office four years later, where he led the enactment of changes in the state's education system, including pioneering standardized tests to measure student progress. He also set up a primary student reading program, reduced class size, created dropout-prevention programs, and established the North Carolina School of Science and Mathematics.

Hunt won reelection easily in 1980, and as his second term progressed it became increasingly clear that this highly popular political figure would become the Democratic challenger to Helms in 1984.

The Republican senator, at this time, was anything but an unbeatable political figure. He had clashed with President Ronald Reagan over spending cuts and a host of legislative issues, despite usually being in agreement on proposals to reduce the size of government. In late 1982 Helms angered members of the Senate when he kept them from recessing for more than a week, while he tried to get improvements in the tobacco program by filibustering against an increase in the federal gasoline tax. His move threatened to keep lawmakers in session through Christmas, and the tactic earned the wrath of senators on both sides of the aisle. "Seldom have I seen a more obdurate and obnoxious performance," said Senator Alan Simpson (R-Wyo.) after the filibuster was broken.[6]

Helms also came in for frequent criticism concerning his role in United States foreign policy, particularly toward Latin America, which he argued needed to stand as a bulwark against creeping Communism in the Western Hemisphere. He had ties to violently authoritarian governments of the era, such as Roberto D'Aubuisson and his ARENA party in El Salvador, which was linked to death squads, and the Guatemalan military, which killed thousands of people suspected of ties to the left, the Argentine junta that led its country to war against Great Britain over the Falkland Islands, and Augusto Pinochet in Chile, among others. Helms organized his own foreign policy staff that in some ways acted as a shadow State Department. In the 1970s and 1980s, he sent aides on covert assignments to Latin America, where they met with anti-Communist leaders—considered by many to be despots—even if the strongmen were not in favor at the White House.

This approach stood in contrast to that of Hunt, 47, who, as noted, had focused on education issues while in office. He was moderate and even relatively conservative on many matters, such as supporting a constitutional amendment to balance the budget, major increases in defense spending, and voluntary prayer in school. One poll in October 1982 showed 51 percent of North Carolina voters would favor Hunt in a senatorial race against Helms, while 35 percent preferred the Republican.[7] Political reporters from national newspapers predicted Hunt would win. "There was kind of a confident feeling in the national media that this is a case of a good New South governor, southern progressive, great record, highly popular in the state, running well ahead of a right-wing ideologue," recalled Will Marshall, Hunt's campaign press secretary.[8]

EARLY AND OFTEN

Helms knew Hunt was likely to present a serious challenge in 1984, and his political machine geared up early for the fight. His campaign began advertising on television eighteen months ahead of the general election and did not stop, except for a one-week cease-fire around Christmas, 1983. Carter Wrenn, for years a captain of the Congressional Club, recalled that Republican political consultant Arthur Finkelstein advised there was little that could be done to change the negative impression of Helms held by some voters. "The strategy that kind of evolved out of that was, 'Look, we never can lift Helms up. We've got to bring Hunt down.' It was really a brutal strategy, but it was really the only option we had left," Wrenn said.[9]

The campaign's early television ads portrayed Hunt as a flip-flopping political opportunist who would bend to the demands of liberal interest groups and who wanted to use the Senate seat as a springboard to a White House run. Many of the ads were 10- and 15-second quick hits on one issue, such as tax cuts, prayer in school, and Reagan's spending cuts. The ads looked cheaply produced and showed Helms talking straight into the camera, spliced next to printed quotes from the governor that showed him taking contrasting sides, at various times, on major issues of the day. Each ended with Helms sneering, in his slightly slurred Southern drawl, "Where do you stand, Jim?"

Another line of Helms ads recounted Hunt's financial support from fundraising trips to liberal enclaves like New York City, Georgetown, and Beverly Hills. Some ads poked fun at "The New York Committee to Elect Jim Hunt" and presented the governor as out of touch with his conservative North Carolina constituency. "It was low-tech, cheap, but in the end, rather effective," Marshall said.

The inexpensive-looking ads were actually the result of the Helms campaign's relatively small bank account by that point. Even though money was coming in quickly, Wrenn recalled, it was also being spent rapidly through the unusually drawn-out political season, in which the Helms team would ultimately produce upwards of 150 television ads (though not all were aired). "We had kind of stumbled in desperation over the chink in Hunt's armor," and the ads helped move poll numbers in the senator's direction, Wrenn said.[10]

The ads offered an early version of the flip-flop charge that was to be hurled so effectively by President George W. Bush's campaign at Senator John Kerry in 2004, which began practically the moment the senator from Massachusetts secured the Democratic presidential nomination. This was certainly not the first race in which wishy-washy/flip-flopper charges had been used. In Senator Adlai Stevenson's (unsuccessful) rematch with President Dwight D. Eisenhower in 1956, Democrats had highlighted the president's seemingly inconsistent statements and policies through an ad campaign asking, "How's that Again, General?" In 1964 GOP presidential nominee Senator Barry Goldwater ran an ad accusing President Lyndon Baines Johnson of trying to have it both ways on a host of issues; and countless other candidates had used similar techniques. However, these prior examples had been sporadic campaign themes. The 1984 Senate race in North Carolina raised the tactic to a high art by defining a political opponent early, setting in stone voters' impressions of him long before they went to the polls.

The commercials shifted the momentum of the race, helping to erase Hunt's double-digit lead by spring 1984. "It was like Chinese water torture, the cumulative effect of these ads,"[11] said Will Marshall, who would go on to found and lead the Progressive Policy Institute, a centrist Democratic think tank in Washington, D.C.

The campaign also took on racial overtones, a persistent theme in Helms's political career. In 1982 Helms had staged a filibuster against an extension of the Voting Rights Act, even though it was supported by 75 senators and endorsed by President Ronald Reagan. And early on, the Helms-Hunt race became ensnared by a proposal in Congress to create a federal holiday to honor slain civil rights leader Rev. Martin Luther King Jr. While in 1983 even Senator Strom Thurmond (R-S.C.), the former staunch segregationist, voted for a federal holiday to honor King, Helms led the fight against it. He went to court to try to force the FBI to open its files on the man the North Carolina senator still considered a Communist or at least to have had Communist associations. Merle Black, professor of political science at Emory University in Atlanta, who in 1984 was teaching at the University of North Carolina, said the MLK issue set the tone of the campaign early. "That was a signal to his North Carolina supporters that the race was on."[12]

In television advertisements, Helms focused on the financial burden of creating a new paid day off for workers. "I fought the Martin Luther King national holiday because it will cost between $5 billion and $12 billion every year, depending on whose estimates you accept," Helms said in one ad. "America doesn't need more holidays; it needs more working days, so that America can produce more and be more competitive in the world market."[13] Though Helms endured much criticism from Democrats and in the media, back home his stance was popular. Surveys showed that 85 percent of white North Carolinians opposed the King holiday.[14]

Critics said the MLK issue shamelessly played the race card. Further suspicion stemmed from ads by Helms that associated the governor with 1984 Democratic presidential candidate Rev. Jesse Jackson, including one showing Jackson years earlier with an outsized "afro" hairdo. Hunt had not endorsed Jackson for president, and the pair had met only once, at the Governor's Mansion in Raleigh, in March 1982. The idea was to woo just enough North Carolinians who would be receptive to this sort of message—white working-class voters, many of them Democrats, who had supported Hunt in governor's races but who would opt for Helms in a more highly charged ideological contest.

FOREIGN POLICY ADVENTURES AND HOT-BUTTON, EMOTIONAL ISSUES

As Hunt's lead evaporated, the governor's campaign decided it needed to ratchet up the heat on the Republican senator. "Helms was savaging us, and we had positive spots on," Will Marshall said. "We could not seem to convey that sense of radicalism to the people of North Carolina."[15] So Helms's foreign policy adventures—particularly his ties to right-wing Latin American strongmen—became a focus Hunt's campaign ads, the first of which ran in May 1984. "When you look at the friends Jesse Helms has around the world, it's no wonder he's made enemies for North Carolina in Washington," Hunt's television ads charged.[16]

One commercial in particular stood out for its dark linkage between Helms and unsavory international figures. It suggested Helms was complicit in right-wing death squads in El Salvador. Aired during the last week of June 1984, the ad opened with the crack of rifle shots in the background, and startling still photographs of bloodied, crumpled bodies. The narrator said sternly, "This is what they do—death squads in El Salvador. Innocent men, women, and children murdered in cold blood. This is the man accused of directing those death squads, Roberto D'Aubuisson. And this [a photo of Helms] is the man whose aides helped D'Aubuisson set up his political party in El Salvador. This is Roberto D'Aubuisson's best friend in Washington, maybe his only friend. Now, Jesse Helms may be a crusader, but that's not what our senator should be crusading for."[17]

Though certainly a hard-hitting move, airing such a graphic ad was risky. The Hunt campaign wanted to nail Helms for siding with heinous dictators, but some campaign staff members felt viewers would find the images of dead bodies jarring and disturbing. These concerns proved prophetic, as polls numbers did not move substantially in favor of the governor once the ad aired. "People felt that [it] had gone over the top." Marshall said. "It was seen as being unfair and grotesque and in questionable taste."[18] And though the Helms campaign had been responsible for the vast majority of negative campaigning for more than a year, the episode provided the senator an opening to play the victim. "It's one thing to attack me on Social Security and taxes and school prayer," Helms complained. "But when Jim Hunt starts involving me with murder, well . . . I'm just absolutely astonished he would stoop that low."[19]

The ad war heated up further in July, when Hunt aired a commercial featuring former Democratic Congressman Richardson Preyer, campaign cochairman, disputing Helms's assertions that the governor had raised taxes. "It's been a campaign of lies and distortion and negative ads by the Helms campaign machine," Preyer said. "The same kind of campaign they've run again and again in this state for years." That prompted Claude Allen, Helms's spokesman, to call the commercial "the second-most low, gutter ad in the campaign [after the El Salvador spot]."[20]

The campaign's tenor degenerated further when the *Landmark*, a Chapel Hill weekly newspaper, published a story raising questions about the governor's sexual orientation. Hunt threatened to sue and demanded a retraction— which he promptly received. The Hunt team suggested Helms's allies were behind the episode, which the senator denied (though the paper benefited from the Republican's campaign advertising).

The race grew even more contentious when late in the campaign the candidates and their henchmen went after each other's war records, or lack thereof. During the third debate of the campaign, on September 23, Hunt criticized the senator for likening veterans' benefits to welfare. Helms responded by chiding Hunt for having missed service in Vietnam, asking the governor, "Which war did you serve in?" Hunt quickly snapped back he was too old to have gone to Vietnam, and had children at the time. He added, "And I don't like you questioning my patriotism."[21] Later in the campaign a Hunt campaign staff member mocked Helms for his stateside service during World War II, when he served as a naval recruiter in North Carolina and Georgia.

With Helms continuing the assault he had launched a year and a half earlier, Hunt was now fighting back on all cylinders. During the debates he attacked Helms relentlessly on Social Security, support for corporate tax breaks, and what he called neglect of education. Other, less high-minded debate exchanges included Helms's jabs at Hunt about using a state-owned aircraft for campaigning, while Hunt questioned whether Helms's political organization, the Congressional Club, had unfairly been provided cut-rate advertising through its subsidiary, the Jefferson Marketing Corporation.

On the final day of the marathon campaign, Helms flew throughout the state and tied Hunt to "homosexuals," "labor union bosses," and "crooks." He said Hunt would win only if he got "an enormous bloc vote"—a code phrase for black voters.[22] Hunt later said he realized the extent of the political beating he had taken on the morning of Election Day, when he was making last-minute voter appeals in Charlotte: A young mother, with her child in tow, told the devout Baptist, "Governor Hunt, we like you, but we're voting for the Christian."[23]

Crucially, Helms had repeatedly tied Hunt to the national Democratic Party. On the campaign trail, in television commercials, and debates, Helms also linked himself with popular President Ronald Reagan, who would carry North Carolina with 62 percent of the vote over Democratic nominee and former Vice President Walter Mondale. After one of the lengthiest and meanest campaigns in modern history, Helms beat Hunt 52 percent to 48 percent.

Certainly President Reagan's 49-state landslide helped bring out to the polls many voters likely to support Helms. "We had a bad case of calendar," said Gary Pearce, a top strategist for Hunt's campaign. "A lot of what happened to us is we got caught in a national tide."[24] Other factors were also at work. Helms's acumen as an attack politician and his ability to portray the race as a choice between an officeholder with fixed convictions and a candidate with fungible principles proved too much for Hunt to overcome. The governor had not effectively answered many of the Helms attacks early on, a reflection of the transition from a gubernatorial race, in which candidates stress technocratic management skills, to a highly charged partisan Senate race run on hot-button ideological issues. The campaign had also bounced around from message to message, without a consistent line of criticism against Helms.

The Helms campaign staffers were also risk takers, willing to pour money into the fight at crucial points even though it would drain most resources. They figured more campaign money could be raised as the race tightened. The Hunt campaign played it more cautiously. Late in the campaign, for instance, New York political consultant Dick Morris came down to North Carolina, armed with polling data showing Helms could actually be vulnerable because of his strict opposition to abortion, even in cases of rape or incest, Pearce recalled. Of course, criticizing an opponent for being too prolife in a conservative-leaning state carried risks. As a compromise, the Hunt campaign ran a few radio ads about the issue but did not turn it into a full-blown television campaign, which would have provided the widest exposure for the new message. Had the Hunt team pounded home the issue, "we might have shaken something loose," Pearce said.[25]

The race offered a foreshadowing of strategies and tactics to come in American politics, including the escalating cost of campaigns, the use of sophisticated television strategies, and the notion of attacking opponents early and often to drive down voters' positive views of them. This Senate race became a political battle of the ages, to the point that it has been used as a case study in Harvard University's Kennedy School of Government, for teaching how to make strategic decisions during high-profile, expensive, and neck-and-neck campaigns.[26]

Hunt, who returned as North Carolina governor from 1993 to 2001, said he learned two important lessons from that epic campaign. Number one, "I would never let anybody start early on me. If they started campaigning, I'd start. Don't give them six months free to be tearing you down. Number two, I learned there are times when you have to fight fire with fire."[27]

SIX YEARS LATER, JUST AS NEGATIVE, SIMILAR RESULT

During the six years after Hunt's defeat, Helms did nothing to moderate his conservative message and approach in the Senate. His power grew with seniority, first as chairman of the Agriculture Committee, a perch of particular importance to North Carolina farmers and tobacco growers, then as ranking member on the Senate Foreign Relations Committee. But as the 1990 election cycle approached there seemed to be less optimism among Democrats that the stalwart conservative could be defeated. Hunt, a political giant in North Carolina, had taken a good run at Helms and come up short. Still, Helms would be at somewhat of a disadvantage in his fourth Senate campaign, because this time he did not have a popular president at the top of the ticket. As the election season progressed and the Democratic field solidified, it became clear North Carolinians would be given a choice of two drastically different candidates. By the time the dust settled on Election Day 1990, residents had witnessed another scorching campaign and several memorable attack commercials.

In the Democratic primary, former Charlotte Mayor Harvey Gantt easily beat local district attorney Mike Easley (a future governor). Gantt, an architect by profession, had an inspiring personal story, but he was hardly the behemoth of North Carolina politics Hunt was. Gantt, then 47, was the first black to attend Clemson University, in South Carolina, and the first black mayor of North Carolina's largest city and financial center. He sought to become the first black elected to the Senate from the South since Reconstruction.

In contrast to Helms's unyielding conservatism, Gantt called for an activist government that would shift spending from the military priorities of the Cold War era to domestic needs. Running with the campaign theme, "It's time for a change," Gantt argued Helms's record as the Senate's most consistent opponent of spending on education, the environment, and health care left him working for his own conservative agenda and against the interests on North Carolina.[28]

To the surprise of many, Gantt succeeded in putting Helms on the defensive, and some polls late in the campaign showed the challenger leading. The precarious political situation prompted Helms to launch a massive media counterattack based on divisive, emotional issues, which painted Gantt as an "extreme liberal." The campaign's most famous ad targeted Gantt's support of affirmative action, an unpopular position among many whites, according to polls and surveys. The spot featured a close-up shot of two white hands holding a job rejection letter and crumpling it, as a narrator intoned, "You needed that job, and you were the best qualified. But they had to give it to a minority, because of a racial quota. Is that really fair?" The narrator continued, "Harvey Gantt says it is. Harvey Gantt supports Ted Kennedy's racial quota law that makes the color of your skin more important than your qualification. You'll vote on this issue next Tuesday—for racial quotas Harvey Gantt, against racial quotas Jesse Helms."[29]

The ad drew national media attention, much of it highly critical of Helms for injecting a "racist" theme into the campaign—a charge the senator denied. "We have not made a racial issue of it," Helms said. "He has, because he's going around encouraging, pleading for a total bloc vote of the black citizens in this state."[30] Republican media consultant Alex Castellanos, the ad's primary creator, said in 1999 that the commercial was fair and issue-based: "The message in that spot's very clear, and that is nobody should get a job, or be denied a job, because of the color of their skin. The vast majority of Americans believe that."[31]

Having been run late in the campaign, the spot has often been portrayed as the clincher in Helms's victory. But like many of the more famous negative campaign commercials over the years, the ad's media attention is out of proportion to its actual effect in moving votes. Years after the 1990 election, Carter Wrenn, one of Helms's former chief political operatives, said that according to internal poll numbers at the time, the "hands" ad, which ran for only a few days at the end of the campaign, moved voters' opinions relatively little. A more effective ad, also with an affirmative action angle, charged that as mayor Gantt profited handsomely in the purchase and resale of a television license by using a federal "minority preference" program. The issue had help sink his mayoral reelection bid in 1987, and in the Senate race three years later, internal polling data in the Helms campaign showed voters were inclined to believe the criticism. The "hands" ad has received the lion's share of attention over the years, Wrenn said, because it dealt with a national issue, affirmative action, while the television license commercial was more localized, a message that resonated with voters.

Beyond any racial aspects, Wrenn said, both affirmative action–related commercials painted Gantt as a liberal, a poisonous label among the North Carolina electorate. "That was an issue that helped show, by North Carolina standards, how far left he was," Wrenn said.[32]

Race was far from the only divisive issue of the campaign. One ad accused Gantt of surreptitiously holding fundraisers in gay bars across the country. A different Helms commercial accused Gantt of running a "secret campaign" in homosexual communities and of being committed to "mandatory gay rights laws," including "requiring local schools to hire gay teachers."

In another ad, parental consent for abortion was front and center. "Should teenage girls be allowed to have abortions without their mothers being informed?" asked the narrator. "Harvey Gantt says 'yes,' Jesse Helms says 'no.'" It concluded, "We can't undermine families." Each ad ended with the narrator sneering, "Harvey Gantt is dangerously liberal. Too liberal for North Carolina."[33]

Gantt tried in vain to throw the negativity back on Helms. Like the senator's previous opponents he argued the toxic message of the commercials aimed to distract from important issues facing North Carolina. "These days you need a warning for your TV screens, because Jesse Helms's ads may be hazardous to the truth," Gantt said in one spot. In another he told viewers, "For 18 years he's been playing on people's fears and killing this state's hopes in the process. This time it's got to stop."[34]

Voters saw it differently. Helms ended up beating Gantt 53 percent to 47 percent. Several reasons accounted for Helms's latest triumph over a hard-charging opponent. The ads centering on affirmative action issues and the Democrat's alleged ties to gays certainly raised his negative ratings among voters. But Gantt also had several built-in disadvantages. He had never before run a statewide race, and he was from Charlotte, North Carolina's largest city, a cause for skepticism among some rural residents. In addition, he had run as an unabashed liberal, which would have hurt under any circumstances in conservative-leaning North Carolina.

The results were largely the same in 1996, during the rematch between Gantt and Helms, by then chairman of the prestigious Senate Foreign Relations Committee. The second time around, on the way to a 53 percent to 46 percent win over Gantt, Helms ran a sort of stealth campaign. He refused to debate, rarely announced his public schedule, and communicated with the press mostly by fax.[35]

A LASTING IMPACT

Helms's victories, starting in 1972 and continuing with his high-profile triumphs over Hunt and Gantt, helped shape campaigns, in North Carolina and elsewhere, into their modern form: long, television-driven, negative, and with relatively few personal appearances by the candidates.[36] A driving force in this transformation was the growth and success of Helms's National Republican Congressional Club, created by Raleigh attorney Thomas F. Ellis in 1973 to retire Helms's $350,000 debt from his successful campaign the previous year. Initially Ellis handed Carter Wrenn a box of cards with 350 names, the first entries in what would become a database of contributors well into six figures.[37] In its heyday the Congressional Club (the name was shortened as the organization's success grew) was America's most successful campaign committee, raising tens of millions of dollars for conservative candidates.

Wrenn recalled that he and Ellis learned the power of television in 1978, in Helms's first reelection bid. During the heated Democratic primary, that party's candidates naturally drew most of the media attention. The Congressional Club decided to run some spots for Helms so folks would not forget he was there, as the general election was only a few months off. The ads helped move Helms's poll numbers up, Wrenn recalled, imprinting on Helms's political aides the importance of television advertising over more traditional grassroots party-organizing methods, such as candidate appearances, distributing posters, and canvassing neighborhoods with yard signs. From then on, Wrenn said, "We just completely changed how we budgeted the campaign expenditures"—with the majority going to television.[38]

The strategy was a departure from Helms's first Senate campaign in 1972, when Ellis would drive him for hours to campaign events that, they would find upon arrival, consisted of "three or four ladies with cookies," Ellis later said.[39]

In a sense, though, Helms's emergence as a leader in political television advertising was not surprising. As a commentator on local television from 1960 to 1972 Helms had specialized in bombastic editorials espousing conservative viewpoints. Some locals dubbed him "an original Rush Limbaugh" for his effective use of modern communications. The style of Helms's commercials, too, was often innovative. In the 1984 race several Helms commercials featured little boxes from Hunt's commercials to play off against what his opponent had said onscreen; this was among the first times the tactic had been used, and within a few years it was common in the campaign industry. And Helms's commercials often used dark colors, harsh sounds, sinister music, and strong words to paint a threatening picture of his opponent.[40] For a politician so many considered a throwback to an earlier era—critics would call him reactionary—Helms's campaign consistently used cutting-edge technological and marketing techniques.

The innovation extended beyond television. The Congressional Club and its maze of allied groups also specialized in hard-hitting direct mail, to both turn out voters at the polls and raise large sums of money months before Election Day. Relying heavily on negative messages, the organization borrowed fundraising techniques from businesses and churches to raise tens of millions of dollars, in relatively small contributions, through mail solicitations across the country. The direct mail solicitations would be sent to hundreds of thousands of people who had previously given to Helms and like-minded candidates. This was a departure from the days in which campaigns relied upon funding from a small cadre of wealthy, "fat cat" contributors.

Leaders of the Congressional Club were pioneers in targeting potential voters through divisive, emotional issues, which Helms would then bring up in campaigns. The fundraising appeals would often use alarmist rhetoric, warning conservatives that militant blacks, homosexuals, labor bosses, and feminists were about to take over the country—lines that would become incorporated into election season through television commercials and stump speeches. "Direct mail needs urgency," Wrenn said. "If there is a villain in the piece that helps," he added, citing the Panama Canal turnover as an issue that motivated conservative donors during the late 1970s.[41] One famous direct mail piece from Helms, requesting campaign contributions, warned recipients: "Your tax dollars are being used to pay for grade school classes that teach our children that CANNIBALISM, WIFE-SWAPPING and the MURDER of infants and the elderly are acceptable behavior."[42] Such hard-hitting direct mail appeals are now standard fare in modern campaigns.

The Congressional Club broke up in the mid-1990s amid disputes between Helms and its leaders over financial and personal issues. But in its prime it had functioned like half of a political party, without the precinct captions and other fixtures of grassroots political organizations. The group grew powerful to the point that in 1985, fresh off Helms's hard-fought victory over Hunt, its leaders even tried to organize a shareholder buyout of CBS, as a way of tempering the television network's perceived liberal bias.

That attempt failed, but the group proved most successful over the years in handpicking often obscure conservative candidates who had limited financial support and helping them to victory. In 1980 the Congressional Club helped oust Democratic Senator Robert Morgan, who lost to Republican John East, a little-known East Carolina University political science professor. East's campaign concentrated on television commercials that dwelt relentlessly on Morgan's alleged views in favor of "the Panama Canal giveaway" and the senator's position on the Occupational Safety and Health Act—stances that the conservative-leaning Morgan claimed on the Senate floor were gross distortions of his record.[43] In 1992, the Helms organization helped defeat Senator Terry Sanford after one term. The former governor, presidential candidate, and veteran Democratic warhorse lost to Republican Lauch Faircloth, who, once in office, served as a chief watchdog and tormentor of President Bill Clinton. (In 1998 Faircloth lost his seat after one term to a rookie Democratic candidate, wealthy trial lawyer John Edwards.)

Much of the ammunition Helms's campaign organization used against Democrats came from issues he helped manufacture: By demanding roll-call votes on measures certain to fail in the Senate he nonetheless put lawmakers on record concerning high-profile issues like AIDS funding, abortion, court-ordered busing, and taxpayer-financed art of questionable taste. Legislative votes on those issues could then be used to hammer candidates in campaigns through direct mail, television ads, and other means. "I wanted senators to take stands and do it publicly," Helms wrote in his 2005 autobiography, *Here's Where I Stand*. "I was willing to leave it to their constituents to decide what would happen next . . . when senators had to run on their record instead of their rhetoric, things really began to change."[44]

Such tactics of campaigning-by-legislation are now a permanent fixture of Congressional operations, and by extension, election seasons. When Republican Senate leaders call for a vote on a proposed constitutional amendment to prohibit gay marriage, it is not because they expect it to actually get the two-thirds majority support necessary; rather it is to put moderate lawmakers from socially conservative states on record voting against it, which could then become a major weapon for opponents in the next election.

Similarly, House Democrats have chafed in frustration at being denied the opportunity to offer amendments on many pieces of legislation flowing through their chamber. Many Democratic lawmakers would like to offer amendments that would repeal the Bush tax cuts for the top one percent of taxpayers and use that revenue to fund education and health-care programs or pay down the national debt. Again, it is not that Democrats actually expected to win adoption of such measures in a Republican-controlled House, but they would like to put GOP members on record voting to maintain "tax cuts for the wealthy," a sound bite that could be repeated endlessly in 30-second campaign commercials.

So long after Helms's retirement from the Senate in 2003, his influence is still being felt in the campaign world.

NOTES

1. David Broder, "Jesse Helms, White Racist," *The Washington Post*, Aug. 29, 2001.

2. Rob Christensen, "Get-Tough Ads? Get Over It," *The* (Raleigh) *News & Observer*, Oct. 20, 2002.

3. Paul Delamar, "Jesse Helms: A Tough Act to Follow," *North Carolina Political Review*, January-February 2002.

4. Helen Dewar, "Hunt, Helms in $21 Million Dead Heat," *The Washington Post*, Oct. 28, 1984.

5. William D. Snider, *Helms & Hunt: The North Carolina Senate Race, 1984* (Chapel Hill: University of North Carolina Press, 1984), 140.

6. Rob Christensen, Carol Byrne Hall, and James Rosen, "Jesse Helms: To Mold a Nation (Three Decades of Political Soul)," *The* (Raleigh) *News & Observer*, Aug. 26, 2001.

7. Snider, *Helms & Hunt*, 94

8. Interview with author, Washington, D.C., Feb. 5, 2005.

9. Interview with author, Raleigh, N.C., Feb. 22, 2005.

10. Interview with author, Raleigh, N.C., Feb. 22, 2005.

11. Interview with author, Washington, D.C., Feb. 5, 2005

12. Interview with author, by telephone, Oct. 5, 2004.

13. Tape courtesy of the Julian P. Kanter Political Commercial Archive at the University of Oklahoma Political Communication Center. [Known hereafter in this chapter as the Kanter Archive.]

14. Rob Christensen, "Hunt-Helms '84 Brawl Makes Other Races Pale," *The* (Raleigh) *News & Observer*, Sept. 19, 2004.

15. Interview with author, Washington, D.C., Feb. 5, 2005.

16. Tape courtesy of the Kanter Archive.

17. Tape courtesy of the Kanter Archive.

18. Interview with author, Washington, D.C., Feb. 5, 2005.

19. Snider, *Helms & Hunt*, 127–28

20. Snider, *Helms & Hunt*, 153.

21. Pamela Varley, "The Helms Hunt Senate Race (D): Case-let Sequels, Phase III, and Post Mortem," John F. Kennedy School of Government, Harvard University, 1986.

22. Christensen, *The* (Raleigh) *News & Observer*, Sept. 19, 2004.

23. Interview with author, Raleigh, N.C., Feb. 22, 2005.

24. Interview with author, Raleigh, N.C., Feb. 23, 2005.

25. Interview with author, Raleigh, N.C., Feb. 23, 2005.

26. Varley, "The Helms Hunt Senate Race," John F. Kennedy School of Government.

27. Interview with author, Raleigh, N.C., Feb. 22, 2005.

28. Peter Applebome, "Helms, Basking in Victory, Taunts 'Ultra-Liberal' Foes," *The New York Times*, Nov. 7, 1990.

29. Tape courtesy of the Kanter Archive.

30. Applebome, *The New York Times*, Nov. 7, 1990.

31. "The :30 Second Candidate," Wisconsin Public Television, 1999.

32. Interview with author, Raleigh, N.C., Feb. 22, 2005.

33. Tapes courtesy of the Kanter Archive.

34. Tapes courtesy of the Kanter Archive.

35. Michael Barone and Richard E. Cohen, The *Almanac of American Politics 2002* (Washington, D.C.: National Journal Group, Inc., 2001), 1133.

36. Christensen, Hall and Rosen, *The* (Raleigh) *News & Observer*, Aug. 26, 2001.

37. John Monk and Jim Morrill, "Rift in Helms Network May Rattle N.C. Politics," *The Charlotte Observer*, Oct. 2, 1994.

38. Interview with author, Raleigh, N.C., Feb. 22, 2005.

39. Kevin Sack, "Public Lives: As Helms Exits, a Conservative Crusader Will Carry On," *The New York Times*, Aug. 25, 2001.

40. James Dao, "Master of Political Attack Ads Is Under Attack Himself," *The New York Times*, Sept. 15, 2000.

41. Interview with author, Raleigh, N.C., Feb. 22, 2005.

42. Michael Kazin, *The Populist Persuasion: An American History* (Ithaca, N.Y.: Cornell University Press, 1995), 259.

43. Peter Ross Range, "Thunder from the Right: President Reagan May Find It Hard to Be Conservative Enough for Senator Jesse Helms and the New Right's True Believers," *The New York Times Magazine*, Feb. 8, 1981.

44. Senator Jesse Helms, *Here's Where I Stand: A Memoir* (New York: Random House, 2005), 65–66.

7

Dole–Gingrich: Going Negative Early and Often

In hindsight, the solid reelection of President Bill Clinton in 1996 looks like a cakewalk. With a resurgent economy and the country at peace, the Democrat never trailed in the polls against the Republican presidential nominee, former Senate Majority Leader Bob Dole of Kansas. Clinton's margin of 379 Electoral College votes to Dole's 159 made for a convincing reelection win.

Two years before, however, during the Democrats' dark days following the disastrous 1994 midterm elections, a second Clinton term seemed almost laughable. House Republicans had won control of that chamber for the first time in forty years, and their Senate counterparts gained back the majority they had lost in 1986. On the campaign trail, GOP candidates had relentlessly criticized Clinton's policies and personal foibles. Then the 1994 elections were cast as a repudiation of his presidency, particularly his enacted tax increases and failed health-care proposal.

Early in 1995, the national spotlight shifted to Speaker of the House Newt Gingrich, father of the "Contract with America," which spelled out the conservative legislation House Republicans promised to vote on during their first 100 days in power. The Georgia Republican and the GOP-controlled House he led succeeded in bringing up for a vote all ten measures mentioned in the contract; even though most passed, many did not become law because they died in the Senate or were vetoed by President Clinton.

The Republicans clearly controlled the national agenda, pushing to limit regulations, reduce taxes, and repeal gun control measures. In April 1995, Speaker Gingrich triumphantly addressed a national television audience to tout the House's accomplishments. Clinton was reduced to reminding reporters during a press conference of his constitutional relevance. Against this backdrop, some pundits suggested fancifully that Clinton not seek the 1996 Democratic nomination, in favor of a party establishment type or elder statesman who could lead the Democrats back to victory. Republican presidential candidates, meanwhile, salivated at the chance to take on the unpopular president, and the GOP primary field grew rapidly.

But little more than a year after the Republican Congress convened, Clinton's fortunes soared again. With great empathy, he had guided the nation through the horrific domestic terrorist bombing of the Alfred P. Murrah Federal Building in Oklahoma City on April 19, 1995. In the fall he turned a series of brutal budget battles with Congressional Republicans to his advantage; coverage largely blamed the GOP for intransigence in negotiations and the government shutdowns that followed. As the economy continued to gain steam after years of outright recession and then slow, sputtering growth, Clinton's political obituaries had been premature.

One weapon in Clinton's arsenal helped his 1996 reelection bid more than anything else: Gingrich, the House speaker and the president's arch political enemy. Even before it became clear who the Republican presidential nominee would be, Clinton advanced his own fortunes tremendously by relentlessly linking GOP candidates generally to Gingrich. The Georgia Republican made for an inviting target. Throughout his congressional career he had proved a ready attack dog on majority Democrats who ran the House. A relentless Clinton critic, as House minority whip he had led his party out of the political wilderness toward the first Republican majority in forty years. But because of poor public relations strategy in the budget standoff, ongoing ethics inquiries, and other reasons, he had become a political liability.

So the Clinton reelection team used the old-school tactic of linking an opponent to another unpopular political figure. The strategy had deep roots. In the 1950 Senate race in California, Republican Congressman Richard Nixon mentioned his opponent, Democratic Congresswoman Helen Gahagan Douglas, and Vito Marcantonio, a far-left wing House member from New York, in the same breath as often as he could. And during the 1976 presidential campaign critics of President Gerald Ford constantly tied him to disgraced former President Nixon, whose resignation under threat of impeachment had paved the way for Vice President Ford's ascension to the Oval Office.

Gingrich now served as the bogeyman. "In 1995 and '96 when I was running the Clinton campaign for reelection, we didn't want to run against Dole," recalled Clinton reelection strategist Dick Morris a decade later. "We wanted to run against Gingrich. So we kept talking about Newt, Newt, Newt."[1] As Democratic warnings of the "Dole–Gingrich" agenda piled up on the television airwaves through the middle months of 1996, the bombastic former backbencher could have easily been mistaken for the Republican nominee's running mate (it was actually former congressman and Housing and Urban Development Secretary Jack Kemp).

In addition, when Dole emerged as the GOP nominee in the spring of 1996, Clinton's campaign, in coordination with the Democratic National Committee, launched an unprecedented early and sustained negative advertising assault on the senator from Kansas. As chapter 6 shows, Senator Helms of North Carolina excelled at negatively defining his 1984 opponent, Governor Hunt, early for voters. On a much wider stage, the 1996 presidential race demonstrated the importance of candidates hammering opponents before most of the electorate even seemed to be seriously paying attention to politics. President George W. Bush's 2004 reelection bid refined that technique further. It is likely to grow in future presidential campaigns.

Through the negative ad campaign Clinton defined the terms of the election and undermined any chance the senator might have had to win, which was already an uphill battle. Clinton became the first Democrat to be reelected since Franklin Delano Roosevelt in 1936, even though Republicans held onto control of Congress.

AN UNLIKELY PAIR

Students of politics knew that the linkage between Senator Bob Dole and Speaker of the House Newt Gingrich was a stretch. The two had led their party's majority conferences in the Senate and House respectively, and each was a conservative. But they had hardly marched in lockstep during the budget battles that took place in the winter of 1995–1996, when congressional Republicans pushed for eventual elimination of the deficit and major cuts in federal spending programs. Gingrich had pursued a more confrontational approach against the president, reflecting the mood of the new Republican majority that had put him in the speaker's chair. Dole, by instinct a dealmaker, had sought a compromise with the president; fellow Republicans saw him as too accommodating.

Democrats made no such distinctions between the two Republican leaders. The lingering budget showdown between President Clinton and congressional Republicans provided plenty of fodder for turning Dole and Gingrich into a tag team. Beginning in spring 1996, the Clinton–Gore reelection campaign ran ads accusing "Dole–Gingrich" of all kinds of dastardly legislative deeds, even though Gingrich was Speaker of the House and not Dole's vice-presidential running mate. One of the most prominent issues was GOP-proposed cuts in Medicare—Republicans argued they were only pushing for a slowdown in the entitlement program's growth rate. In a typical Democratic television spot, the narrator intoned in a serious voice, "The Dole–Gingrich budget tried to cut Medicare $270 billion . . . President Clinton cut taxes for millions of working families. The Dole–Gingrich budget tried to raise taxes on eight million of them."[2]

Meanwhile, Gingrich was becoming politically damaged goods. In early 1996 Clinton vetoed a Republican-approved deficit-reduction package, and budget negotiations collapsed. When the Republican congressional leadership declined to pass a temporary spending measure, in what turned out to be a mistaken belief that the president would be forced to agree to their terms, the federal government shut down temporarily. Polls showed a majority of the public blamed congressional Republicans for the impasse, due to their proposed rollbacks in federal spending programs.[3] By January 1996, Gingrich's personal approval rating had fallen below 25 percent; he would never recover the political power he had had after the historic 1994 election landslide.[4] Crucially for Democrats, the evening news and cable shows repeatedly showed Dole and Gingrich walking into the White House for budget negotiations. "They really started pounding on them as the dastardly twins," recalled Rick Davis, deputy campaign manager of the Dole '96 campaign.[5]

The Democratic negative ads continued even after Dole resigned as Senate majority leader in June 1996 to concentrate on his presidential campaign.

"The president bans deadly assault weapons," asserted one ad. "Now Dole resigns, leaves gridlock he and Gingrich created."[6]

The anti-Gingrich ads extended beyond the presidential races to Democratic House campaigns, which tied GOP opponents to the unpopular speaker. Just as in the caricature of Dole by Democrats, Republican congressional candidates were frequently shown in pictures with Gingrich, portrayed as mindless clones bent on polluting the environment, balancing the budget on the backs of the poor, and evicting elderly people from nursing homes. Gingrich himself estimated that out of about 75,000 political spots aired that year, ten percent criticized him.[7]

Using the speaker of the House as the centerpiece of a negative advertising campaign was not unprecedented. In October 1980, the National Republican Congressional Committee spent several million dollars running a national generic party ad showing a Lincoln Town Car running out of gas, as a lookalike of Democratic House Speaker Tip O'Neill was dazed and confused about the direction the country was headed. The message was designed to be a broadside against congressional Democrats, linking them with what many voters considered the incompetent leadership of President Jimmy Carter's administration.[8] The ads mocked the House speaker as overweight, haggard, and out of gas. Such an effort was minor compared to the linkage created sixteen years later between Dole and the first Republican House speaker in forty years.

A COORDINATED EFFORT

Dole got caught on the receiving end of a massive Democratic advertising blitz that began more than a year before Election Day, long before it was clear he would be the Republican nominee. During the summer of 1995 the Clinton campaign began airing $2.4 million in campaign ads, many of them in such swing-state cities as Fresno, Tampa, and Raleigh. These commercials, largely run under the radar screen of the national media, were positive "issue ads" that would allow Clinton to dictate the national agenda before Republicans knew what had hit them.[9] But a series of ads also blasted congressional Republicans and were often coordinated efforts with the Democratic National Committee (DNC).

The negative spots intensified once Dole emerged as the Republican nominee. Many of the DNC spots used the Clinton campaign's linkage strategy. In one DNC ad released in May 1996, the narrator said, "America's values—Head

Start, student loans, toxic cleanup, extra police, protected in the budget agreement, the president stood firm. Dole–Gingrich's latest plan includes a tax hike
on working families."[10] Though the sponsor was different, this message was
virtually indistinguishable from the one being offered by president's team.
The Dole–Gingrich message, combined with the Democrats' fatter wallet,
made for a potent weapon against the Republican candidate. (The coordination between the Clinton campaign and DNC would later be the source of
embarrassing hearings on the Democrats' campaign finance schemes for the
1996 elections, which revealed a series of questionable sources for the money.)

Dole's ability to fight back was hampered by his acceptance of matching
funds from the taxpayers to help pay for his Republican primary campaign.
Under this system, Dole and Clinton, like all major-party presidential candidates in recent decades up to that point, accepted money from the federal
treasury, which "matched" a percentage of their own fundraising. So they
could take that money, candidates agreed to abide by state-by-state spending
caps. By spring 1996, Dole had reached his primary-season spending caps. His
next infusion of cash would not come until he officially accepted the Republican nomination in August 1996. So in late spring and early summer he had
to campaign on a shoestring, while the unchallenged Clinton-Gore reelection
campaign was flush with primary cash—to the tune of $37 million—and the
Democrats hammered away at the presumptive Republican nominee through
negative ads.

At the time it was unheard of for presidential candidates to decline federal
matching funds, which would have allowed them to finance primary campaigns through privately raised money and spend as much as they wanted.
Had the Dole campaign declined federal matching funds, it could have raised
$100 million, recalled Rick Davis, Dole's deputy campaign manager. "Bob
Dole never had trouble raising money," he added, "and he was still majority
leader" while running in the Republican primaries.[11]

Dole was forced to spend almost all of his allotment for the primary season
simply fighting off his GOP opponents. Then came the onslaught of the Democrats' Dole–Gingrich ads, which introduced an aggressive air war against the
Republican during what had traditionally been considered a dead period. Previously, candidates had spent this time between the end of primary season and
the summer conventions consolidating their party bases, to make sure they
got a good turnout in November. The presumptive party nominees "never re-

ally paid much attention to each other," Davis said. "There wasn't actual voter contact directed at attacking the opponent."[12] Even during the heated 1988 presidential campaign, in which the campaign of Vice President George H. W. Bush's campaign relentlessly criticized Massachusetts Governor Michael Dukakis, the attacks did not begin in earnest until midsummer. As president running for reelection four years later, Bush waited until August 17, 1992, to say Bill Clinton's name. And President Ronald Reagan, on his way to a landslide victory in 1984, did not mention Democratic nominee Walter Mondale by name until October 12 of that year.[13]

For the Dole campaign, whether to accept primary matching funds was never really in doubt because of the campaign mores at the time. The matching-funds system was part of the post-Watergate campaign finance laws that aimed to make candidates less reliant on large individual contributions. Tradition mandated that to decline matching funds and rely solely on private money would violate the spirit if not the letter of the law. At the very least such a move would certainly trigger a barrage of negative news stories, which would suggest the candidate was using a technicality to evade campaign-finance limits. Clinton later said his campaign advisers had urged him to decline matching funds, but he didn't feel it was right. Of course, the unusually tight coordination with the DNC provided significant financial resources to the president's campaign.

"POSITIVE NEGATIVES"

Though Dole was at a financial disadvantage and on the defensive for crucial months after securing the Republican nomination, he wasn't a hapless victim of a mean Democratic smear machine. The former Senate majority leader was known for his hard-edged campaign style. During his stint as Republican National Committee chairman from 1971 to 1973, Dole was a tough partisan for the GOP, particularly as a vocal defender of President Richard Nixon before much of the damaging information about Watergate emerged. In Dole's 1974 reelection bid, his Senate career was threatened by a strong challenge from Democrat William Roy, a two-term House member and OB/GYN practitioner. Dole labeled his opponent an "abortionist" and in a debate late in the campaign challenged the doctor on how many times he had performed the procedure.[14] Occurring the year after the *Roe v. Wade* Supreme Court decision,[15] the Senate race marked one of the first times that abortion was politicized in a congressional campaign.

Senator Dole's runs for national office had included a series of nasty political barbs. As the running mate of President Gerald Ford in 1976, he memorably labeled World War II and the Korean conflict "Democrat wars," in reference to the commanders in chief whose watch they had begun under. In 1988 he famously admonished his Republican presidential primary rival, Vice President George H. W. Bush, to "stop lying about my record."

Throughout the 1996 presidential primaries Dole was not afraid to heap criticism on the policies and proposals of fellow GOP aspirants, such as Senator Phil Gramm of Texas, former Governor Lamar Alexander of Tennessee, publisher Steve Forbes, and others. The primary season reinforced the notion that Dole was a tough guy. Dole hid his fun side, which would be on abundant display during the years after he left office. Having participated in clinical trials for Viagra after being treated for prostate cancer in the early 1990s, he starred in a commercial for the drug in 1999, he then appeared in a Pepsi spot that lampooned the Viagra ad. At the 2000 Republican National Convention, Dole got more attention for his appearance on *Comedy Central* than for his speech.

The ads against Dole in 1996 were not personal or focused on "character issues." Democrats stuck to attacking Dole on public policy grounds, whether Medicare, Medicaid, education, or the environment. At the same time many of Clinton's ads argued that the president had a positive agenda on those issues. In fact the Clinton-Gore campaign in 1996 raised the use of "positive negative" ads to a new art form, in which criticism of the opponent was sandwiched between praise for the candidate running the commercial. This fist-in-a-velvet-glove approach allowed the Clinton campaign to get its licks in against the Republican without taking the blame for running negative ads.

Take the television ad "Drums," in which slogans quickly flashed across the screen while a menacing-sounding percussion instrument beat ominously in the background. The text read: "Newt Gingrich. Bob Dole. Dole–Gingrich. Against family leave. Against a woman's right to choose. Dole. Gingrich. Cutting vaccines for children. Against Brady Bill and assault weapons ban. Against higher minimum wage. Cutting college scholarships." Those negative slogans took up about 15 seconds. Then, to the sound of a catchy, fast-moving, optimistic-sounding drum riff, the next half of the commercial proclaimed: "Clinton–Gore. Brady Bill signed. Higher minimum wage signed. College tuition tax deductible. Clinton/Gore. $500 per child tax credit. Clean air and water. Internet access for schools. Economic growth. Ten million new jobs. When it comes to America's future, which drummer do YOU want to march to? Vote Clinton–Gore."[16]

A similar approach worked well in the ad "Surgeon." It featured wide-eyed children discussing their distant professional ambitions, including desires to be a doctor, civil engineer, astronaut, and airline pilot. Then the viewer learned that Clinton supported a $1,500 tuition tax credit, making $10,000 of college tuition tax deductible and "all college more affordable." Dole–Gingrich, meanwhile, had tried to cut scholarships, and, according to the commercial, wanted to dismantle the Department of Education. The contrasts could not have been clearer. Because much of the commercial was set to bright, cheery music and only a few seconds devoted to the opponents, the viewer hardly might have thought of it as a negative ad, even though it very much was.

The positive/negative approach extended to the campaign trail and candidate debates. During the second and final debate between the two presidential aspirants, Clinton was asked if Dole's age—he would be 73 upon inauguration—disqualified him from the White House. "I don't think Senator Dole is too old to be president. It's the age of his ideas that I question," Clinton responded.[17] In one stroke Clinton had shown respect to an elder statesman while leveling criticism at his opponent. This line also effectively played off President Ronald Reagan's highly effective remark in a 1984 debate against Democratic nominee Walter Mondale, "I will not make age an issue in this campaign. I'm not going to exploit for political purposes my opponent's youth and inexperience."[18]

LESSONS LEARNED

Though Republicans lost the 1996 presidential election soundly, it offered important strategic and tactical lessons for later campaigns. Presidential candidates realized that accepting federal matching funds meant that they did not have the resources to fight back against drawn-out political attacks.

And the 1996 campaign demonstrated the importance and effectiveness of presumptive nominees setting the agenda themselves, going after the opponent long before the general election season. In that regard, Bush in 2004 began to define John F. Kerry negatively almost immediately after the senator from Massachusetts emerged as the de facto Democratic nominee. Bush ran his first attack ad March 4—two days after Kerry's victories in the "Super Tuesday" primaries effectively clinched the Democratic nomination. By the end of May 2004, the Bush-Cheney campaign had bought 49,050 spots in the hundred top media markets; three-quarters of Bush's ads were negative.[19] The strategy helped soften up Kerry for the general election campaign and center the debate on issues that were favorable to Bush, such as national security and fighting the war on terror.

The negative campaign against Kerry was comprehensive and coordinated. Through the television ads, news releases, websites, e-mail, and statements by Bush spokesmen and surrogates, the Bush-Cheney campaign drove home the message that Kerry had "flip-flopped" on Iraq, support for the military, taxes, education, and other matters. Chastised in some quarters for this unprecentedly early onslaught of negativity, the Bush campaign argued the president was responding to heaps of criticism that Democratic presidential candidates piled on his record during the primaries.[20] The coordinated negative campaign worked effectively to drive up Kerry's negative ratings.

The Republicans also learned about the power of linkage to unpopular politicians. Gingrich's high profile in 1996 had played into the Democrats' strategy by providing them a prominent target. Eight years later, Democrats tried a similar tactic by linking GOP candidates with House Majority Leader Tom DeLay of Texas. Though he was popular with his Republican colleagues, DeLay had taken a severe public relations beating. The House ethics committee had admonished him several times, for enlisting the help of federal aviation officials in a redistricting dispute, for the appearance of linking political donations and legislation, and for suggesting that he'd support the candidacy of a Republican lawmaker's son in return for a vote for a Medicare prescription drug benefit. At the same time, the district attorney in Travis County, Texas, had indicted three of DeLay's political associates in a corporate campaign donation controversy, though at the time the investigation never appeared to touch on DeLay himself.

During the 2004 election cycle, Democrats tried to paint Bush, Republican congressional candidates, and the House majority leader as one in the same. But DeLay kept a relatively low profile on the campaign trail. Unlike Gingrich, whose exuberant ego had kept him in the spotlight throughout the 1996 campaign, DeLay quietly helped raise money for fellow Republicans from behind the scenes. His lack of public prominence meant that Democrats were unable to get traction on the issue.[21] The GOP picked up seats in Congress, at the same time President Bush won reelection. "He let them take their hits, and he sat down and shut up," said Rick Davis, the veteran Republican political consultant. "He helped Bush. If he had gone out there and sort of engaged the enemy, that's exactly what they wanted."[22]

And while in 1996 Clinton mastered the art of linking his political opponent to an unpopular figure, he himself had previously been on the receiving end of an onslaught of negative associations. During the 1994 midterm elections Clinton proved to be a severe handicap for many Democrats, particularly in the South. One of the GOP's more popular tactics included "morphing" commercials, in which Democratic candidates turned into Clinton. The technique first garnered widespread attention in spring 1994, when Republican Ron Lewis won a special election to a traditionally Democratic U.S. House seat in Kentucky after an ad showed Democrat Joe Prather electronically "morphing" into Clinton. Candidates in other races followed suit, and similar comparisons played out in dozens of successful Republican campaigns across the country. A slew of Republican ads in the days before the November 1994 elections maintained that select House and Senate Democrats cast the "deciding vote" for President Clinton's deficit reduction measure the previous year, which included tax increases on upper-income earners.[23]

Even the most moderate Democrats could not escape Clinton's shadow. In an open seat Senate race in Oklahoma, Democratic Congressman David McCurdy ran against fellow House member James Inhofe. McCurdy, first elected to his seat from southwest Oklahoma in 1980 at age 30, had long been considered a rising star, and when his opportunity for political advancement finally came, he seemed to fit the state's general mold of a conservative Democrat. Yet no matter what he said or did on the campaign trail that year, he could not shake his association with Clinton, particularly because the two had been leaders together in the centrist Democratic Leadership Council. McCurdy had even made a nominating speech for Clinton at the 1992 Democratic National Convention. No matter how much the Democratic Senate candidate tried to point out differences with the president, Inhofe could top it. A virulent Clinton critic, Inhofe voted against the Family and Medical Leave Act, the Brady Bill, mandating a waiting period for handgun purchases, the 1993 budget and economic stimulus pack, the North American Free Trade Agreement, and the assault weapons ban.[24] An Inhofe commercial showed

McCurdy's face morphing into Clinton's (it didn't help that the pair shared a striking physical resemblance, with a big shock of graying hair and wide smile.) Inhofe won, 55 percent to 40 percent.

In a different context, in 2000 President Clinton again became part of a negative political linkage strategy, this time tagged with his heir apparent, Vice President Al Gore. Republicans hung Gore with "Clinton fatigue," lingering negative associations from the president's behavior in the Monica Lewinksy scandal two years earlier. On the day the House impeached Clinton in December 1998, Gore called his boss one of the nation's best presidents. In summer 2000, in Texas Gov. George W. Bush's speech accepting the Republican presidential nomination, he referenced the Democratic incumbent. "Our current president embodied the potential of a generation. So many talents. So much charm. Such great skill . . . So much promise. . . . Instead of seizing his moment, the Clinton-Gore administration has squandered it. . . . And now they come asking for another chance."[25]

Gore tried to align himself with Clinton's policies but distance himself from the president's personal problems. Gore succeeded only partially in fending off the linkage. Despite Clinton's eagerness to campaign, Gore kept his boss at arm's length, afraid he would hurt more than he would help. Clinton arguably could have shored up support for Gore in strategic Electoral College targets, such as the president's home state of Arkansas. Gore lost that state to Bush by the relatively small margin of about 50,000 votes (51 percent to 46 percent), and its six Electoral College votes would have been enough to make him the winner of the presidency.

In 2002, Senator Inhofe of Oklahoma once again used the image of the 42nd president as a punching bag, when he faced former Governor David Walters. The Democrat had run into trouble during his one term in office, from 1991 to 1995; in October 1993, he pleaded guilty to a misdemeanor count of violating campaign finance laws during his 1990 campaign, and in exchange the prosecution dropped eight felony counts. So an Inhofe ad featured the former president and Oklahoma governor, represented by actors in a classroom setting. "Listen, David, people forget about scandals," a smiling, bubbly "Clinton" told his students. "You had the eight-felony indictment. Heck, we were both nearly impeached." A more serious narrator then jumped in with, "They were ineffective governors of neighboring states. Bill Clinton has raised thousands of East Coast liberal dollars for Walters, and they are most remembered for scandal."[26] Once again, Inhofe prevailed, sailing to re-election 57 percent to 36 percent.

Bill Clinton was not the only one in his family to become a target of negative political linkage. His wife, New York Senator Hillary Rodham Clinton, became a source of tension for Republican candidates jockeying for the Texas Republican gubernatorial nomination in 2006. Senator Kay Bailey Hutchison was actively considering a Republican primary challenge to Governor Rick Perry. His campaign, attempting to portray her as left-leaning, hired a video crew to tape her and Senator Clinton on stage together at a women's history museum in Washington, D.C., in March 2005. The tape showed Clinton saying she was "delighted that Kay is my partner on so many important fronts." Perry supporters circulated the video via e-mail. A few days later, the tables were turned when a Hutchison campaign staffer released a 1993 letter in which Perry, then Texas agriculture commissioner, commended then-First Lady Clinton for her efforts on health-care reform.[27]

The linkage tactic, perfected by President Bill Clinton's 1996 reelection team, remains a tried and true method of negative campaigning, particularly when the opposition is a divisive political figure. It is likely to only increase as advances in digital technology have made it easier for ads to morph photographs and to employ other visual gimmicks. The strategy has proved among the toughest for candidates to combat, because they are tacitly forced to answer for the actions of others.

The Clinton campaign against Dole had other long-term effects on political strategies as well. The memory of Clinton's success in defining Bob Dole negatively so early, because the Republican lacked the resources to fully defend himself, contributed to later candidates' decisions to forgo matching funds and raise more money on their own. Texas Governor George W. Bush was the first major-party nominee to do so when he secured the Republican presidential nod in 2000. "I'm mindful of what happened in 1996," Bush said as his campaign opened. "I'm not going to let it happen to me."[28]

Multimillionaire publisher Steve Forbes, a Republican rival largely financing his own campaign, also rejected matching funds that year. On the Democratic side, in 2000, Vice President Al Gore accepted the federal matching money, which limited him to a total of $33.5 million to spend during the primary season. That cap allowed the Republicans to launch months of negative advertising against Gore—and positive commercials about Bush—before the vice president officially accepted the Democratic nomination and received a fresh infusion of federal money.

By 2004 the notion of matching funds seemed almost quaint. Despite lacking primary opposition, President Bush declined matching funds and raised $270 million, six times the $45 million overall limit available to candidates who opted into the public financing system. On the Democratic side, former Vermont Governor Howard Dean, at the height of his popularity in fall 2003 and flush with campaign cash from prodigious Internet fund raising, rejected the public money. That decision caused Senator John Kerry of Massachusetts, the eventual nominee, to follow the same course; he showed his own fund-raising prowess by raising $235 million before accepting his party's nod.[29]

These decisions, the legacy of Clinton's strategy against Dole in the 1996 race, ratcheted up the costs of presidential campaign exponentially and had a direct effect on their negative tone. They eliminated the traditional lulls in the campaign cycle and invited candidate attacks earlier and earlier.

NOTES

1. Transcript from "The O'Reilly Factor," FOX NewsChannel, April 14, 2005.

2. Ruth Marcus and Charles R. Babcock, "System Cracks Under Weight of Cash," *The Washington Post*, Feb. 9, 1997.

3. Eric Patashnik, "Congress and the Budget Since 1974," in *The American Congress: The Building of Democracy*, ed. Julian E. Zelizer (New York: Houghton Mifflin Company, 2004), 683.

4. Major Garrett, The *Enduring Revolution: How the Contract with America Continues to Shape the Nation*, (New York: Crown Forum, 2005), 127.

5. Interview with author, Alexandria, Va., Feb. 10, 2005.

6. Tape courtesy of the Julian P. Kanter Political Commercial Archive at the University of Oklahoma Political Communication Center. [Known hereafter in this chapter as the Kanter Archive.]

7. Darrell M. West, *Air Wars: Television Advertising in Election Campaigns, 1952–1996* (Washington, D.C.: Congressional Quarterly, Inc., 1997), 168.

8. Glen Bolger, "'Top Gun Comes to Politics," *Roll Call*, May 23, 2005.

9. Marcus and Babcock, *The Washington Post*, Feb. 9, 1997.

10. Tape courtesy of the Kanter Archive.

11. Interview with author, Alexandria, Va., Feb. 10, 2005.

12. Interview with author, Alexandria, Va., Feb. 10, 2005.

13. Martin Kasindorf and Mark Memmott, "'04 Slugfest May Appeal to, Not Repel, Voters," *USA Today*, March 12, 2004.

14. Transcript, PBS's *Frontline*, "The Choice '96," Oct. 8, 1996. (http://www.pbs.org/wgbh/pages/frontline/shows/choice/)

15. 410 U.S. 113 (1973).

16. Ad courtesy of The American Museum of the Moving Image's "The Living Room Candidate: Presidential Campaign Commercials 1952–2004" (http://livingroomcandidate.movingimage.us/index.php).

17. Transcript of the second Clinton-Dole presidential debate, Oct. 16, 1996, University of San Diego, San Diego, Calif., from the Commission on Presidential Debates (http://www.debates.org/pages/trans96b.html).

18. Paul F. Boller, Jr., *Presidential Campaigns: From George Washington to George W. Bush* (New York: Oxford University Press, 2004), 371.

19. Evan Thomas and the Staff of *Newsweek, Election 2004: How Bush Won and What You Can Expect in the Future* (New York: PublicAffairs, 2004), 67.

20. Dana Milbank and Jim VandeHei, "From Bush, Unprecedented Negativity: Scholars Say Campaign is Making History with Often-Misleading Attacks," *The Washington Post*, May 31, 2004.

21. DeLay became a top Democratic target again in 2005, when on Sept. 28 he was forced to relinquish his leadership post, after the first of two indictments for alleged involvement in money laundering related to 2002 Texas legislative elections. DeLay was indicted in Austin, Texas, by a Travis County grand jury, on criminal charges of conspiracy to violate election laws in 2002. Soon after, he was also indicted on charges of money laundering by another grand jury. In accordance with House Republican Conference rules, DeLay stepped down from his position as House majority leader. He publicly denied the charges, saying that they were a partisan move by Travis County District Attorney Ronnie Earle. Amid the political and legal

proceedings, Democrats took fresh aim at DeLay in advance of the 2006 midterm elections, tying him to what they called a broader "culture of corruption" surrounding the operating style of the GOP congressional majority and the Bush White House.

22. Interview with author, Alexandria, Va., Feb. 10, 2005.

23. Christopher J. Dolan, "Two Cheers for Negative Ads," in *Lights, Camera, Campaign!*, ed. David A. Schultz (New York: Peter Lang, 2004), 51–52.

24. Philip D. Duncan and Christine C. Lawrence, *Politics in America 1996: The 104th Congress* (Washington, D.C.: Congressional Quarterly, Inc., 1995), 1071–72.

25. Boller, *Presidential Campaigns*, 407.

26. Video courtesy of Strategic Perception, Inc., Hollywood, Calif.

27. Kelley Shannon, "Texas May See GOP Clash Over Governorship," *Associated Press*, April 11, 2005.

28. Jonathan D. Salant, "With $30 Million in the Bank, Bush Gives Up Federal Funds," *Associated Press*, July 16, 1999.

29. Norman Ornstein, "BCRA Works, So Let's Focus on Presidential Fund-raising Now," *Roll Call*, Feb. 16, 2005.

8

The Politics of Fear: Negative Campaigning in the Post-9/11 World

In what was expected to be a routine legislative day in the U.S. House of Representatives, Congressman Peter DeFazio, Democrat of Oregon, took to the floor early one Tuesday morning to lambaste Republicans' Social Security and tax policies. "The tax cuts are the thing that is putting us in the hole," DeFazio argued in the routinely partisan manner of the closely divided House. The federal government could not afford the tax rebates it had just distributed: "Cash the check quickly," he advised. "It might bounce soon."[1] The issue of fiscal responsibility was sure to be a major cudgel for Democrats to hammer Republicans with in the run-up to the midterm elections, which would take place 14 months later.

Shortly after DeFazio finished his speech, on Sept. 11, 2001, Capitol police evacuated the building, as members of Congress quickly scattered like everyone else inside; many were left milling about on the Capitol lawn, frantically punching in keys on cell phones, Blackberries, and Palm Pilots to get a read on the chaotic situation. As word spread about the twin attacks on the World Trade Center in New York City it seemed Washington, D.C.—and possibly the Capitol itself—could be the next target of what was obviously a coordinated terrorist plot. Their worst fears seemed to be confirmed when they looked toward the west and saw smoke rising, the aftermath of the jet that had just crashed into the side of the Pentagon.

As the hours passed and the enormity and horror of the terrorist attacks became clear, members of Congress received intelligence briefings that quickly pointed to Osama bin Laden and his al-Qaeda network as the perpetrators of the assaults. These terrorists needed to get a message, lawmakers decided: To demonstrate that democracy and open society would not be deterred by the nation's enemies, members of Congress convened on the Capitol's east side. As the sun set on the most prominent symbol of democracy, a faint smell of smoke wafted from the still-smoldering Pentagon, across the Potomac River from Virginia to Washington, D.C., and toward the Capitol dome. On that somber Tuesday night the tough partisan rhetoric that had permeated the hallowed House and Senate chambers only hours earlier now seemed a distant memory. Elected officials as disparate ideologically as House Majority Leader Dick Armey, the conservative Texas Republican, and Congresswoman Maxine Waters, the firebrand liberal from South Los Angeles, stood arm in arm with colleagues to sing "God Bless America" in an unprecedented show of bipartisan unity. Party labels had quickly disappeared, as the nation tried to make sense of the worst terrorist attacks in American history, which had resulted in nearly 3,000 deaths.

In the days and weeks immediately after the tragedy, an array of bipartisan legislation moved quickly through Congress. Though a few legislators did voice concerns, the House and Senate quickly concurred on a financial relief package for New York City, a victims' compensation fund package for those who lost relatives and loved ones in the terrorist attacks, and a measure to prop up the near-bankrupt airlines. The resolution authorizing force to respond to the attacks, soon acted upon in the Afghanistan war to uproot al-Qaeda and evict the ruling Taliban regime, passed nearly unanimously (only one House member dissented, Democrat Barbara Lee, who represented Berkeley, Calif.) The Patriot Act, an anti-terror law that beefed up law enforcement powers, passed in October 2001 with strong bipartisan support, only weeks after the attack.

The anthrax attacks on several Senate and House offices and scares about further contamination only unified Congress further. Senator Bill Frist of Tennessee, a doctor who as chairman of the Senate Republicans' campaign organization openly sought to turn Democrats out of office, now advised them on how best to respond to health threats to themselves and their staff members.

On the House side, Speaker Dennis Hastert (R-Ill.) conferred regularly with Minority Leader Dick Gephardt (D-Mo.); prior to September 11 they had been barely on speaking terms. The top House leaders also huddled together with President George W. Bush at the White House, where they hashed out emergency bipartisan legislative proposals, joined by Senate Majority Leader Tom Daschle (D-S.D.), and Senate Minority Leader Trent Lott (R-Miss.).Under these stressful circumstances the working relationships became so tight that when Bush entered the House chamber to deliver a joint address to Congress on September 20, he hugged Daschle, formerly his political nemesis. Republicans and Democrats stood as one; neither side would politicize the sorrowful events.

Fast-forward a year to fall 2002, when the political atmosphere regarding terrorism-related issues had changed dramatically. An image of Osama Bin Laden, the mastermind of the September 11 attacks, and video of Iraqi dictator Saddam Hussein would be used in a Georgia U.S. Senate campaign commercial to seemingly suggest one candidate was less than resolute in fighting the war on terror. Questions of who could best protect America from terrorists, previously off-limits in political discourse, became fodder for 30-second campaign ads, like other partisan issues such as tax cuts, health care, guns, and gay rights.

Democrats blame a television ad in the Georgia Senate race for ushering in a new era of negative campaigning, based on the politics of fear. Republicans contend the television spot in question has been wildly misconstrued and that the defeated side has successfully played the victim in a political race it lost fair and square. "The Democrats could not believe they were defeated, so they had to try to pick something out other than themselves and their policies and their votes to blame it on," said Tom Perdue, a Republican media consultant and creator of the commercial.

Whatever one's perspective on its propriety, the use in political commercials of images showing the nation's enemies and the 9/11 attacks is a practice unlikely to dissipate as long as the United States and the world face major terror threats. "This is the new Communism, the new Cold War," said Democratic strategist Jamal Simmons, a reference to the white-hot political issue of the early 1950s that tripped up many a candidate during an era of fear and paranoia.

A SLOW CREEP

As weeks and months passed after the terrorist attacks, fissures in the bipartisan unity of Capitol Hill began to emerge. Citizens across the country sought to return to some sense of normality, and Congress began to take up a regular order of business. On issues such as tax cuts, trade, and energy, old-style partisanship slowly began to reassert itself. The biggest threat to bipartisan cooperation seemed to be the tendency on both sides of the aisle to repackage controversial programs under the frame of "antiterrorism."[2] In the House, majority Republicans pushed through a series of tax and trade policies disliked by Democrats, and members of the minority party delicately voiced opposition.

Partisan rancor rose as the White House and Congress began grappling with complex and difficult questions of how best to prevent future attacks against an enemy clearly willing to take drastic measures to achieve its destructive goals. What had served as an unwritten truce between the Republicans and Democrats began to fray in January 2002, when senior White House political advisor Karl Rove told Republican National Committee members that the administration's handling of terrorism could be an important theme for the party to trumpet in the November midterm elections. "Americans trust the Republicans to do a better job of keeping our communities and our families safe," Rove said. "We can also go to the country on this issue because they trust the Republican Party to do a better job of protecting and strengthening America's military might and thereby protecting America."[3]

The remarks were striking because only days before President Bush himself had suggested that terrorism not be a campaign issue. At a town hall meeting on January 14 in Ontario, California, the president had said, "It's time to take the spirit of unity that has been prevalent when it comes to fighting the war and bring it to Washington, D.C."[4]

Not surprisingly, congressional Democrats immediately pounced on Rove's comments as a violation of the informal political truce that had held since September 11. "Democrats will continue working with the president to win the war on terrorism—regardless of how cynically White House officials use the war to help the Republican Party," said Congressman Martin Frost of

Texas, the House Democratic Caucus chairman. "America cannot afford to allow partisan politics to have any role in the war effort."[5]

Divisions over who could best lead the fight against terrorism issue grew that spring, when information emerged indicating the Bush administration had been warned in August 2001 that Osama bin Laden's associates might be planning airline hijackings. As lawmakers and the press raised questions about whether the administration had seen intelligence raising the possibility of a large-scale attack on American soil, White House Press Secretary Ari Fleischer suggested the matter "crosses the lines" of legitimate political comment.[6]

And Democrats ratcheted up criticism of the White House amid reports over a fundraising technique of questionable taste: For $150 the Republican Senate and House campaign committees offered a series of three photographs of President Bush that included one of him talking on the telephone with Vice President Dick Cheney just hours after the 9/11 attacks. Democrats argued the photo was being used to capitalize on a national tragedy, while Republicans said it was an honest portrayal of the president at work.

THE GEORGIA STORY

It was against this backdrop of slowly creeping partisanship that the 2002 U.S. Senate race in Georgia became so prominent in the political fight over who could best protect the nation from future terrorist attacks. That Georgia would be the center of political action would have been difficult to predict early in the 2002 election cycle, simply because the race was not thought to be particularly competitive. Democratic Senator Max Cleland looked relatively safe for reelection. In a post-9/11 world, when national security and strength were foremost on the minds of Americans, Cleland embodied patriotism, sacrifice, and love of country. As a young man he had volunteered for Army service in Vietnam. In the field he lost both legs and his right arm when a loose grenade exploded. Piecing his life back together, he returned to Georgia and embarked on what would be a successful political career: He won a seat in the state Senate at age 28, the youngest person to serve in that body; he was secretary of Veterans' Affairs in the administration of President Jimmy Carter; and Georgia voters elected him four times as secretary of state.

After being elected to an open Senate seat in 1996, Cleland compiled a relatively moderate voting record, at least compared to his more liberal brethren in the Democratic Caucus. In May 2001 Cleland had voted for Bush's tax cuts.

In October 2002 he voted to authorize the use of force against Iraq, which put him on the same side of the issue as the president, a very popular figure in Georgia. And in his 2002 reelection bid Cleland had the support of Zell Miller, Georgia's junior senator, who was bitingly critical of most other Democrats in Washington.

Cleland's Republican opponent in 2002 was Congressman Saxby Chambliss, who represented a Moultrie-based district in the south-central part of the Peach State. Most professional political analysts considered Chambliss the underdog, due in part to Cleland's seemingly moderate Senate voting record and his veteran status (a bad knee had allowed Chambliss to avoid service in Vietnam). The small-town lawyer had come to Congress as a member of the Republican class that helped sweep the party to power in the House in 1994. He had risen steadily there, earning a high-ranking position on the House Budget Committee. But when the time came to hand out chairmanships after the 2000 elections Chambliss was passed over to lead that panel. Further to Chambliss's dismay, a redistricting map drawn by state Democrats carved up his political base; to win reelection he likely would have had to run against a fellow Republican House member in a primary. Instead he chose to run for the Senate against Cleland.

The Democrat's hold on the seat was not as secure as it initially seemed. After all, Cleland had narrowly beat his Republican opponent in 1996, 49 percent to 48 percent, and Georgia had strongly favored Bush over Vice President Al Gore in the 2000 presidential election. In addition, each remotely competitive Senate seat would be hotly contested: In a 50–49 Senate (with one Democratic-leaning Independent), the Democrats' majority hung by a single seat.

As the race heated up in summer 2002, Chambliss sought to paint Cleland as a liberal Democrat out of touch with Georgia voters. Chambliss tied Cleland as much as possible to the Democratic Senate majority, which the Republican argued was obstructing the president's agenda. Chambliss ramped up his criticism with a series of 10-second spots that mentioned Cleland's opposition to an amendment banning aid for schools that barred the Boy Scouts, his votes against the partial-birth-abortion ban, his support of school clinics passing out morning-after pills without parental permission, and his vote against confirmation of Attorney General John Ashcroft, among others.[7]

Each of the issues got raised in commercials in different media markets around Georgia. Once the ads ran, Cleland had to respond to disparate questions by reporters about these Republican-oriented issues. To an extent, the attacks diverted Cleland away from his own campaign agenda, which included emphasis on Social Security and health care. "Their whole line was, 'Max Cleland's too liberal for Georgia,'" said Matt McKenna, the Democrat's campaign research director. "Our whole response to that was, 'Max Cleland's a consensus builder, he voted for the tax cut; he's going to support the president when he's right and oppose him when he's wrong. But Georgia's always going to come first.'"[8]

Still, Chambliss's criticisms revolved around conventional partisan campaign issues that did not distinguish this Senate race from other contests around the country. Added into this mix was homeland security, the issue that a year before had been off-limits in politics but now helped stoke Chambliss's electoral fortunes.

Because of legislative infighting among Republicans and Democrats in the Senate, Cleland began to look increasingly vulnerable on the homeland security issue. Shortly after the September 11, 2001, terrorist attacks, President Bush created the position of director of homeland security, an executive-branch job, answerable to the president. Democrats had pushed to expand the position to become part of the Cabinet, a job that would require Senate confirmation. The Homeland Security Department would also have its own budget authority, and its power would be expanded to take in several existing federal agencies.

The proposal initially came from a Democratic senator, Joseph Lieberman of Connecticut, and Bush resisted it. Eventually, though, the president came around and embraced the proposal with gusto, except for one element: He said personnel provisions of the Democratic bill did not leave enough flexibility to hire and fire workers, which when dealing with sensitive national security issues needed to be done quickly and with minimal obstacles. With a slim Senate majority, Democratic leaders decided to block Bush's version of the Homeland Security Department plan because it did not include a provision guaranteeing labor rights for federal workers. Cleland went along, opposing the limited degree of flexibility over work rules the new department would have.

Cleland's decision to side with the majority Democrats gave Chambliss an opening to declare his opponent more interested in the fortunes of labor unions than in standing with Bush in beefing up homeland security. In mid-October Chambliss ran an ad that opened with a montage of military images, including U.S. fighter planes and soldiers. In the screen's top left appeared Osama Bin Laden, the 9/11 mastermind, staring off to the side; in the bottom right was Iraqi dictator Saddam Hussein, shaking hands with one of his generals. A single, menacing piano chord sounded over and over. Then, after the images of the international villains dropped from the screen, over a grainy black-and-white picture of Cleland, the narrator intoned, "As America faces terrorists and extremist dictators, Max Cleland runs television ads claiming he has the courage to lead." The narrator continued, "He says he supports President Bush at every opportunity, but that's not the truth." The narrator added, "Since July, Max Cleland has voted against the president's vital homeland security efforts eleven times." The ad ended with the narrator saying, "Max Cleland says he has the courage to lead, but the record proves he's just misleading."[9]

The ad created an immediate uproar. For Democrats, using terrorists' images in a campaign commercial—for any purpose—crossed a line of fairness and good taste. "To put my picture up there with Saddam Hussein and Osama bin Laden and insinuate I'm not fighting hard enough for national security, I just find that this is an incredible low in Georgia politics," Cleland said shortly after the ad aired.[10]

Yet the "Courage" ad did not compare Cleland and the notorious terrorist and dictator, even indirectly; rather it contended that the Democrat was shading the truth when he claimed to fully support some of President Bush's efforts in the war against terrorism. But coming just a little more than a year after the terrible events of September 11, 2001, images meant a lot; feelings were still raw and emotions easily stirred. The ad drew instant national media attention and harsh denunciations, mostly from Cleland surrogates.

As word of the ad spread, computer users rapidly downloaded the commercial on the Internet. Television networks replayed the ad repeatedly, earning it tremendous amounts of "free media," through numerous stories and punditry segments. Virtually all debated the appropriateness of an ad that showed pictures of both a candidate and the nation's enemies—though not at the same time, and not in comparison.

Tom Perdue, the Republican media consultant who created the commercial, said homeland security was not originally planned as an issue in Chambliss's 2002 Senate campaign; the focus instead would be on domestic and social issues, where the Republican seemed in line with the conservative Georgia electorate. After the terrorist attacks House leaders had named Chambliss chairman of the Intelligence Subcommittee on Terrorism and Homeland Security. Because of this sensitive position, to run on homeland security issues, Perdue said, "It would look very much like Saxby was using the 9/11 tragedy to help himself personally and politically." Perdue recalled discussing the issue with Senator Bill Frist, the Republican campaign chair, for whom he had worked in the Tennessean's successful 1994 campaign. At that point in the election cycle, around spring 2002, Frist had encouraged all Senate campaigns to stay away from ads relating to September 11, out of concerns of propriety, and concern about the perception of exploiting the tragedy.[11]

What changed that political calculus, Perdue said, was a Cleland ad showing himself with Bush, saying he had voted with the president on homeland security issues eleven times. Some of those votes had taken place in committee and some on the Senate floor (the picture of Bush and Cleland together was taken during tax cut negotiations in 2001). Chambliss's campaign felt the senator's claim dramatically misrepresented his real voting record; so now homeland security issues were back on the table.

Perdue said the Courage spot was entirely fair and accurate, since it was based on Cleland's votes. He came up with the concept for the now-famous ad while driving his pickup truck alone from his Atlanta home to the Nashville editing studio in early October 2002. Upon arrival, the voice talent in South Carolina was ready, and by phone recorded the narration.

As for the commercial's controversial images, the pictures of Saddam Hussein and Osama bin Laden were never intended to draw a comparison with Senator Cleland, Perdue said. The images were included "to show that the world is a dangerous place still. These were horrible dictators. There is absolutely no way anybody, I mean anybody, can legitimately say that those pictures were intended to reflect on Cleland's patriotism. What kind of fool would challenge his patriotism?"[12]

The campaign shipped the ad to Georgia television stations, and it began running on Thursday, October 10. Less than a day later, a national outcry ensued among critics. Democrats put out a national e-mail campaign, urging supporters to flood the Chambliss campaign with calls of complaint. "Their goal was to create so much controversy in our own campaign we would pull the ad," Perdue said. Cleland himself went on CNN's *Inside Politics* to decry

the commercial's contents. Here and in other forums, the senator, a triple am-
putee from his Vietnam war wounds, said his opponent questioned his patriotism. "The attack leveled against me disrespects everything I have worked for
throughout my life," Cleland said. He called the ad "the most vicious ex-
ploitation of a national tragedy and attempt at character assassination I have
ever witnessed. . . . My opponent not only attacked my honor, he attacked the
very fiber of my being."[13]

The Cleland campaign spread the same message to reporters. "We went
into nuclear mode," said campaign spokesman Jamal Simmons, who was in
Florida that weekend attending the wedding of a close friend. He spent most
of the time in his hotel room working on his laptop computer, with a cell
phone in hand, frantically relaying the campaign's message to the media.[14]

Democrats were not the only ones to complain about the ad's tone. Senator John McCain of Arizona, a Vietnam veteran and longtime prisoner of war,
called it "worse than disgraceful." A fellow Republican senator and Vietnam
veteran, Chuck Hagel of Nebraska, said it was so "beyond offensive" that "it
made me recoil."[15] Hagel at one point prepared to cut a television commercial
in Cleland's defense, to the point that a script was readied, though that plan
never materialized. Even conservative commentator Patrick Buchanan called
the spot "pretty raw," adding, "I don't think anyone questions Max Cleland's
courage."[16]

Yet while the protestations did include explanations about the individual
votes the senator had taken on homeland security legislation, Cleland's campaign could not get past the fact that civil service protections for workers
seemed like a higher priority than passing the administration's Homeland Security Department plan. "He couldn't answer his votes," Perdue said. "He
couldn't argue the fact that he had voted against the president eleven times."[17]

Simmons said in hindsight that it was clear the Cleland position lent itself
to a 30-second attack ad. "We were in a tough position because of the homeland security vote, and trying to make a very nuanced argument about why
the Homeland Security Department" needed to have civil service protections,
he said.[18]

Still, the Democrats' outcries and protests meant the images in the ad had
become a distraction to the Republican's campaign. So over the weekend one
of Perdue's associates edited the ad, to delete the pictures of the international
villains, and replaced them with images of aircraft carriers and submarines:

"To still denote the same thing—that the world is a dangerous place," he said.[19]

Democrats wanted the commercial pulled entirely, as they continued to argue that it impugned Cleland's patriotism. "We thought it was offensive and had no place in the discussion," said Matt McKenna, the campaign's research director.[20] On this point, the Chambliss campaign did not back down, and the newly revised ad, minus the disputed images, began running that Monday, October 14.

The controversy over the ad was a net plus, Perdue said. It "became the focus, so that everybody who saw the ad also saw the votes and the documentation of the votes." He added, "The more Cleland screamed, the more people wanted to see the ad. The more the national people showed it, the more people talked about the ad. You couldn't go to a barbershop in Georgia without that ad being talked about."[21]

Though the commercial came in for tremendous criticism outside Georgia, in the Peach State voters did not seem outraged. To many voters, the senator did indeed look more interested in protecting labor unions than backing Bush's efforts on homeland security. Taking the union line in the conservative-leaning state was just about political suicide. For many it seemed as if Cleland was at the beck and call of Senate Majority Leader Tom Daschle, who by then was a reviled figure among many Republicans. "In retrospect, that was clearly a mistake," said Simmons. "What we should have done is signed up with the Homeland Security bill that President Bush was pushing, declared victory on it, and taken a hit from the unions." In addition, the vote in favor of Bush's plan would have seemed consistent with Cleland's other stances on national security. The approach should have been, "We had already voted for the [Iraq] war. We are 'in for a penny, in for a pound,'" Simmons said.[22]

Late in the election cycle national Republican strategists began to target the Georgia Senate race as a possible pickup opportunity, and President Bush visited the state six times in support of Chambliss, who, with his stately head of white hair, seemed typecast for the role of Southern senator. Meanwhile, a Chambliss mailer juxtaposed Cleland with Democratic Senators Ted Kennedy, Mass., and Hillary Rodham Clinton, N.Y., which further undercut Cleland's claim that he stood apart from the national Democratic party and supported President Bush.[23] Chambliss beat Cleland solidly, 53 percent to 46 percent, helping Republicans win enough Senate seats to reclaim the majority, with a 51 to 49 margin.

While the commercial criticizing Cleland had earned tremendous attention, it had less to do with Cleland's loss than is often portrayed in news stories. "Nobody's smart enough to create one ad that can turn a campaign,"
Perdue said. "You just take advantage of your circumstances."[24] When the spot
ran in mid-October, Chambliss's candidacy was already on the rise. Political
events outside the Senate race helped: In the Georgia governor's race that year,
the Democratic incumbent Roy Barnes had made changes to the state flag,
which minimized its Confederate emblem, an issue that would depress
turnout for the governor and by extension the remainder of the Democratic
ticket. In the same vein, Cleland's loss was tied, in part, to the sorry fortunes
of Georgia Democrats on Election Day 2002, which included the surprise defeat of Barnes, the loss of two new congressional seats expected to go Democratic, and the felling of several prominent state legislators.

If anything, the Courage ad had the potential to backfire, given the Republican's avoidance of military service during Vietnam. "I think it will go down
as one of the biggest gambles in the history of modern American politics, for
a guy like Chambliss to make that charge of a guy like Max," said Matt
McKenna.[25]

The greatest benefit Chambliss derived from the ad may have been the success his campaign had in throwing the Cleland side into disarray. Rather than
running the campaign on issues the Democrat wanted to discuss, such as Social Security and health care, it had to respond to the Republican opponent;
oftentimes that is just what negative ads are designed to do.

The Cleland campaign also assumed that voters would equate his military
service with being on the right side of modern national security issues. In the
past, though, candidates' military service has often appeared to be a relatively
minor issue for voters. In 1992 then Arkansas governor Bill Clinton, who
avoided serving in the Vietnam War, easily defeated President George H. W.
Bush, a decorated World War II veteran. Clinton accomplished the same feat
four years later against Senator Bob Dole, a World War II veteran who carried
permanent injuries. Only in Senator John Kerry's 2004 campaign, as the Democratic presidential nominee, did a candidate's military service get turned
against him, a subject to be discussed in the next chapter.[26]

In hindsight, it is clear that the Cleland campaign should have relied less on
surrogates and put the senator out front to show the full fury of his reaction.
Simmons, the campaign spokesman, recalled running into the late Maynard

Jackson, a former Atlanta mayor and Democratic elder statesman, shortly after the election. He said, "What I don't understand is, how come ya'll never sat Max Cleland in front of the camera, or in one of those debates, and had him say, 'Saxby Chambliss, if you ever question my patriotism one more time, I'm going to hop up out of this chair and whoop your ass with the one good arm I've got left.'"[27]

After his defeat, Cleland become a political martyr figure for Democrats, the victim of what they considered an unconscionable smear on a patriot who had literally given his body defending his country. The mythology of Cleland's defeat became a rallying cry for the party in 2004, when the wheelchair-bound former senator appeared often on the presidential campaign trail with Kerry.

TERROR ADS GROWN EXPONENTIALLY

What seemed shocking in 2002—running images of terrorists and dictators in campaign ads—was a more routine part of the political landscape by the 2004 election cycle. Several candidates that year lambasted opponents as being soft on terror, and, despite the outcry in the Georgia Senate race two years before, they had no qualms about using images of Osama bin Laden and other terrorists in campaign ads. The comparisons were often more direct than they had been two years previously, making the Courage ad look rather tepid. In fact, in 2004 bin Laden took a starring role in several key Senate and House races around the country.

Candidates who used this tactic had a mixed record of success. In Colorado, Democratic Senate candidate Ken Salazar, the state attorney general, ran a television spot that criticized his Republican opponent, beer magnate Pete Coors, for not supporting the death penalty for terrorists. Coors opposed the death penalty on moral grounds based on his own religious beliefs. Still, he made clear throughout his Senate campaign that he would have shed no tears had bin Laden been killed in battlefield operations or other military actions. Salazar's ad opened with a close-up of the al-Quaeda leader, while the narrator said, "Osama bin Laden. Should he face the death penalty for murdering 3,000 Americans?" The ad showed a picture of Coors dressed in a tuxedo. "Pete Coors says 'no.' Unbelievable," concluded the narrator.[28] Colorado voters seemed to agree with Salazar's perspective. He won the Senate race with 51 percent of the vote, to 47 percent for Coors, a rare bright spot for

Democrats in an election cycle that saw the GOP Senate majority grow from 51 to 49 to 55 to 45.

One 2004 Republican Senate candidate who did not benefit much from linking his opponent to the al-Qaeda leader was George Nethercutt of Washington. The five-term congressman was initially expected to be a tough opponent against Democratic Senator Patty Murray, who had compiled a generally liberal voting record in her twelve-year Senate career. Nethercutt was considered a giant-slayer among Republicans for his 1994 defeat of the sitting Speaker of the House, Democrat Tom Foley. Moreover, it seemed Murray had handed her opponent a golden campaign issue through her comments, two years earlier, about the roots of terrorism. In December 2002, during a meeting with high school students in Vancouver, Washington, she seemed to attribute bin Laden's popularity in Afghanistan and other places to what she called his generosity toward the poor: "He's been out in these countries for decades, building schools, building roads, building infrastructure, building day-care facilities, building health-care facilities, and the people are extremely grateful. He's made their lives better. We have not done that," Murray said.[29]

At the time the comments triggered a few days of negative stories in the Washington press, but the controversy soon faded away. Not surprisingly, her words surfaced again when her reelection race heated up. In late September 2004 Nethercutt's campaign began running an ad that opened with footage of the rubble of the World Trade Center. It then interspersed her controversial taped comments; Nethercutt's voice chimed in at the end, declaring, "Winning the war on terror means fighting terrorists, not excusing them."

But Murray was expecting this line of attack, and she wasted no time in defending herself. The senator immediately held a joint press conference with former Senator Cleland to condemn the ad; she said the comment was taken out of context. Then in a conference call with reporters she said, "George Nethercutt's ad is a lie, and he knows it. I have always said Osama bin Laden is an evil terrorist who is responsible for the deaths of thousands of Americans." But she then turned the table on her opponent, chastising him for seemingly using a national tragedy for political purposes. She aired an ad that asked "what kind of politician would use Osama bin Laden and images of 9/11 to get elected?"[30] Voters seemed to agree; Murray won reelection walking way, earning 55 percent to Nethercutt's 43 percent.

Running images linked to the 9/11 attacks worked effectively in a different context in the 2002 Oklahoma governor's race. Throughout that year, former GOP Congressman Steve Largent was thought to be the frontrunner. Oklahoma had long trended Republican, and Largent, a Hall of Fame wide receiver from his professional football days with the Seattle Seahawks, seemed in line with the state's conservative tendencies. In the general election, he matched up against Democratic state Senator Brad Henry, who was virtually unknown statewide and did not even enter the race until late June. Also in the contest was an independent candidate, Gary Richardson, an attorney who had twice run for Congress as a Republican.

Largent's whereabouts on September 11, 2001, became a campaign issue: Though Congress was scheduled to be in session on that day, Largent was in Idaho bow hunting, and out of touch with the rest of the world. He later said he planned the hunting trip as his last opportunity to get away before embarking on a grueling gubernatorial bid. His timing was bad, as the isolation of the Idaho forest meant he did not hear about the attacks until two days later. Nonetheless, on September 11 his staff managed to issue a statement for him, including direct quotations from the congressman. Largent later had to apologize for his office creating statements that were obviously not his own, though he noted the quotes were in line with what he *would* have said had he been available for comment.

Richardson seized on Largent's absence that tragic day: The third-party candidate ran an ad that accused Largent of being AWOL from Congress when he was needed. As Alan Jackson's "Where Were You When the World Stopped Turning" played, the screen filled with photos of the World Trade Center on fire and the towers collapsing. The announcer intoned, "We'll never forget where we were." The ad then focused on Largent's reaction to the accusations that he was negligent in office; it cut to a clip of the former congressman responding angrily to a local television interviewer who questioned his whereabouts that day. "That's bullshit [bleeped out]. No, no, I'll accept about 'Where were you on, you know, 9/11.'" Then in Richardson's attack ad, the announcer chimed in again: "Largent was hunting in Idaho, out of touch while Congress was in session. But to Largent: "That's bullshit [bleeped out]."[31]

Richardson also ran negative ads against Henry, the Democrat; but the attacks linking Largent and the images from September 11 were far more damaging. The Republican nominee lost narrowly to Henry, 43.3 percent to 42.6 percent, with 14 percent for Richardson.

BETTER EQUIPPED TO FIGHT TERROR

Candidates stoking fears about potential future terrorist acts played out most prominently in the 2004 presidential race, the first since the attacks of September 11, 2001. Organizations officially independent of the Bush and Kerry presidential campaigns used this tactic most aggressively. The Progress for America Voter Fund, a Republican-leaning group, ran a television ad that suggested Kerry could not adequately defend the nation against terrorists. The spot began by showing 9/11 plot leader Mohammed Atta, Osama bin Laden, and other terrorists, while the announcer said, "These people want to kill us." It then presented images of the attack on Russian schoolchildren in Beslan, Russia, the March 2004 attack on a Spanish commuter train, and firemen in the smoking rubble of the World Trade Center after September 11, 2001. The ad claimed Kerry had "a 30-year record of supporting cuts in defense and intelligence."[32] Democrats quickly and loudly protested that the ad had several factual errors, noting that since taking office in 1985 he had supported $4.4 trillion in defense spending, including a sizable increase in 2002.[33]

And though the sharpest-edged ads came from outside groups, the campaigns themselves were not shy about using the terror issue as a wedge for attracting voters, or, more precisely, repelling them from the opposition. Take a Bush campaign ad that showed wolves in the woods moving menacingly toward the camera. The announcer said Senator Kerry had supported budget cuts in intelligence in the 1990s "so deep they would have weakened America's defenses. And weakness attracts those who are waiting to do America harm." Again the Kerry team sought to deflect the charges. "They have stooped so low now that they are using a pack of wolves running around a forest trying to scare you," said Senator John Edwards of North Carolina, the Democratic vice-presidential nominee.[34]

Of course the use of terrorism threats as a campaign issue was not limited to the airwaves. On the stump candidates openly suggested that the country would be less safe if their opponent were elected. Vice President Dick Cheney received widespread attention for employing this tactic when he seemed to suggest that a Kerry victory would make another terrorist attack more likely. "It's absolutely essential that eight weeks from today, on November 2, we make the right choice, because if we make the wrong choice, then the danger is that we'll get hit again, that we'll be hit in a way that will be devastating from the standpoint of the United States,"[35] Cheney said on September 7, 2004 at a campaign event in Iowa. He later softened the statement, but to many the message seemed clear.

Cheney made other sharp-elbowed verbal attacks on the campaign trail; at various points he suggested that if the Massachusetts senator had been president in recent history, the Soviet Union would not have fallen, a nuclear-armed Saddam Hussein could be in control of the Persian Gulf, and the United States might have ceded its national defense to the United Nations. Cheney cited Kerry's opposition to some Cold War weapons systems and to the 1991 Persian Gulf War, and to statements Kerry made in the early 1970s calling for U.N. approval before deploying U.S. forces.[36]

House Speaker Dennis Hastert (R-Ill.) took a similar tack on the campaign trail in September 2004 when he said al-Qaeda leaders probably wanted Kerry to win the election.[37] At a Republican fundraiser, Hastert said, "I don't have data or intelligence to tell me one thing or another [but] I would think they would be more apt to go [for] somebody who would file a lawsuit with the World Court or something rather than respond with troops." Asked whether he believed al-Qaeda would be more successful under a Kerry presidency, Hastert said: "That's my opinion, yes."[38]

The tactic brought considerable critical press scrutiny on Bush. A September 25, 2004, *New York Times* editorial, recalled in this book's opening chapter, accused the president's campaign of indulging in "despicable" and "un-American" politics and of conducting "an organized effort to paint [Kerry] as a friend to terrorists.[39] A *Washington Post* story made a similar finding: "President Bush and leading Republicans are increasingly charging that [Kerry] and others in his party are giving comfort to terrorists and undermining the war in Iraq—a line of attack that tests the conventional bounds of political rhetoric."[40]

Such criticism was largely off the mark. No one in the Bush campaign ever actually challenged Kerry's patriotism, as Democrats repeatedly claimed or called Kerry "a friend to terrorists" or said he's "giving aid and comfort to the enemy," as the *Times* charged elsewhere in its editorial.[41] Rather, the president's campaign contended Bush was a better terror-fighter than Kerry and that al-Qaeda knew it.

Nor was the Bush campaign the only one to stoke fears about terrorism. Kerry, the Democratic National Committee, and surrogates often warned during the latter stages of the campaign that a second Bush term could lead to greater casualties and another Vietnam-like quagmire in Iraq, a military draft, and a secret call-up of reservists.[42]

In an inverse of Bush's arguments, the Democrats also suggested Osama bin Laden could go uncaptured and remain a threat to the United States if Kerry were not elected. The line of attack sharpened as the campaign drew to a close and Kerry ran as an increasingly vocal critic of the war in Iraq; he argued that the invasion—which he voted to authorize—had actually undermined the hunt for bin Laden and other terrorists. One Kerry ad blamed Bush for "the Iraq quagmire" and pointed out that "the Pentagon admits terrorists are pouring into Iraq."[43]

Democrats not on the Kerry campaign payroll went even further. "A mushroom cloud over any American city is the ultimate nightmare, and the risk is all too real," Senator Edward Kennedy of Massachusetts said in a speech at George Washington University in late September. "The war in Iraq has made the mushroom cloud more likely—not less likely—and it should never have happened," added the Democratic elder statesman.[44]

The 2004 presidential race certainly did not introduce the now-common candidate tactic of suggesting opponents were favored by enemies of the United States. It only took the practice to a new level. In some ways these salvos were just a ratcheting-up several notches of tactics used in previous campaigns, from Lyndon Johnson's portrayal of Barry Goldwater as likely to start a nuclear conflict or President Jimmy Carter's caricature of Ronald Reagan as a warmonger in 1980.[45]

And in 1972, Vice President Spiro Agnew skewered South Dakota Senator George McGovern, the Democratic presidential nominee, for advocating peace negotiations in Vietnam. "Even Neville Chamberlain did not carry a beggar's cup to Munich—as George McGovern proposed to carry to Hanoi," Agnew said.[46] The Nixon/Agnew ticket cruised to a forty-nine-state romp over McGovern and his running mate, Sargent Shriver. In 1980, a "Democrats for Reagan" television ad (an arm of the Republican nominee's campaign) claimed Ayatollah Khomeini had basically endorsed President Jimmy Carter for reelection, as the Iranian hostage crisis dragged on. Said the narrator: "In a copyrighted story in the *New York Times* on October 27, William Safire wrote, 'The smoothest of Iran's diplomatic criminals was shown on American television this weekend, warning American voters that they had better not elect Ronald Reagan. Ayatollah Khomeini prefers a weak and manageable American president, and has decided to do everything in their power to determine our election result.'[47] Voters seemed to agree with Reagan's interpretation of events, as he won forty-four states over incumbent Carter.

TERRORISM-RELATED ISSUES AND THE CAMPAIGN TRAIL, GOING FORWARD

As the events of 9/11 recede further into the past, whether emotionally charged symbols and language continue to be used effectively in campaigns will likely depend on the mood of the nation at the time of each election cycle. Anti-Communism as a tool of negative campaigning reached a white-hot intensity in the late 1940s and early 1950s; charges that opponents were "soft" on the Russians were a dominant theme in American politics. Anti-Communism served as an effective political issue for the ambitions of Richard Nixon, Wisconsin Senator Joe McCarthy, and scores of other, less prominent officeholders.

Yet the effectiveness of charging or implying political opponents were Communists or Communist sympathizers softened over time. Nixon, for instance, found the charge fell flat in his 1962 bid for California governor. In the political wilderness after his narrow loss to President John F. Kennedy two years earlier, Nixon sought to be the Golden State's chief executive as a way of keeping his political fortunes alive and remain in the public spotlight. In a bid to oust Democratic Governor Pat Brown, Nixon brandished the weapon that he had used so successfully in his meteoric political rise, anti-Communism, accusing the governor of paying insufficient attention to the Red threat. But the potency of such Red Scare charges had faded by then. Hugh Burns, a conservative Democrat from California's Central Valley, who was president of the state Senate and chairman of its Un-American Activities Committee, declared that no new anti-Communist laws had been enacted while Brown was governor because none were needed. Nixon's broadsides were among several conservative standbys he used against Brown, including high taxes and cumbersome regulations, but each failed, and the former vice president got crushed by the popular governor.[48]

Events of the 1968 presidential race further reflected the diminution in effectiveness of raw red-baiting. Nixon, having resurrected himself politically and now the Republican presidential nominee, chose as his running mate Spiro Agnew, who was known to always be ready with a colorful quip to slam political opponents. Shortly after getting the nod as Nixon's running mate, the Maryland governor called the Democratic nominee, Vice President Hubert Humphrey, "squishy-soft on Communism." Such a notion seemed laughable to many; as LBJ's understudy, Humphrey had been a stalwart supporter of the war in Vietnam, a position that brought about considerable opposition and criticism from within his own party. Rather than helping the Republican ticket, Agnew apologized for the comments, saying he was unaware of the historical implications of such remarks.[49]

Similarly, the effectiveness of labeling political foes soft on terror will no doubt evolve and change in the decades following September 11, 2001. How comfortable Americans feel about national security will guide the extent to which they reward or punish at the polls candidates who use terror-related issues as a form of negative campaigning. If the Middle East remains unstable, al-Qaeda leaders are still at large, and Americans in general feel insecure, campaign ads with horrifying pictures and tough-talking stump speeches are likely to be effective. But if the foreign situation settles down and Americans feel more comfortable with the course of world events, this approach will not have as much resonance.

In the elections immediately following the 9/11 attacks, Republicans generally found an effective balance between reminding voters about that day's tragic events and convincing them that they were better prepared to prevent future attacks. In his 2004 reelection bid Bush rarely shied away from invoking September 11, often interjecting it into answers from unrelated questions. And at the Republican National Convention in late summer 2004, speeches and public memorials were able to effectively showcase what GOP strategists found to be Bush's perceived greatest strength: resolve in the face of terrorism.[50] The oft-criticized approach was vindicated by the election results, when Bush won clear Electoral College and popular vote majorities.

Still, in the near future, at least, references to the events of September 11 in a political context will remain a touchy subject. Baltimore Mayor Martin O'Malley found that out in February 2005, after he drew a loose comparison between Bush's proposed cuts in urban aid and the terrorist strikes on New York and the Pentagon, just outside Washington, D.C., three and a half years earlier. "Back on September 11, terrorists attacked our metropolitan cores, two of America's great cities. They did that because they knew that was where they could do the most damage and weaken us the most," O'Malley said during a press conference at the National Press Club, in Washington, D.C. "Years later, we are given a budget proposal by our commander-in-chief, the president of the United States. And with a budget ax, he is attacking America's cities."[51] Newspaper editorialists and, less surprisingly, Republicans, conservative talk-show hosts, and bloggers immediately blasted the mayor for politicizing a national tragedy. O'Malley, positioning himself for a Maryland gubernatorial bid the next year, had to backtrack on the remarks.

More prominently, Bush White House Deputy Chief of Staff Karl Rove stirred a wave of Democratic condemnation when in June 2005 when he accused liberals of responding with restraint and timidity to the 9/11 terrorist attacks. In a speech to the New York State Conservative Party Rove said no issue better illustrated the philosophical difference between liberals and conservatives than national security. "Conservatives saw the savagery of 9/11 and the attacks and prepared for war," Rove said. "Liberals saw the savagery of the 9/11 attacks and wanted to prepare indictments and offer therapy and understanding for our attackers." In his remarks Rove also referred to MoveOn.org, some of whose members shortly after 9/11 individually expressed through an online petition opposition to military action in Afghanistan. Democrats accused Rove of impugning their patriotism and demeaning the memories of 9/11 victims.[52] Rove and by extension the Bush administration took several days of media pounding for the remarks, at a time that the president's handling of the Iraq situation was under increased criticism and scrutiny.

The episodes demonstrated that when candidates and political operatives link opponents, even indirectly, with America's worst enemies, national security, and the fateful events of 9/11, the references bring torrents of criticism, risks that can easily offset potential political gains.

NOTES

1. *The Congressional Record*, Sept. 11, 2001, H5493.

2. Gail Russell Chaddock, "Cracks Are Now Showing in Congress's Unified Surface: Leaders of Both Parties Scramble to Bridge Deep Divisions on Energy Policy, Tax Cuts and Trade," *The Christian Science Monitor*, Oct. 12, 2001.

3. Richard L. Berke, "Bush Adviser Suggests War as Campaign Theme," *The New York Times*, Jan. 19, 2002.

4. Berke, *The New York Times*, Jan. 19, 2002.

5. "Statement of Democratic Caucus Chair Martin Frost," Jan. 21, 2002 (www.house.gov/frost/pr02/pr020121-apology.htm).

6. Edwin Chen, "Bush Defends Handling of Hijack Threat: White House Takes to Task Critics of the President's Pre-Sept. 11 Response. Democrats Say the Issue Is Information and Not Partisanship," *The Los Angeles Times*, May 18, 2002.

7. Michael Barone and Richard E. Cohen, *The Almanac of American Politics 2004* (Washington, D.C.: National Journal Group, Inc., 2003), 461–62.

8. Interview with author, by telephone, May 5, 2005.

9. Tape courtesy of the Julian P. Kanter Political Commercial Archive at the University of Oklahoma Political Communication Center [Known hereafter in this chapter as the Kanter Archive].

10. Jeffrey McMurray, "Ad Uses Saddam, Bin Laden to Question Cleland's Record," *Associated Press*, Oct. 10, 2002.

11. Interview with author, by telephone, Feb. 16, 2005.

12. Interview with author, by telephone, Feb. 16, 2005.

13. William M. Welch, "Republicans Using Iraq Issue to Slam Election Opponents," *USA Today*, Oct. 13, 2002.

14. Interview with author, Washington, D.C., May 10, 2005.

15. Bob Kemper, "Loyalty to Bush Helps Chambliss Rise: Ad Attacking Cleland Still a Sore Point," *The Atlanta Journal-Constitution*, Feb. 6, 2005.

16. Jim Tharpe, "Negative Ads Dog Senate Race: Candidates Spend Millions to Sully Each Other's Names," *The Atlanta Journal-Constitution*, Oct. 26, 2002.

17. Interview with author, by telephone, Feb. 16, 2005.

18. Interview with author, Washington, D.C., May 10, 2005.

19. Interview with author, by telephone, Feb. 16, 2005.

20. Interview with author, by telephone, May 5, 2005.

21. Interview with author, by telephone, Feb. 16, 2005.

22. Interview with author, Washington, D.C., May 10, 2005.

23. Charles S. Bullock III, "It's a Sonny Day in Georgia," in Larry J. Sabato, ed., *Midterm Madness: The Elections of 2002* (Lanham, Md.: Rowman & Littlefield Publishers, Inc., 2003), 183.

24. Interview with author, by telephone, Feb. 16, 2005.

25. Interview with author, by telephone, May 5, 2005.

26. Mark Z. Barabak, "The Democrats' 'Poster Boy': Max Cleland, Who Lost His U.S. Senate Seat to a Republican in 2002, Says He's Ambivalent about Personifying His Party's Anger," *The Los Angeles Times Magazine*, July 18, 2004.

27. Interview with author, Washington, D.C., May 10, 2005.

28. Chris Cillizza, "Bin Laden's Face Pops Up in Ads," *Roll Call*, Oct. 6, 2004.

29. Jim Brunner, "Murray Weak on Terror, Ad Claims," *The Seattle Times*, Sept. 30, 2004.

30. Cillizza, *Roll Call*, Oct. 6, 2004.

31. Tape courtesy of the Kanter Archive.

32. "Bush Ad Twists Kerry's Words on Iraq," *Factcheck.org*, Sept. 28, 2004.

33. Howard Kurtz, "Ad Invokes Terror Threat to Assail Kerry: Democrat Quick to Respond with Commercial Decrying Pro-Bush Group's Tactics," *The Washington Post*, Sept. 26, 2004.

34. Richard W. Stevenson, "Bush Attacks Kerry as Weak on Security," *The New York Times*, Oct. 23, 2004.

35. Janet Hook, "Campaigns Accentuate the Negative: Attacks by Both Parties Have Taken Incivility to a New Level This Year, Analysts Say," *The Los Angeles Times*, Oct. 17, 2004.

36. Michael Laris, "Cheney Conjures a Worse World Had Kerry Led It," *The Washington Post*, Oct. 24, 2004.

37. Hook, *The Los Angeles Times*, Oct. 17, 2004.

38. Dana Milbank, "Tying Kerry to Terror Tests Rhetorical Limits," *The Washington Post*, Sept. 24, 2004.

39. "An Un-American Way to Campaign," a *New York Times* editorial, Sept. 25, 2004.

40. Milbank, *The Washington Post*, Sept. 24, 2004.

41. Morton Kondracke, "Despite New Charges, Democrats Still Lead in Low-Blow Department," *Roll Call*, Sept. 30, 2004.

42. Jim VandeHei and Howard Kurtz, "The Politics of Fear: Kerry Adopts Bush Strategy of Stressing Dangers," *The Washington Post*, Sept. 29, 2004.

43. Ad courtesy of The American Museum of the Moving Image's "The Living Room Candidate: Presidential Campaign Commercials 1952–2004" (http://livingroomcandidate.movingimage.us/index.php).

44. Michael Janofsky, "Kennedy Denounces Bush Policies as Endangering the World," *The New York Times*, Sept. 28, 2004.

45. VandeHei and Kurtz, *The Washington Post*, Sept. 29, 2004.

46. Francis X. Clines, "Spiro T. Agnew, Point Man for Nixon Who Resigned Vice Presidency, Dies at 77," *The New York Times*, Sept. 16, 1996.

47. Ad courtesy of The American Museum of the Moving Image's "The Living Room Candidate: Presidential Campaign Commercials 1952–2004" (http://livingroomcandidate.movingimage.us/index.php) [Known hereafter in this chapter as The Living Room Candidate].

48. Ethan Rarick, *California Rising: The Life and Times of Pat Brown* (Berkeley: University of California Press, 2005), 242.

49. Stephen J. Whitfield, *The Culture of the Cold War*, 2nd ed. (Baltimore: The Johns Hopkins University Press, 1996), 229.

50. Mark Silva, "Convention Uses 9/11 to Define Presidency," *The Chicago Tribune*, Aug. 30, 2004.

51. Lori Montgomery, "O'Malley Likens Bush's Proposed Cuts to Sept. 11 Attacks," *The Washington Post*, Feb. 9, 2005.

52. Dan Balz, "Democrats Call for Rove to Apologize," *The Washington Post*, June 24, 2005.

9

Opening the Floodgates: Campaign Finance "Reform" and the Rise of Negativity

During the heated 2004 campaign season, television viewers in Ohio, Florida, and other presidential battleground states learned that Senator John Kerry had once accused American servicemen in Vietnam of committing war crimes. Viewers were also told, in another commercial, that a former officer in the Alabama Air National Guard and his friends never saw George W. Bush at their unit in 1972, when he was temporarily assigned there.

Such accusations, hurled against Kerry by the Swift Vets and POW's for Truth (originally known as the Swift Boat Veterans for Truth) and toward Bush by Texans for Truth, made liberal use of facts on the public record. But the ads didn't tell the whole truth. In testimony before a Senate committee in 1971, Kerry did not accuse specific people of war crimes; he said he was describing atrocities alleged by other veterans. And Bush pointed to his honorable discharge from the Air National Guard as evidence that he had fulfilled his service.

Such nuances and finer points were lost on many television viewers. That was exactly the point. The ads played on viewers' emotions and aimed to drive true believers to the polls on Election Day. The spots were among a slew of hard-edged television attacks aired during the 2004 presidential election cycle, the first to operate under the rules of the 2002 Bipartisan Campaign Finance Reform Act (BCRA), also known as McCain-Feingold, for its sponsors, Senators John McCain (R-Ariz.) and Russ Feingold (D-Wis.).

Notably, neither Bush nor Kerry sponsored the ads. Instead, they came from independent groups bankrolled by wealthy individuals who wanted to affect the election outcome. Ironically, their donations were the very things BCRA sought to block, or at least reduce. Unlimited fat-cat donations simply shifted from national party organizations—the Republican National Committee and Democratic National Committee—to private groups that aimed not just to support their favored candidate but to tear down the opposition with the bluntest possible words and images as well.

The biggest recipients of the campaign cash were 527 groups, named for the federal tax code provision that governed their operations. These organizations eagerly threw out charges and criticized the opposition more virulently than the candidates themselves did. Bush's campaign did not criticize Kerry for his decorated service while in Vietnam because that could have easily brought a backlash, considering the president had stayed stateside during the war. The Swift Vets, Kerry's key critics among the 527 groups, felt no such restraints. "The Bush campaign would never have said the things the Swift Boat Vets said," noted Chris LaCivita, the group's chief strategist. "If people want to complain about 527s, thank McCain-Feingold."[1]

The new, complex campaign finance rules—upheld virtually in their entirety by the U.S. Supreme Court[2]—helped spawn a dramatic increase of negative campaigning over the airwaves, on the Internet, and through direct mail. The 527s ratcheted up the shrillness, nastiness, and outright distortions in political ads, all the while injecting massive sums of money into the political process. According to a postelection study by the nonpartisan Campaign Finance Institute, 527 committees raised $405 million in 2004, up dramatically from the $151 million they collected in 2002.[3] GOP Senator Trent Lott of Mississippi—who had voted against BCRA—called contributions to 527s "sewer money" after the election.[4]

During debate over BCRA in 2001, many legislators said they supported the campaign finance proposal, in part, to deal with the proliferation of negative campaigning. "The unlimited contributions which have come into campaigns, directly and indirectly, have been one of the major sources for the horrendous amount of negative attack ads which are inflicted upon our constituents in most of these elections," declared Senator Carl Levin, Democrat of Michigan. Senator Ron Wyden, Democrat of Oregon, similarly lamented "the explosive growth of negative political commercials that are corroding the faith of individuals in the political process."[5]

The linchpin of BCRA was a prohibition on political parties against collecting the unlimited "soft money" contributions from individuals, corporations, and unions, none of which were regulated by federal election laws. The soft money previously allowable was ostensibly meant to encourage "party-building" activities, but not specific candidates. In reality, though, there was a loophole that let wealthy contributors give six-, seven- and even eight-figure contributions to the parties, which then used the money to support individual candidates. This system became a primary source of gathering tens of millions of dollars from big givers during the fall presidential campaigns, when direct contributions to candidates are prohibited. They were also used to support congressional candidates in key battleground states during off-year elections.[6] Such donations had grown to dominate presidential and congressional races in the 1990s. BCRA, however, did nothing to restrict the 527 committees from collecting the huge donations that previously had gone to the Democratic National Committee and Republican National Committee.

CANDIDATES GET OUTSIDE HELP

The stakes in the 2004 election were huge: Executing the global war on terror in the post–9/11 world; a costly, divisive war in Iraq; and an economy in recovery that still lost hundreds of thousands of jobs. Adding to the intensity was the near even split between registered Republicans and Democrats, lingering bitterness over the disputed 2000 election, and the deep, personal dislike many Democrats had for the president, along with the disdain Republicans held for the Democratic challenger.[7]

So it was no surprise that big money would find a way into the system, especially to opponents of the legislation who predicted just such an outcome. Recent campaign history showed outside organizations would seek to fill in the gaps where candidates were limited in collecting donations. The 527s that proliferated during the 2004 election cycle were only the latest type of independent-expenditure group to be active in national politics. During the 1980 election cycle, the National Conservative Political Action Committee

(NCPAC) spent more than $1 million on independent-expenditure ads in an effort to defeat several Democratic U.S. senators. After sending out millions of direct mail pieces and running scores of television commercials knocking the Democratic incumbents, NCPAC succeeded wildly; the Republicans won control of the Senate for the first time in 26 years. NCPAC also ran several independent ads in favor of Republican presidential candidate Ronald Reagan that criticized President Jimmy Carter's handling of the Iranian hostage crisis and other matters. And the most memorable ad of the 1988 presidential election—one that linked Democratic nominee and Massachusetts Governor Michael Dukakis with furloughed criminal Willie Horton—came from an independent group called the National Security Political Action Committee. (The independent ad showed a picture of Horton, who was black, while a spot by the campaign of Vice President George H. W. Bush focused solely on the Massachusetts prison-furlough program and did not feature the criminal's image or name.)

Even two of the Supreme Court justices whose decision upheld the constitutionality of BCRA acknowledged that large amounts of money would still find a way into the political system, which Congress would eventually have to regulate again: "[We are] under no illusion that this will be the last congressional statement on the matter. Money, like water, will always find an outlet. What problems will arise, and how Congress will respond, are concerns for another day," wrote John Paul Stevens and Sandra Day O'Connor.[8]

Such commentary on the effectiveness of limiting campaign contributions was prescient. Rich people who wanted to participate in politics were not likely to throw up their hands and move on to something else, simply because they could not write big checks to the RNC or DNC. Individuals with deep pockets generally did not need another luxury car, private airplane, diamond ring, or lavish European vacation. Instead these well-heeled individuals were intent on having a voice in public-policy issues. By banning the use of large soft-money donations to party organizations, BCRA essentially made 527s the only conduit for unregulated, unlimited contributions.[9]

During the early stages of the 2004 election cycle, Democrats dominated the 527 scene, as party strategists saw their main fundraising source evaporate before their eyes. The new soft-money ban included corporate and union donations, which had long been a mainstay of the Democratic Party. In the summer of 2003, Harold M. Ickes, a former deputy chief of staff to President

Bill Clinton and a leading Democratic strategist, feared that McCain-Feingold would give President George W. Bush and the Republicans, with their far bigger base of wealthy and upper-middle-class supporters, a huge advantage over the Democratic nominee. Worse still, Ickes figured, the Democratic nominee would probably be broke after a grueling primary season (as Republican Bob Dole had been in 1996), and unable to defend himself against a barrage of negative ads from GOP sources.[10]

So Ickes came upon the idea of creating a group of connected 527 organizations, which would operate in battleground states, where the presidential election would likely be decided.[11] Ickes joined forces with Ellen Malcolm, founder of Emily's List, a fundraising group for Democratic women candidates who favor abortion rights, and former AFL-CIO political director Steve Rosenthal. They created several interlocking 527 groups and tapped big-time liberal donors who might have given to the DNC in years past. On paper, their plan seemed to work brilliantly: In 2004, tens of millions of dollars flowed from wealthy donors to liberal independent groups. Five donors spent about $78 million combined to defeat the president: Billionaire hedge fund manager and philanthropist George Soros, Hollywood producer Stephen L. Bing, and Peter B. Lewis, founder of Progressive car insurance, and the California investors Herbert and Marion Sandler.[12]

Conservatives were slow to get into the 527 game because, in part, during the early part of the election season Bush was amassing a record war chest that ultimately reached $270 million. Many potential contributors did not see the need to give further. Republicans also filed aggressive challenges to the efforts of Democratic 527s, contending they were improperly coordinating with the Kerry campaign, among other arguments. These challenges largely fell flat. After the Federal Election Commission declined to seriously crack down on the fundraising practices of Democratic 527s during the 2004 election cycle, Republicans started forming their own groups to support Bush and hammer Kerry.

With Democratic-allied groups millions of dollars ahead in fundraising and leading the air war in television commercials, Republican-leaning donors decided to try to level the playing field. That was the intention of Texas oil tycoon T. Boone Pickens, who gave $2 million to the Swift Vets and POW's for Truth (he also contributed $2.5 million to another Republican-oriented group, Progress for America.)[13] The contribution to the Swift Boat Vets was necessary, he told *Texas Monthly*, to counter the multimillion-dollar sums being poured into independent campaigns aimed at defeating Bush, particularly from the likes of George Soros. "This legislation was supposed to take big money out of political campaigns, which is how it should be," Pickens said. "But once we were stuck with playbook, we didn't have a choice. . . . I figured if 527s were going to be a part of the process, we'd have to play our part, too."[14] Other major contributors to Republican 527s included Carl H. Lindner Jr., chairman of American Financial Group, and Alex G. Spanos, owner of the San Diego Chargers National Football League team.[15]

The new campaign finance rules proved so porous in terms of allowing large donations to reach the political system that the measures congressional sponsors later sued the FEC to force stricter regulations, as intended under the law.

GOING MUCH FURTHER

Many of the independent groups' ads were striking for their vitriol, anger, and accusatory tone. Strategists at the Bush and Kerry campaigns knew a backlash would follow if their ads crossed a line of negativity voters did not find acceptable. While the candidates had to exercise such restraint, the independent groups had almost no accountability and could basically say whatever they wanted. If an ad went too far, the candidate could simply dissociate himself and let the independent group take the blame. Kerry accused Bush of hiding behind the Swift Vets in challenging his record of valor in Vietnam. "He wants them to do his dirty work," Kerry asserted, a charge the president's campaign denied.[16] Bush went on to credit Kerry's military service, providing modest cover.

Like the spots once sponsored by political parties, the independent groups' commercials could not explicitly advocate for or against a candidate, because that would have to be paid for in "hard money." The maximum allowed in this category was $4,000: $2,000 in the primary and $2,000 for the general election. The ads never said, "Vote for John Kerry," or "Vote for George W. Bush"—or even anything explicitly about elections. Instead, they focused on the candidates' histories, policies, and personal foibles.

In tone, the outside groups were much more likely to connect the dots in a conspiratorial fashion and draw the worst possible conclusions about the opposition. "You had both sides feeling essentially the world was going to turn into a black hole if the other side won," said Brooks Jackson, director of

FactCheck.org, an authoritative website that monitors the veracity of campaign ads.[17]

The negative ads from the independent groups were sometimes based on policy issues, but a number used ad hominem attacks. One ad, aired during the Democratic primary season by the antitax Club for Growth, labeled former Vermont Governor Howard Dean a "tax-hiking, government-expanding, latte-drinking, sushi-eating, Volvo-driving, *New York Times*–reading, body-piercing, Hollywood-loving, left-wing freak show." And a spot from the conservative Citizens United labeled Kerry "another rich liberal elitist from Massachusetts who claims he's a man of the people."[18]

When policy was mentioned, the rhetoric often did not match the facts. One issue Democrats liked to attack Bush on was the loss of jobs to overseas workers. An ad by the Media Fund, a leading Democratic 527, showed a displaced worker fuming that "when President Bush says he's going to help companies outsource jobs, it's infuriating." Bush never made that statement. What he had said was, "The best way to deal with job creation and outsourcing is to make sure our businesses are competitive here at home."[19] Bush had even suggested he knew people in America were looking for work "because jobs have gone overseas." (Still, the line of attack was not completely unfounded. In March 2004, Treasury Secretary John Snow said, "You can outsource a lot of activities and get them done just as well, or better, at a lower cost."[20])

The most memorable independent ads picked heart-wrenching issues that easily stirred up strong feelings. One television spot, financed by the leftist MoveOn.org PAC, opened with the sound of laughter at a media dinner in Washington, D.C., where a tuxedo-clad President Bush made light of the search for Iraqi weapons. Then Brooke Campbell of Kirksville, Mo., described what happened thirty-six days after that event. "My brother died in Baghdad on April 29," she said. "I watched President Bush make a joke, looking around for weapons of mass destruction. My brother died looking for weapons of mass destruction."[21]

Some independent ads drew a firestorm of criticism—and free media. A different MoveOn.org PAC commercial showed an American soldier sinking chest-deep into sand, as he tried to keep his rifle above his head, apparently surrendering. That commercial, run in September 2004, noted that more than 1,000 soldiers had been killed and that billions of dollars had been spent on the war. The narrator concluded, "George Bush got us into this quagmire. It will take a new president to get us out."[22] Republicans pounced on a commercial that showed an American soldier surrendering, to the point that Kerry verbally distanced himself.

On the opposing side, a hard-hitting ad by the conservative Progress for America Voter fund (PFA) showed pictures of Osama bin Laden and Mohamed Atta, the lead hijacker on September 11, as the announcer declared, "These people want to kill us . . . Would you trust Kerry against these fanatic killers? President Bush didn't start this war, but he will finish it."[23] PFA President Brian McCabe said after the election, "We think we helped define the debate, the public policy debate on the war on terror. We created a favorable image of President Bush's public policy agenda, while at the same time raising doubt about Senator Kerry's ability to lead the war on terror."[24] Similar ads took aim at the previous Democratic president, Bill Clinton. The pro-Republican organization Citizens United made a television spot with footage of various al-Qaeda terrorist attacks staged during Clinton's years in office, then asked rhetorically: "So who is responsible for leaving us vulnerable to terrorists?"[25]

Arguably no ads were more memorable—or controversial—than those run by the Swift Vets. The group consisted of Vietnam veterans who patrolled the Mekong Delta in Swift boats similar to those that Kerry piloted. Kerry had tried to inoculate himself on national security issues by making his heroism in Vietnam the centerpiece of his nominating convention and a reason he was fit to be commander in chief.[26] To critics, that strategy opened Kerry up to the torrent of criticism about his military service that followed.

The Swift Vets wanted to destroy Kerry's heroic image and raise questions about his ability to lead the nation during a time of war. Their ads started with an initially small media buy, $500,000, in Wisconsin, Ohio, and West Virginia. But cable shows played the ads repeatedly, and pundits chewed them over on air for weeks. Senator Kerry's critics furiously e-mailed the spots to anyone they could. Even criticisms of the Swift Vets' charges helped increase their exposure. "We wanted to generate controversy," said Chris LaCivita, the Swift Vets' chief strategist.[27] That strategy succeeded wildly. The ads had the effect of confronting Kerry on one of his perceived strong issues, said LaCivita, a combat Marine veteran from the Gulf War, who said he was drawn to the group by their disgust with Kerry for criticizing active-duty troops after he returned from Vietnam.

The commercials were a milestone in the history of negative campaigning in presidential politics. Candidates had long been chastised for avoiding combat service, whether it was Grover Cleveland for hiring a substitute during the Civil War or Bill Clinton for pulling strings to avoid going to Vietnam. But the Swift Vets' ads in 2004 marked the first time a candidate's active-duty military service had been used *against* him during a campaign, rather than in his own favor.

Under the old system, these hard-hitting ads would not likely have been run by the Bush campaign or the GOP, LaCivita said. Even though the parties were often willing to go further than the candidates themselves, they might have demurred from having to endure the criticism that accompanied the Swift Boat ads questioning Kerry's military record. Similarly, the Kerry campaign or DNC would likely have been reluctant to run an ad sponsored by a liberal group that tied Bush's policies to the poisoning of pregnant women. So the outside groups were much less accountable to the public than the previous recipients of the large soft-money donations, the RNC and DNC.

BCRA did achieve some of its goals. The RNC and DNC had to wean themselves off the large unlimited contributions (that instead went to 527s and other independent groups) and rely instead on small donors. Indeed, the 2004 election saw dramatic growth in individual contributions to candidates and political parties. From 2000 to 2004, the DNC increased its individual contribution revenue to $356 million from $111 million, while the RNC's cash intake jumped to $344 million from $186 million. Presidential candidates raised $234 million in 2000, while in 2004 they collected $631 million.[28]

These increases were tied, at least in part, to another provision in BCRA. In the absence of soft money, the law doubled individual contribution limits from $2,000 to $4,000 per election cycle per candidate. It also raised the aggregate individual contribution limit per election cycle to $95,000. So just because the parties could not collect soft money, a lot of cash still flowed into their coffers, only in smaller donations from many more individuals than had previously been the case.

STAND BY YOUR AD

BCRA also took aim at the tone of political advertisements. The "stand by your ad" provision (SBYA), adopted as an amendment to the act, aimed to create a direct linkage for television viewers between the ad they were watching and who made it. Candidates now have to identify themselves and approve the ad in their own voice. In television ads, they must make the statement to the camera, or their image must accompany a voiceover. "I think that would have the very beneficial effect of making candidates think twice before hurling accusations that perhaps are exaggerated or unfounded against an opponent," said Senator Susan Collins, Republican of Maine, during the March 2001 Senate consideration of BCRA. "I believe it would help elevate the political debate, and it would help curb some of the egregious negative ads that offend all of us."[29]

In practice, however, there is little evidence that candidates are willing to blunt their attacks on opponents simply because they have to verbally endorse their own commercials. Most candidates want to win more than they want to look like nice guys. And savvy political consultants have found ways to turn the requirement to their advantage, or at least neutralize its downside. One approach that became common in 2004 had the candidate offering the disclaimer at the beginning of a commercial. The screen went to black for a few frames, and then proceeded to a typical negative spot. Shortly after Senator Kerry clinched the Democratic nomination in spring 2004, the Bush campaign ran an a commercial that featured the president's disclaimer up front; it then launched into charges that Kerry had supported more than 350 tax increases and was soft in the war on terror.

Another increasingly common technique was to split a 30-second commercial into two roughly 15-second spots, one negative and one positive, with the disclaimer in the positive portion. The first part often showed a grainy black and white, unflattering picture of the opponent, with menacing music and a stern narration of the candidate's shortcomings. In the second half, where the disclaimer was placed, the candidate running the ad was shown perhaps with family members or walking on a beach with their dog.

Candidates quickly adopted the technique of using the tagline requirement to spin their own messages. During the 2004 Democratic presidential primary season, the former governor of Vermont looked into the camera and said, "I'm Howard Dean, and I approve this message because it's time to take our country back." Senator John Edwards of North Carolina authorized a commercial for his Democratic presidential bid by citing foreign trade: "I approve this message because I want to export American products, not American jobs."

Kerry noted at the end of one of his ads, "I approved this message because it's time to roll back the Bush tax cuts for the wealthy, crack down on corporate corruption, and put opportunity in the hands of all Americans."[30]

In some cases in congressional races, candidates even managed to turn the candidate disclaimer—meant to foster high-minded campaigning—into barbed comments against opponents. In South Dakota, Democrat Congresswoman Stephanie Herseth closed a television attack ad on her Republican opponent with, "I approved this message because I'm committed to a truthful campaign. It's clear that Larry Diedrich is not."[31]

The requirement has not tangibly changed the ads' tone or messages. "We saw just as many that were pretty direct, and pretty negative," said Jim Margolis, who produced John Kerry's primary campaign advertising. "The tone wasn't markedly different than other years."[32] Fred Davis, an ad maker for the Bush-Cheney 2004 campaign, said the SBYA rule ate up precious time in campaign spots that could have been used to inform voters about the candidates' policies and positions. At one point Davis spent two hours filming President Bush, trying to devise ways to make the self-endorsement sound seamless. "You would not believe how much effort went into [figuring out] how to get the seated president of the United States to not look weird giving that little disclaimer at the end or the beginning," he recalled.[33]

But there is some reason to believe that candidates would still rather not be associated with certain negative spots, a central premise behind the SBYA measure. In 2004, many of the nastiest commercials moved from television to the Internet, where no "stand by your ad" provision applied (a subject discussed in chapter 12). In spring 2004, the Bush-Cheney campaign website ran an ad highlighting Kerry's votes to curb military spending during his nineteen years in the Senate. The spot cautioned viewers that the Democratic president candidate "repeatedly opposed weapons vital to winning the war on terror." Had that ad run on television, it would have required a shot of Bush endorsing the video, or the president's photograph, combined with a Bush voiceover. And while the Bush-Cheney television ads that questioned Kerry's fitness to be commander in chief were plenty tough, most were not nearly as explicit as those on the Internet.

Congressman David Price, Democrat of North Carolina, said the intent of the provision he sponsored is often misunderstood. The measure was meant to encourage personal responsibility on behalf of candidates and organizations running campaign ads. Whether the tone is positive or negative, viewers at least know who is paying for it. "There's no category of ad that we have sought to get off the air," he said. "Whether or not the ads lessen the level of negativity in campaign commercials, viewers have more information than they used to about who is sponsoring the commercial."[34]

When the SBYA rule took effect along with the rest of BCRA, existing disclaimers consisted of minute type at the bottom of the television screen, said Price. That level of disclosure was ineffective in disclosing who was behind ads. Now, "voters are going to have more knowledge, and therefore may act on that knowledge," said Price, first elected to his Raleigh-area district in 1986. He argued the political system is still better off with the disclosure regulations. "There is still a greater brand ID than there was before," he said.[35]

NOTES

1. Interview with author, Washington, D.C., Jan. 27, 2005.

2. *McConnell v. Federal Election Commission*, 540 U.S. 93 (2003).

3. "Curtailing Big Checks," a *Washington Post* editorial, March 31, 2005.

4. Glen Justice, "McCain Calls for New Limits on Money to Political Groups," *The New York Times*, Feb. 3, 2005.

5. *The Congressional Record*, March 22, 2001, S2692.

6. The Center for Responsive Politics, Glossary of Terms (www.opensecrets.org/pubs/glossary/softmoney.htm).

7. David Nather, "The $4 Billion Campaign: Better, or Just Louder?" *CQ Weekly*, Oct. 30, 2004.

8. American Bar Association, Case Summaries, 2003–2004 term (www.abanet.org/publiced/preview/summary/2003–2004/f2.html).

9. James V. Grimaldi and Thomas B. Edsall, "Super Rich Step into Political Vacuum: McCain-Feingold Paved Way for 527s," *The Washington Post*, Oct. 17, 2004.

10. *NewsHour with Jim Lehrer*, PBS, March 26, 2004.

11. Lisa Getter, "With 527s, New Power Players Take Position: Through the Creation of These Independent Organizations, at Least 45 Individual Donors Have

Contributed $1 Million or More in This Election," *The Los Angeles Times*, Nov. 1, 2004.

12. Byron York, *The Vast Left Wing Conspiracy: The Untold Story of How Democratic Operatives, Eccentric Billionaires, Liberal Activists, and Assorted Celebrities Tried to Bring Down a President—and Whey They'll Try Even Harder Next Time* (New York: Crown Forum, 2005), 8.

13. The Center for Responsive Politics, www.opensecrets.org, T. Boone Pickens Contributions to 527 Committees 2004 Election Cycle (www.opensecrets.org/527s/527indivsdetail.asp?ID=11001162782&Cycle =2004).

14. Pamela Colloff, "Sunk: When the Swift Boat Veterans for Truth Capsized John Kerry's Presidential Campaign, Much of the Unfriendly Fire Came from Texas. Here's How, in Their Own Words, Another Band of Brothers—and a Few Sisters— Changed History. Or, at Least, Rewrote It," *Texas Monthly*, January 2005.

15. Grimaldi and Edsall, *The Washington Post*, Oct. 17, 2004.

16. "Kerry: Bush Lets Groups Do 'Dirty Work,'" *Associated Press*, Aug. 19, 2004.

17. Interview with author, by telephone, Jan. 5, 2005.

18. Mark H. Rodeffer, "Stand by Your Ad: How Candidates Having to Endorse Their Own Television Advertisements Is Changing Media Strategy," *Campaigns & Elections*, June 2004.

19. Dana Wilkie, "Truth Be (Not) Told: Watchdog Groups Say Misstatements, Distortions by Both Candidates Plague President Race, Making It Difficult to Separate Fact from Fiction," *San Diego Union-Tribune*, Oct. 4, 2004.

20. John Byczkowski, "Treasury's Snow Says Jobs Coming," *The Cincinnati Enquirer*, March 30, 2004.

21. Howard Kurtz, "Ads Aiming Straight for the Heart: Independent Groups Spend Millions on Hard-Hitting Spots," *The Washington Post*, Oct. 27, 2004.

22. Glen Justice, "Political Group's Antiwar Ad Draws Ire of the Bush Campaign," *The New York Times*, Sept. 17, 2004.

23. Thomas B. Edsall, "After Late Start, Republican Groups Jump into the Lead," *The Washington Post*, Oct. 17, 2004.

24. The Annenberg Public Policy Center of the University of Pennsylvania, "527s in 2004: Did They Make a Difference." Panel discussion at the National Press Club of Washington, D.C., Dec. 6, 2004.

25. Glenn Garvin, "Hardball Ads Are Effective—and Win Elections," *The Miami Herald*, Sept. 20, 2004.

26. David B. Magleby, J. Quin Monson, and Kelly D. Patterson, eds., *Dancing without Partners: How Candidates, Parties and Interest Groups Interact in the New Campaign Finance Environment* (Provo, Utah: Center for the Study of Elections and Democracy, Brigham Young University, 2005), 8.

27. Interview with author, Washington, D.C., Jan. 27, 2005.

28. Magelby, Monson, and Patterson, *Dancing without Partners*, 1, 6.

29. *The Congressional Record*, March 22, 2001, S2692.

30. Rodeffer, *Campaigns & Elections*, June 2004.

31. Kelly D. Patterson, Kristina Gale, Betsey Gimbel Hawkins, and Richard Hawkins, "I Approved This Message: A Study of Political Disclaimers," *Campaigns & Elections*, May 2005.

32. Interview with author, Washington, D.C., Feb. 18, 2005.

33. Interview with author, by telephone, March 16, 2005.

34. Interview with author, Washington, D.C., Feb. 9, 2005.

35. Interview with author, Washington, D.C., Feb. 9, 2005.

A Double-Edged Sword: When Negative Campaigning Backfires

In fall 2002 Felix Grucci Jr. seemed a safe bet for reelection to his Long Island–based congressional seat. The freshman Republican represented a district where GOP voter registrants outnumbered Democrats by more than 50,000. Grucci had looked after the interests of constituents and he was running against an opponent with no political résumé. In addition he sported a well-known last name in the local area; the Grucci family had long been active in the fireworks business.

Still, as the 2002 midterm election season progressed Grucci sensed trouble on the political horizon. The 1st District had had a volatile voting history in recent years. Republican Michael Forbes won the seat in the 1994 GOP landslide that gave Republicans control of the House for the first time in forty years. He voted generally conservatively, but over the years his enthusiasm for the GOP agenda waned; in 1999 he switched parties, earning the wrath of House Republicans and making him a major target in 2000. That year Forbes unexpectedly lost (by thirty-five votes) the Democratic nomination to Regina Seltzer, a little-known elderly woman. Seltzer was then defeated by Grucci in the general election by a wide margin (55.5 percent to 40.6 percent).[1]

So when Grucci's 2002 Democratic opponent, Timothy Bishop, mounted a stronger than expected challenge, Grucci decided to go negative. A former town supervisor in Brookhaven, Grucci had earned his political spurs in the rough and tumble world of Long Island politics, and running an attack ad seemed natural. Instead the decision turned out to be a politically fatal mistake.

In late September, Grucci launched a radio ad accusing Bishop, provost of Southampton College on Long Island, of falsifying rape statistics on campus and "turning his back on rape victims." The commercial's woman narrator said, "After sexual assaults on campus continued, Tim Bishop was asked by students to promote better school security. He said to students, quote, 'I can't tell you that you're safe here. I can't tell your parents that you're safe here.'"[2]

The problem for Grucci was that the ad was based on a discredited report in the college's newspaper. It turned out that the 1994 article was so error-ridden that the editors voluntarily retrieved every copy of the newspaper they could find; Bishop's alleged quote was deemed false. Officials with Long Island University, which runs the college, sued to stop the ad from airing; a judge ruled it could run but could not name the school.[3]

Despite these massive factual errors in the student newspaper article, Grucci refused to take the ad off the air or admit the mistake, arguing that there had never been a correction in print. He quickly came in for strong criticism by his Democratic opponent for knowingly peddling false information in a campaign commercial. "Mr. Grucci's radio ad is just not true," Bishop said in his own radio spot. "Grucci's latest attack crosses the line, and I'm not going to stand for it. He accuses me of not caring about rape. As the father of two college-age daughters, I'm disgusted Mr. Grucci would sink so low."[4]

Bishop's rejoinder had hit the mark with voters, and polls showed the Republican's support sinking. It quickly became apparent that Grucci had blundered badly. The House Democrats' campaign machine saw an opening and began to pour money into the race. Soon the airwaves were filled with ads hammering Grucci for not recanting the charges against Bishop. They also criticized Grucci on environmental issues, saying his family's fireworks business was linked to chemical contamination of local drinking water.

Grucci's self-inflicted wound proved too deep to overcome. He lost by 2,752 votes out of a little more than 167,000 cast. And he was one of just three Republican incumbents defeated for reelection that year.[5]

Grucci's political plight demonstrates the dangers and risks in going negative on an opponent. If negative campaigning is not carried on judiciously and with discretion, it can backfire on a candidate just as easily as it can help. Scores of other candidates have learned the hard way that it can be detrimental to turn up the heat too high on an opponent. "You've got to measure all sides of the question," said legendary Republican consultant Stu Spencer. "You always run an element of risk."[6]

OLD NEWS

Negative campaigning has often backfired when candidates dredged up embarrassing incidents from opponents' pasts that had already been reported extensively and were long in the public domain. Lisa Quigley found out as much in 2004 when she sought the Democratic nomination in the California's 20th Congressional District, based in the state's Central Valley. She had served as chief of staff for Democratic Congressman Calvin Dooley, who was retiring after fourteen years in Congress. Quigley faced off in the primary against Jim Costa, a veteran of the state legislature.

Though Quigley, a Merced native, had Dooley's support, Costa's name had been on the ballot many times before. Voters were familiar with the legislative record of a man who had served sixteen years in the state Assembly and eight in the state Senate, before term limits forced him from office in 2002. While she focused on education and environmental issues, he touted his long record in Sacramento pushing through laws to help agriculture and expand health care coverage. With his wide name recognition, Costa led throughout the race leading up to the March 2004 primary, in the Fresno-to-Bakersfield district.

The Quigley campaign banked on the fact that not all of Costa's publicity over the years was positive. In 1986, Sacramento police arrested Costa for soliciting a police decoy posing as a prostitute. Costa apologized to his constituents, pleaded no contest, served three years of probation, and paid a $160 fine. In 1994, police investigating a break-in at Costa's Fresno home found a small amount of marijuana, which Costa strongly denied was his. Police confirmed that fingerprints on the box containing trace amounts of marijuana were not Costa's, and no charges were ever filed.[7]

The long-ago episodes resurfaced in a 2004 Quigley television commercial, which slammed her Democratic primary rival. The ad opened with unflattering newspaper headlines and the voiceover: "Jim Costa was arrested and convicted of a crime so inappropriate for daytime TV, we won't say it." The ad also mentioned the marijuana incident, and, in a more conventional line of political attack, portrayed him as a legislator who took large amounts of special-interest money, voted against the interests of his district, and became "part of the Sacramento mess."[8]

Not surprisingly, the run-ins with law enforcement had received extensive local media coverage years before, when they occurred. By 2004 they were old news. Since the 1986 incident voters had endorsed Costa on the ballot about a dozen times. On the campaign trail, Costa shrugged off the attacks, calling them a sign of a desperate politician. A Costa spokesman called the ad "the equivalent of a Hail Mary pass in football." The congressman from a neighboring district, Democrat Dennis Cardoza, sided with Costa, his former colleague in the state legislature. Cardoza told Quigley in a letter that he was "gravely concerned and disturbed by the negative and personal tone your campaign has taken." *The Fresno Bee* withdrew its endorsement of Quigley, criticizing not only her ad as below-the-belt politics but also her suggestion at one point that Costa should submit to a drug test, as she was willing to do. As the political damage mounted, Quigley desperately defended the ad. "Voters want to know that the person they send to Washington shares their values" and will work on their behalf, she said. "This is the contrast that we provide."[9]

Voters thought otherwise, making clear they were not interested in hearing about warmed-over charges and long-ago brushes with law enforcement. Costa crushed Quigley in the Democratic primary, earning 73 percent of the vote. He captured the seat in the general election (defeating state Senator Roy Ashburn) and became the district's new congressman.

The episode illustrates how voters are often turned off to negative campaigning when it recycles old and dated information. Absent new revelations, candidates contemplating this form of mudslinging have often done better keeping the information bottled up. Tony Sanchez in Texas learned a similar lesson in 2002 when he ran for governor. The multimillionaire Laredo businessman was the Democratic nominee against Republican Governor Rick Perry, the former lieutenant governor who assumed the office when George W. Bush won the presidency. Back in 2000 Lt. Governor Perry received some unfavorable publicity when the vehicle he was traveling in from San Antonio to the Capitol in Austin got pulled over for speeding. A police car dashboard camera captured his reaction: The blurry video showed an agitated Perry urging a state trooper to "let us get down the road."[10] The driver got a warning for going 20 miles over the speed limit.

The video received widespread news coverage in Texas at the time. In the gubernatorial campaign, Sanchez decided to dredge up the video again—in October 2002, more than two years after the incident. Sanchez ads, aired late in the campaign, implied that Perry had used his official position to bully the state trooper out of ticketing his car. One ad repeated the scene in which Perry said, "Why don't you just let us get down the road?" while an announcer listed state problems that the then-lieutenant governor was allegedly ignoring. The ad ended, "Rick Perry. We didn't elect him. Let's just let him get on down the road."[11] But the ad contained no new information, and the traffic stop had previously received extensive media coverage. So by the time the Sanchez campaign rehashed the video again, it seemed to Texas voters like old news. If anything, the reaction was more negative against Sanchez for airing the footage once again, than about the contents of the video. "After the first 50 viewings, every driver in the state was muttering: 'Why doesn't Sanchez just stick it in his ear?'" noted the *Austin Chronicle*, an alternative newspaper.[12]

Not that Perry sat on his hands in reaction. He ran a series of hard-hitting ads against the Democratic nominee. One commercial featured two retired Drug Enforcement Administration agents suggesting that alleged money laundering at Sanchez's Laredo savings and loan was indirectly responsible for the murder of a DEA agent in Mexico.[13] Sanchez refuted the charges, but it made little difference. The electoral landscape was already working in Perry's favor, as Texas was a heavily GOP state. In a strong Republican year nationally, Perry cruised to victory over Sanchez 58 percent to 40 percent.

SIMPLY NOT CREDIBLE

Negative campaigning has worked most effectively when a candidate's attacks, charges, and accusations play into preconceived notions about the opposition. In effect it has ratified in voters' minds doubts they already had about the candidate. Negative campaigning has often failed when those seeking office have hurled out charges that did not square with the opposition's voting record or stands on issues, as demonstrated in 2004 during the fight for the Republican nomination in North Carolina's 5th Congressional District.

The Republican stronghold district in the state's western regions came open when GOP Congressman Richard Burr ran (successfully) for the U.S.

Senate. Because the district leaned Republican, the winner of the Republican nomination was virtually assured of election to Congress. Eight candidates ran in the Republican primary; on Election Day, July 20, Winston-Salem City Councilman Vernon Robinson finished narrowly ahead of state senator Virginia Foxx. But because nobody received 40 percent of the primary vote, a runoff was needed to determine the GOP nominee.

Robinson had run an aggressive primary campaign against his multiple opponents, notable for its intense level of name calling. Former Congressman Jack Kemp (R-N.Y.), who had endorsed Robinson at the outset of the campaign, was so displeased with the candidate's tactics that he rescinded the endorsement weeks before the primary Election Day.[14] The gloves came off further during the campaign for the August 17 runoff, when it was just Robinson and Foxx. They shared similar conservative views on issues, such as favoring tax cuts, trimming federal spending, and opposing abortion. Robinson aimed to distinguish his candidacy by proclaiming himself a "black Jesse Helms" (he sought to become the first black Republican elected to the House from the Old South since the post–Civil War Reconstruction era).

And seeking to portray himself as the most conservative candidate, in ads Robinson compared his opponent to Senator Hillary Rodham Clinton (D-N.Y.), and tried to cast her as a left-wing feminist. His campaign accused Foxx of supporting the failed Equal Rights Amendment, tax increases, and racial quotas, and said she took money from "the homosexual lobby"—a reference to a small contribution Foxx had received from a gay rights group during a legislative campaign a decade earlier. But these charges did not square with reality. In the state senate Foxx had voted a strongly conservative line. Among other things, she had opposed same-sex marriage and abortion, supported limiting class-action lawsuits against businesses, and was a member of the NRA. His negative critiques of her were wildly off-mark and lacking credibility. Her name had been on the ballot several times in recent years, when voters had affirmed her for office, so they were clearly familiar with her record.

Robinson also ran a series of ads and made statements that did not directly criticize Foxx but that caused many potential supporters to question whether he possessed a temperament suitable for service in Congress. One ad took aim at illegal immigration, a sensitive issue in a state with one of the fastest growing Latino populations in the nation. In Robinson's spot the narrator said: "The aliens are here, but they didn't come in a spaceship. . . . They sponge off the American taxpayers. . . . They've even taken over the DMV. These aliens commit heinous crimes."[15] On the stump, Robinson targeted the district's most conservative voters by expressing outrage about gay rights groups and those thought to be hostile to mixing religion and public office. He paid $2,000 from his own pocket to erect a granite marker of the Ten Commandments outside the Winston-Salem City Hall and called gay marriage "a slippery slope to complete paganism."[16]

While the district did have a conservative bent, Robinson's actions made him appear unhinged. The local press savaged Robinson for his negative campaigning. The *Winston-Salem Journal*, in an editorial endorsing Foxx, called Robinson "negative and divisive" and wrote, "sending Vernon Robinson to Washington to represent the 5th District would be worse than sending no one at all."[17] Robinson made no apologies for his tactics and likened himself to Helms, the state's controversial former senator.

After running a relatively low-key primary campaign, Foxx went negative herself to counter Robinson's tactics. She ran an ad calling Robinson a "master of the big lie." A direct mail piece her campaign sent out suggested that Robinson was under criminal investigation for campaign finance irregularities, though a local prosecutor declared that to be untrue. But the brunt of the attacks came from Robinson's campaign, and in the end voters sent the message that his campaign tactics were unacceptable. Foxx ended up receiving 55 percent of the runoff vote to Robinson's 45 percent. Robinson's campaign offers a cautionary tale about candidates needing to understand public perceptions of an opponent's voting record and hurling charges that come across to voters as credible, not outlandish.

PLAYING THE VICTIM

Those on the receiving end of negative campaigning are sometimes able to turn their situations to their advantage. Depending on how the damaging information is released, the candidate being attacked has the opportunity to play the victim. That was the case in the 2004 open seat race to represent New York's 29th Congressional District, which stretches over broad swaths of the state's southwestern section. The seat came open when 18-year incumbent Amo Houghton, a moderate Republican, decided to retire. In the GOP-leaning district, Randy Kuhl, a state legislator for 24 years, easily won the Republican nomination. With Houghton's endorsement in hand and running in a district that favored Republicans, the veteran politician was expected to cruise to victory in the general election, against his Democratic opponent, Samara Barend, who had previously worked on Capitol Hill as an aide to the late Senator Daniel Patrick Moynihan.

Kuhl did not get a free ride, though, and his biggest troubles did not involve disputes with his opponent over public policy issues. Instead, controversy stemmed from charges made by Kuhl's ex-wife in divorce papers that, by law, were supposed to be sealed. She contended that at a dinner party in 1994 he had pulled two shotguns on her and, as could be expected from divorce papers, made several other unflattering statements and allegations about the lawmaker.[18] Somehow the negative information from Kuhl's divorce records found its way into the local media, and her statements in the legal documents clearly reflected poorly on the Republican candidate.

But rather than respond to the substance of the accusations, Kuhl discussed process. He stressed that the divorce papers had been distributed illegally; he charged the Barend campaign with being responsible for disseminating the information. It was an invasion of privacy, Kuhl said, and he called for legal action against the people in Barend's campaign responsible for obtaining and making public the sealed divorce records. A Steuben County district attorney's investigation led authorities to Jonah Siegellak, Barend's campaign manager, as the leaker of the damaging information. The documents apparently got into the hands of the Barend campaign when a worker in the Steuben County clerk's office accidentally released them to a researcher, along with papers that were public, such as police records relating to Kuhl's 1997 arrest for drunken driving.

Siegellak and other members of Barend's staff initially denied having anything to do with the release of the documents, and the candidate defended her campaign workers. Barend went so far as to tell the *Elmira Star-Gazette* editorial board that she had her campaign staff's "word of honor" that it was not involved.[19] Still, after several weeks of mounting evidence and public pressure, Siegellak admitted leaking the papers to the media. Local press coverage quickly turned against Barend for engaging in below-the-belt politics. The *Star-Gazette* chided her for failing to take decisive action by firing Siegellak, even after he admitted his complicity in the episode. "Barend has allowed her credible candidacy to degenerate into a muddy campaign where voters in this race—especially the undecided—are left no choice but to question her ability to manage a campaign and, by implication, the rigors of a congressional term," the paper wrote.[20] Houghton, the outgoing congressman, chimed in against the Democrat. "Divorce, by its very nature, is very contentious," he said. "To have that thing ripped open is just absolutely to me unconscionable. Now that the finger has been pointed at the people in the campaign, not to have somebody fired is unbelievable."[21]

Kuhl came out of the controversy as a sympathetic figure whose privacy rights had been violated. He won the race 50 percent to 41 percent. There is evidence that voters were turned off by the negative tone of the campaign. Kuhl beat Barend by 136,883 votes to 110,241, while Conservative Party candidate Mark Assini got 17,272 votes, and Independence nominee John Clampoli, who lived outside the district and did not campaign, earned 5,819 votes[22]—unusually high totals for third-party candidates. It is likely that Kuhl would have been victorious anyway, as he sported the endorsement from Houghton, an enormously popular figure in the district, which already favored Republicans. But the challenger's clumsy attempt at surreptitious negative campaigning destroyed any chance she had of an upset. (The Barend campaign did avoid legal jeopardy, as the Steuben County district attorney declined to press criminal charges, saying divorce papers' disclosure was inadvertent, since they were part of a search of other documents that were public.)

Occasionally candidates on the receiving end of an attack can literally go before the electorate and grovel their way to victory. Such was the case of Senator Charles Percy, Republican of Illinois, back in 1978, during his hotly contested bid for a third term. The Chicago wunderkind businessman-turned-politician faced off against Alex Seith, a relative political novice whose highest-profile political position had been a seat on President Jimmy Carter's advisory board on ambassadorial appointments.[23] A graduate of Yale and Harvard Law School, on issues such as tax cuts and advocating an end to federal aid to education Seith (the Democrat) was considerably more conservative than Percy, a scion of the GOP's moderate wing.

Polling showed weak support for a two-term senator, with many voters unenthusiastic about the prospect of voting for him again. Still, Seith had low name recognition and eight campaign staff members, compared to Percy's more than forty advisors. And with a smaller war chest to work with (less than $1 million against Percy's more than $2.4 million), Seith's campaign team aimed to knock Percy off balance with targeted advertising.[24]

The campaign found an opening in the July 6 debate between the candidates. On a question about agriculture, Percy mentioned Earl Butz, secretary of agriculture under Presidents Richard Nixon and Gerald Ford, and said, "I wish he were secretary of agriculture still today," referring to Butz's free-market policies. However, Butz hadn't merely retired after Ford's defeat: He had been fired during the 1976 presidential campaign after *Rolling Stone* magazine reported on an extremely racially insensitive and indecorous joke he told on *Air Force One*. Percy's slip had not featured prominently in press accounts of the debate, but after an article in a Bloomington, Illinois, paper recorded Percy calling "for a return to the Earl Butz era in farming and a return to power of the former secretary of agriculture himself," the Seith campaign pounced.[25]

Seith's advisers thought they could benefit by stoking up anger at Percy from groups across the political spectrum: His seeming praise for Butz would annoy farmers who liked the former agriculture secretary and remembered his earlier call for Butz's removal. Percy's statement would also appall black voters, when reminded of circumstances under which Butz was forced from office.

Tony Schwartz, the New York–based consultant who produced Lyndon Johnson's "Daisy Girl" spot in 1964, was on the Seith team. Schwartz developed a 60-second anti-Percy ad to appear on radio stations in predominantly black communities. In the ad, the narrator said, "Do you think Senator Percy is a friend of black people? Well, remember Earl Butz? He was that secretary of agriculture who made a racist and sexually obscene joke about blacks. We can't repeat his words on the air, of course, but they were so offensive that he had to resign. Maybe you are wondering what that's got to do with Senator Percy. Just this—Senator Percy said of Earl Butz. 'I wish he were secretary of agriculture today.' Still today, Senator Percy? Percy wants the black vote, and with friends like this, you don't need enemies. Because Charles Percy tolerates the Earl Butz insult to blacks, more and more people are getting behind Alex Seith for the United States Senate."[26]

Percy complained that the ad depicted him as a racist, while in fact he had called for Butz's resignation the moment he learned of the Cabinet secretary's impolitic joke. The senator had significant backing: Mike Royko of the *Chicago Sun-Times*, one of the most influential journalists in the state, lambasted Seith in print, while boxing champ Muhammad Ali and the Reverend Jesse Jackson cut radio ads on the Republican's behalf. During an October 17 debate, Seith was forced to acknowledge that Percy had deplored the Butz joke, and did not imply the incumbent was a racist.[27] For the rest of the campaign, Percy shifted the issue from his Butz remark (which hadn't been particularly well covered or well known) to whether Seith's campaign had twisted his words and crossed the line of campaign decorum. Percy at one point called Seith an "ineffectual puppet" of Tony Schwartz: "If you can buy into an election with this tactic and this below-the-belt technique with a hired gun from New York, save us then from the future, if television and radio can be used for that purpose."[28]

At campaign's end, Percy ran an emotional television ad in which he looked into the camera, seemingly on the verge of tears, and pleaded with voters: "The polls say many of you want to send me a message," Percy said earnestly, in the hastily produced commercial shown statewide in the days before the election. "But after November 7, I may not be in the Senate any longer to receive it." He continued, "Believe me, I've gotten the message, and you're right. Washington has gone overboard, and I'm sure I've made my share of mistakes. But in truth, your priorities are mine, too—stop the waste, cut the spending, cut the taxes."[29]

Using a minor radio ad that implied that he was dishonest and possibly racist, Percy managed to shift the focus of the campaign from his own record as senator to his opponent's negative tactics and portrayed himself as honest and unfairly battered. Facing a possible upset, Percy pulled off a 53 to 47 percent victory over Seith.

More than a quarter century later, Seith's campaign manager, Garry South, said the episode taught him to vet carefully each word in every single spot, for the potential of giving inadvertent messages or perceptions that could sink a candidate.[30]

While Percy's beg for forgiveness among the voters of Illinois worked in 1978, it came back to haunt him during his next reelection bid, in 1984. His Democratic opponent, Paul Simon, a 10-year congressman from downstate Illinois, used the concession in an ad, asking if Percy had really gotten the message. "Paul Simon means never having to say you're sorry," went the tag line. That time Percy lost the election 50 percent to 48 percent.[31]

Perhaps the most prominent "victims" of negative campaigning in recent times were Mary Cheney and her parents, Vice President Dick Cheney and his wife, Lynne. The Second Family were given an opportunity to draw sympathy

in fall 2004 after a questionable comment by Senator John Kerry of Massachusetts about the Cheney daughter's sexual orientation, during the third and
final presidential debate, in Tempe, Arizona. The controversy grew out of
Kerry's response to a question from debate moderator Bob Schieffer of CBS
News. Schieffer indicated that both candidates opposed legalization of gay
marriage and wondered how they had arrived at that position. He asked: "Do
you believe homosexuality is a choice?" Bush responded, "I just don't know. I
do know that we have a choice to make in America, and that is to treat people
with tolerance and respect and dignity." Then Kerry chimed in: "We are all
God's children, Bob. And I think if you were to talk to Dick Cheney's daughter, who is a lesbian, she would tell you that she's being who she was; she's being who she was born as. I think if you talked to anybody, it's not choice."[32]

Immediately after the debate critics, starting with the Cheneys themselves,
blasted Kerry's comments as gratuitous, mean, and out of bounds. The sexual
orientation of the vice president's daughter, they said, had nothing to do with
the question at hand. The day following the debate the vice president called
himself "a pretty angry father" and Kerry "a man who will do and say anything
to get elected." Lynne Cheney said Kerry was "not a good man" and accused
him of a "cheap and tawdry political trick." Kerry tried to explain the remark
by arguing he "was trying to say something positive about the way strong families deal with the issue."[33]

That explanation did little to mollify critics, particularly since it came
shortly after Kerry's running mate, Senator John Edwards of North Carolina,
had also mentioned her sexual orientation, during his debate with Cheney.
"This second time around, the gratuitous insertion of Cheney's daughter into
an answer slipping around a hot-button social issue revealed that is was part
of a deliberate Kerry campaign strategy," wrote William Safire in the *New York
Times*. He continued: "One purpose was to drive a wedge between the Republican running mates. President Bush supports a constitutional amendment
limiting marriage to a union of a man and a woman; Cheney has long been
on record favoring state option, but always adds that the president sets administration policy."[34]

Criticism compounded when Kerry's campaign manager, Mary Beth
Cahill, in a television interview labeled the Cheney daughter as "fair game."
Polls immediately after the debate showed a two-to-one disapproval of the
Democrats' raising of the issue. Overnight focus groups showed what had

been a neck-and-neck race between Bush and Kerry moving slightly toward the president. A *Washington Post* poll showed that by a two to one margin, likely voters said Kerry's reference to Mary Cheney's homosexuality was "inappropriate," including more than four in ten of Kerry's supporters and half of all swing voters. Just a third thought the remark was appropriate.[35]

Of course, Kerry's narrow loss cannot be attributed to any one statement, action, or episode during the long, heated, and complex campaign. But his debate remark about the sexual orientation of the vice president's daughter certainly did more harm than good.

NEGATIVE CAMPAIGNING AND SMALL STATE POLITICS

Negative campaigning works least effectively in small-population states or districts. There voters can often feel a personal connection to their elected leader, and an attack on a candidate is viewed almost like a slap in the face to a family member. Nowhere is negative campaign tactics shunned more than Delaware. The state is just 100 miles long and 35 miles wide, making it the second smallest after Rhode Island. The state has only three counties—two when the tide is in, as residents joke. With its 830,000 or so residents, Delaware enjoys the usual stable of elected officials—two U.S. senators, one U.S. House member, governor, lieutenant governor, and other statewide officeholders. There are 41 members of the state House and 21 members of the state Senate, along with city councils in the three largest municipalities, Wilmington (75,000 people), Newark, and Dover (about 30,000 each).

With all these offices in such a small state, residents even vaguely involved in business and civic life are likely to know many, if not most, of their elected officials on a first-name basis. Residents expect to see their elected representatives, including federal officeholders, back home for ribbon cuttings, Little League playoffs, barbecues, and other such activities. Candidates meet on a regular basis with firefighters, police, teachers, civic association leaders, along with civic, arts, and public health groups. "It's pretty difficult not to run into somebody you know on a regular basis," said state representative Joseph DiPinto, a Republican who was first elected to the legislature in 1986.[36]

That has led to a long-term tradition of candidates in Delaware shying away from strongly negative campaign tactics, which are a staple of political contests in larger states. "Basically, people try to be civil," said Wilmington Mayor James Baker.[37] Residents' familiarity with their politicians means they often have friends on both sides of the aisle. "It's really tough to have long-term, ongoing anger" at former political opponents, DiPinto said.

Delaware voters often punish candidates who do not stay positive. In 1990 Senator Joseph Biden, chairman of the Judiciary Committee, sought a fourth term. He was coming off a short-lived run for the 1988 Democratic presidential nomination, which flamed out after questions were raised about plagiarism from a speech by a British politician. His Republican opponent in the Senate race was M. Jane Brady, a deputy state attorney general. Brady recycled the charges from the presidential campaign. She distributed 40,000 copies of videotape that replayed some of Biden's worst moments. At the time Brady was unapologetic about the tone of her campaign. "I've never known character not to be an issue," she said.[38] Still, Biden crushed his opponent 62 to 36 percent. While the senator's enduring popularity was undoubtedly an important factor in his typically large reelection margin, voters had also demonstrated disdain toward overtly negative campaign tactics. (Voters did not keep a lasting grudge against Brady; in 1994 she won the first of three terms as state attorney general.)

The state's political culture is embodied by Return Day, the celebration in Georgetown on the Thursday after an election. In this ritual, which began in the 1790s, the winners and losers are thrown together in a parade to close out the campaign hostilities. The winning and losing candidates each ride together in a horse-drawn carriage or antique car. Later the candidates and party leaders literally bury a hatchet in a container of sand taken from a local beach. "People use it as a healing process,"[39] said Dale Wolf, a former Republican lieutenant governor, who served as governor in January 1993 (Wolf filled the last three weeks of Republican Governor Michael Castle's term after he resigned to assume the U.S. House seat he had won in November).

Though losing political candidates across the country often make a perfunctory concession call to the winner on Election Night, only in Delaware do they ride together in a car days after the election. Compare this ritual to the refusal of losing 2004 Illinois Senate candidate Alan Keyes (R) to offer a former concession to the winner, Barack Obama (D). Despite losing the race by more than forty points Keyes maintained his opponent stood for "a culture evil enough to destroy the very soul and heart of my country"[40] and was not worthy of a concession call. That is not a statement likely to be made by a candidate in Delaware, at least one looking for a future in elected office.

Even Delaware candidates involved in high-profile races with national political implications are relatively restrained in attacking opponents, because going at them too hard can easily backfire. Consider the 2000 U.S. Senate race. It featured titans of Delaware politics: Democratic Gov. Tom Carper, who challenged Republican Sen. William V. Roth, a thirty-year incumbent and chairman of the powerful Senate Finance Committee. Carper won election to the U.S. House in 1982 by defeating an incumbent, a rare feat in Delaware politics. He served for ten years before being elected governor in 1992, when he switched jobs with Republican Michael Castle. By 2000 Carper had exhausted the state's two terms allowable as governor, and he launched a challenge against Roth. The senator for years had a key role in shaping national trade and tax policy, including a tax-deferred individual retirement account that made his a household name.[41] Roth had been a leader, with then-Rep. Jack Kemp (R-N.Y.) in major tax-cutting efforts of the 1970s and 1980s. He ascended to chair of the Senate Finance Committee in the mid-1990s and was among the most powerful members of Congress when he sought reelection in 2000, to a sixth term. "Each man had compiled an enviable record of electoral success and enjoyed very high approval ratings," University of Delaware political science professor Joseph A. Pika wrote after the election. "Voters were accustomed to supporting both of them, not choosing between them."[42]

In most other states a campaign between two of a state's leading politicians would be considerably negative. But in Delaware's peculiar political culture neither side went after the other with more than mild criticism. Not that the candidates avoided challenging each other. The governor pointed out his differences with Roth on issues, but in a polite way. Television ads were used more extensively in this Senate campaign than in other contests, as partisan control of the Senate hung in the balance and outside groups on both sides took a keen interest in the race.

In one commercial Carper sat in what looked like his kitchen, talking into the camera, and said, "I'm Tom Carper. I respect Bill Roth, but we disagree on some very important issues." He then ran through a list of public policy concerns he would focus on as a senator, including a patients' bill of rights and using the federal budget surplus that existed at the time to pay off the national debt. "As your senator, I will cast the votes that Bill Roth has not, and that's why I am running for the U.S. Senate," Carper concluded.[43]

This was undoubtedly a comparative ad that sought to frame the incumbent in a less-favorable light. But it was a long way from commercials and rhetoric elsewhere that have tacitly compared opponents to Osama Bin Laden, Saddam Hussein and other international villains. Such tactics would almost certainly have been unacceptable to the Delaware electorate. "Carper had to be polite to [Roth]," said Basil Battaglia, former chairman of the Republican Party of Delaware. "He would have paid the price" had he turned up the heat more.[44] And although the Democrat did not directly make a point of it overtly, age became a factor, as challenger Carper, 53, was a generation younger than incumbent Roth, 79. On Election Day voters decided to retire Roth involuntarily. Carper won 56 percent to 44 percent for the longtime senator.

Delaware's electoral politics stand in marked contrast to contests in other states. Take the 2000 U.S. Senate race in Missouri, when Democratic Governor Mel Carnahan sought to unseat GOP Senator John Ashcroft. Long foes in state politics, the pair went negative against each other early. Carnahan, completing his second four-year term as governor, sought to paint Ashcroft as extremist on issues like Social Security, Medicare, gun control, and prescription-drug coverage. Ashcroft, meanwhile, claimed Carnahan's tenure had led to failing urban schools, crumbling and dangerous highways, rampant methamphetamine problems, and record-high state taxes.[45] Beyond the policy realm, the race included ugly insinuations of racism. Ashcroft came under attack for blocking black Missouri Supreme Court Justice Ronnie White from moving to the federal bench, and Carnahan was forced to apologize for appearing in blackface during a comedy skit in the 1960s.[46] The Ashcroft–Mel Carnahan fight came to an abrupt and tragic end just weeks before Election Day when the governor, his son, campaign workers, and pilot were killed in a plane crash. Voters elected Carnahan posthumously, and his wife Jean took office in his place. Ashcroft was later confirmed U.S. attorney general in the Bush administration.

KNOWING THE ELECTORATE

Even in states significantly larger than Delaware, such as Iowa, politicians must beware of local political mores that frown upon negative campaigning. The presidential campaigns of former Vermont Governor Howard Dean and Congressman Richard Gephardt of Missouri were both mortally wounded there during the 2004 caucuses after they went after each other with a series of stinging attack ads.

In the months leading up to the caucuses it appeared as if Iowa would be a showdown between Dean, then riding high as the Democratic front-runner, and Gephardt, the former House minority leader, whose long-standing ties to organized labor were thought to provide an edge. As caucus day approached the pair began aiming increasingly negative television spots at each other: Dean went after Gephardt for helping craft the Iraq war resolution in October 2002 and for voting in favor of an $87-billion spending bill to fund operations in the violence-prone nation. Gephardt's ads played upon his frequent charge that Dean backed Republican efforts to cut the growth of Medicare in the mid-1990s.

Iowa voters rejected these tactics. Dean finished third, deflating what had once been a front-running candidacy. Gephardt came in fourth and dropped out of the presidential race the next day, ending his political career. Perhaps the biggest beneficiaries were those who stayed largely above the fray: Senator Kerry, the first-place winner, and Senator John Edwards, who insisted on running a positive campaign and finished a surprising second. Each ended up on the national ticket, with Kerry the presidential nominee and Edwards later named his running mate.

NOTES

1. University of Virginia Center for Politics, Larry Sabato's Crystal Ball; Nov. 3, 2004 (www.centerforpolitics.org/crystalball/2004/house/?state=NY)

2. Rick Brand, "At War Over 'Rape' Ads: A Claim by Grucci Prompts Bitter Dispute in Campaign," *Newsday*, Oct. 1, 2002.

3. Michael Barone and Richard E. Cohen, *The Almanac of American Politics 2004* (Washington, D.C.: National Journal Group, 2003), 1105.

4. Brand, *Newsday*, Oct. 1, 2002.

5. Grucci did eventually return to Washington; his family business, Gruccis of New York, produced a fireworks extravangza on the national Mall the day before President Bush's second inaugural, in January 2005.

6. Interview with author, Palm Desert, Calif., Nov. 27, 2004.

7. Cyndee Fontana, "Quigley Ad Heats Up Campaign: Costa Camp Calls Move 'Sleazy' Attack; Quigley Says It's Conduct That's 'Sleazy,'" *The Fresno Bee*, Feb. 27, 2004.

8. Fontana, "Quigley Ad Heats up Campaign."

9. Fontana, "Quigley Ad Heats up Campaign."

10. Juan A. Lozano, "Sanchez Ad Shows Perry's Police Tape," *Associated Press*, Oct. 23, 2002.

11. Lozano, "Sanchez Ad Shows Perry's Police Tape."

12. "News Top 10s," *The Austin Chronicle*, Jan. 3, 2003.

13. "News Top 10s."

14. Josh Kurtz, "Robinson's Negative Tactics Could Cost Him Votes, Support," *Roll Call*, July 22, 2004.

15. Lynn Bonner and J. Andrew Curliss, "No Apologies in 5th District," *The* (Raleigh) *News & Observer*, Aug. 19, 2004.

16. Jim Morrill, "Foxx, Robinson Stuck in a Mud of Rhetoric," *The Charlotte Observer*, Aug. 15, 2004.

17. Peter E. Harrell, "Foxx Wins Bruising GOP Runoff in North Carolina's 5th District," *CQ Today*, Aug. 18, 2004.

18. Jack Jones, "Barend Demotes Campaign Boss; Amo Houghton, Others Criticize Release of Opponent's Divorce Records," *Elmira Star-Gazette*, Oct. 26, 2004.

19. "A Slack Campaign: Candidate Barend Has Lost Her Credibility Because of Staffer's Role in Kuhl Controversy," *Elmira Star-Gazette* editorial, Oct. 26, 2004.

20. "A Slack Campaign," *Elmira Star-Gazette*.

21. "A Slack Campaign," *Elmira Star-Gazette*.

22. New York State Board of Elections, General Election Results, Certified Dec. 6, 2004.

23. "Alex R. Seith Wants to Be U.S. Senator: He Believes He Can Beat Percy and Offers Proposals on State-Federal Revenue and on Foreign Affairs," *Illinois Issues*, Dec. 1977.

24. Garry South, "Anatomy of a Spot," in *Target '82: Politics and the Media—A Working Seminar, for the Democratic National Committee*, 34.

25. South, "Anatomy of a Spot," 4–7.

26. South, "Anatomy of a Spot," 10. (Radio ad text reproduced with permission of Garry South.)

27. Robert G. Kaiser, "It's Playing in Peoria: Who Is Alex Seith, and Why Is He Saying Those Terribly Effective but Outrageously Inaccurate Things about Charles Percy?" *The Washington Post*, Nov. 3, 1978.

28. South, "Anatomy of a Spot," 19.

29. Kaiser, *The Washington Post*, Nov. 3, 1978.

30. E-mail to author, March 24, 2005.

31. Victor Kamber, *Poison Politics: Are Negative Campaigns Destroying Democracy?* (New York: Insight Books, 1997), 217.

32. Transcript of The Third Bush-Kerry Presidential Debate, Oct. 13, 2004, Arizona State University, Tempe, Ariz., from the Commission on Presidential Debates (www.debates.org/pages/trans2004d.html).

33. James Rainey and Susannah Rosenblatt, "Kerry's Reference to Mary Cheney Hits a Nerve," *The Los Angeles Times*, Oct. 15, 2004.

34. William Safire, "The Lowest Blow," *The New York Times*, Oct. 18, 2004.

35. Richard Morin, "Singling Out Mary Cheney Wrong, Most Say; 2 in 3 Polled Find Kerry's Comments 'Inappropriate,'" *The Washington Post*, Oct. 17, 2004.

36. Interview with author, Wilmington, Del., Nov. 12, 2004.

37. Interview with author, by telephone, Nov. 18, 2004.

38. Celia Cohen, *Only in Delaware: Politics and Politicians in the First State* (Newark, Del.: Grapevine Publishing LLC, 2002), 362.

39. Interview with author, Wilmington, Del., Nov. 12, 2004.

40. Eric Zorn, "Candidates Need to Concede a Lack of Good Manners," *The Chicago Tribune*, Dec. 16, 2004.

41. Matthew Tully, "Delaware's Roth Banking on Seniority to Fend Off Carper," *CQ Weekly*, Aug. 5, 2000.

42. Joseph A. Pike, "The 2000 Delaware Senate Race," American Political Science Association's *Journal of the Profession*, June 2001.

43. Tape courtesy of the Julian P. Kanter Political Commercial Archive at the University of Oklahoma Political Communication Center.

44. Interview with author, Wilmington, Del., Nov. 12, 2004.

45. Kevin Murphy, "Carnahan Outlines Senate Campaign Strategy against Incumbent Ashcroft," *The Kansas City Star*, June 21, 2000.

46. Patti Davis, "Missouri Heavyweights Slug It Out in Heated Senate Race," *CNN.com*, Sept. 28, 2000.

Hitting the Mark: Negative Campaigning Efforts That Just Plain Worked

Bill McCollum looked on track for his political comeback a month before Election Day for the Florida U.S. Senate primary in summer 2004. Polls showed the former ten-term congressman with a comfortable lead over his closest rival for the Republican nomination, former Housing and Urban Development Secretary Mel Martinez. Sure, some Republican activists were irked at McCollum's loss in his U.S. Senate bid back in 2000, the same year President George W. Bush eked out a win in the Sunshine State. But McCollum still seemed like a good fit for the conservative Republican electorate. During his career in the U.S. House from 1981–2001, representing central Florida, McCollum had compiled a staunchly conservative voting record on tax cuts, gun control, and social issues, which should have pleased the party activists who dominated voting in the Republican primary, to be held in late August 2004. Further, McCollum had led a task force on terrorism before September 11, 2001, and was acknowledged as an expert on related issues, an important credential in the post–9/11 world.

In Congress and on the campaign trail, however, McCollum had taken stances on the issues of "hate crimes" and stem cell research that deviated

slightly from conservative orthodoxy. Specifically, he had supported legislation that would have increased penalties against people who committed violent acts against gays and lesbians because of their sexual orientation. And on
stem cell research he backed proposals to allow scientists to study leftover em-
bryos that would otherwise be discarded, which researchers believed could
eventually unlock cures for a variety of diseases. McCollum, who called himself a product of the Reagan revolution, said he agreed with former First Lady
Nancy Reagan that the medical research could accelerate the finding of cures
for Alzheimer's and other life-threatening diseases. Martinez, meanwhile, supported the near blanket ban on federal funding for research on embryonic
stem cells imposed by President Bush during his first year in office, contend-
ing the practice marked the destruction of human life.[1]

McCollum's positions were not good enough for conservatives who opposed the idea of increasing penalties for violent crimes just because they were
committed against gay people (they argued a crime should carry the same
penalty no matter what the motivation). This most conservative element of
the Republican coalition also viewed any form of stem cell research as the
taking of a life, period. These social issues provided a crucial opening for
McCollum's leading primary opponent to paint him as insufficiently conservative, through an aggressive—and effective—negative campaign.

The idea of McCollum as anything but right-leaning was a laughable notion
to those who had followed the political career of the consistently conservative
former House manager in President Bill Clinton's 1999 impeachment trial. In
fact, it was McCollum who was originally viewed as the right-winger in the primary race. A millionaire trial lawyer from Orlando, Martinez faced some skepticism from Republicans who wanted to limit lawsuit awards. And he had served
in the nonpartisan position of chairman of Orange County government in the
Orlando area, in a manner that won praise from across the political spectrum.

The Bush White House had handpicked Martinez to run, in part because
he was considered more centrist than McCollum, during a presidential election year in which Florida would again be a battleground.[2] As a teenage
refugee from Cuba who had earned significant financial and political success
in the United States, Martinez also offered a bridge to Florida's large Hispanic
population.

But instead of steering a middle course, Martinez went hard right during
the closing stage of the Republican primary season. To hammer home Mc-

Collum's record on hate crimes, the Martinez campaign unleashed a direct mail advertisement during the final week of the race that attacked McCollum for taking positions "to appease certain political constituencies, including the radical homosexual lobby," and sent out a mailing that called McCollum "the new darling of the homosexual extremists."[3] A television commercial accused the former congressman of sponsoring a bill "granting homosexuals special rights."[4] The Martinez campaign also arranged a conference call by conservative and religious leaders, who challenged the former congressman's conservative credentials on hate crimes and stem cell research, including former presidential candidate Gary Bauer, the Traditional Values Coalition and the National Right to Life PAC.

The potential potency of these issues quickly became clear, as large blocs of the conservative-leaning Republican primary electorate were still undecided about whom to vote for. Former Senator Connie Mack, a Republican revered in party circles, wrote to 15,000 state GOP activists, saying Martinez's campaign "sunk to a new low in Florida politics" by launching a "mean-spirited, desperate and personal attack" that would "only hurt our party and doom us in November." Even Governor Jeb Bush prevailed on Martinez to pull the ad that charged McCollum with "granting homosexuals special rights." Martinez did take down the ad—but not before its message got through loud and clear to Republican primary voters.

The aggressive tactics also drew tremendous outcry in the press. The editorial page of *The St. Petersburg Times*, a prominent Florida newspaper, withdrew its endorsement of Martinez. "The *Times* is not willing to be associated with bigotry," its editorial said. "No matter what else Martinez may accomplish in public life, his reputation will be forever tainted by his campaign's nasty and ludicrous slurs of McCollum in the final days of this race."[5]

McCollum himself tried to ward off the attacks, calling the television commercial on hate crimes "an ad of hate and bigotry." During a debate, McCollum dramatically pulled a negative Martinez flier out of suit-coat pocket, saying it "accuses me of catering to the radical homosexual lobby." He told Martinez, "That is just despicable. It's nasty. It's not true. It's absolutely incorrect."[6]

Despite the criticism, the attacks helped gin up conservative anger at McCollum, and survey numbers reflected the shift. A month before the election, a Mason-Dixon poll showed McCollum leading Martinez 29 percent to 24 percent among Republicans likely to vote in the primary.[7] Other polls bore similar results. But by the weekend before Election Day, Martinez led McCollum 33 percent to 27 percent, according to the updated Mason-Dixon poll. Martinez ended up winning the primary with 45 percent of the vote to McCollum's 31 percent, with several other Republican candidates trailing further. Martinez went on to win the general election narrowly against a competitive Democratic candidate, and replaced retiring Senator Bob Graham (D).

The negative campaigning seemed to make the most difference with undecided voters in the Republican primary, which broke strongly toward Martinez. Whether or not the television ads and mailers attacking McCollum on cultural issues were decisive in the race is impossible to tell. It is always difficult to credit one advertising campaign with having turned the tide of an election. Other factors, including a Martinez television commercial that showed him with President Bush, clearly helped. But the shift in poll numbers coincided with Martinez's negative onslaught against McCollum, and must be credited with having a major impact on the race.

Martinez's successful effort to define his opponent offers a good illustration about why candidates and political consultants use negative campaigning. It often works. Yes, as demonstrated in the previous chapter, negative campaigning can backfire on candidates if they are sloppy with language used, misunderstand the electorate, and don't brace themselves for the backlash and fallout. But when executed and timed correctly, negative campaigning —particularly television ads and direct mail pieces—can work to devastating effect on the opposition.

UNEARTHING A FLIP-FLOP

As California Governor Gray Davis geared up for reelection in 2002, former Los Angeles Mayor Richard Riordan looked to be a formidable general election foe—if, as expected, he won the Republican nomination. The Democratic governor and Riordan shared moderate positions on many social issues, and public opinion polls suggested Riordan was viewed as having had been a very successful mayor in Los Angeles, from 1993 to 2001 (though an L.A. mayor had never been elected governor). Crucially, the candidates also shared a base of Southern California campaign contributors; if a more appealing candidate came along, well-heeled individuals might turn off the financial spigots to Davis and back the challenger.

Davis had once been in a stronger position politically. After a career climbing the ranks of state government, the highly disciplined Davis had secured the Democratic nomination for governor in 1998 after his primary opponents spent millions attacking each other on television. Davis, then lieutenant governor, remained relatively untouched, and their squabbling damaged each other so much that he was able to cruise past them. After winning a 20-point victory in the 1998 general election over a lackluster Republican opponent, Davis early in his first term had been hailed as an innovator in education and other policy areas, to the point he received a glowing profile in *TIME* magazine and was mentioned as a future presidential candidate. Things began to sour, however, when the state's botched electricity deregulation scheme, passed in 1996, began to produce power shortages, rolling blackouts, and increasing financial problems for California's giant public utility companies in late 2000. As his 2002 reelection bid loomed, Davis also was burdened with the national economic turndown and the bursting of the Silicon Valley's dot-com bubble, which dropped state revenues by $17 billion, the biggest decrease since World War II, leading to huge budget deficits.

Davis appeared open to a strong challenge. In addition to considering him responsible for the state's public policy problems, many viewed him as interested solely in his own political advancement, a perception fueled by a frantic fundraising schedule during his first years in office. Sensing a threat from Riordan in the general election, the Davis team sought to soften up the former Los Angeles mayor, who ran for the GOP nod against rookie candidate Bill Simon, a wealthy businessman who had lived in California for only 12 years, and Secretary of State Bill Jones, a veteran state officeholder.

Riordan was a multimillionaire businessman and lawyer who sported the backing of the Bush White House and virtually the entire California Republican Party establishment. His matchup in the fall against Governor Davis seemed inevitable. So Davis's campaign launched what would become a $10-million ad blitz during the other party's nominating fight, with the intent of weakening the former L.A. mayor for the general election. "We decided he could not go through a Republican primary untouched," recalled Garry South, the governor's chief political strategist.[8]

A $10,000 expenditure nearly a decade before provided the Davis campaign an ace card. In 1993 South had worked for Michael Woo, a Democratic local politician who squared off against Riordan in the mayoral runoff. Acting on a tip, South came across a tape of an appearance by Riordan, then a civic activist, on a small cable station in West Los Angeles in 1991. After prolonged negotiations, South persuaded the tape's owner to sell it to the Woo campaign for $10,000. During the interview featured on the tape, the future Los Angeles mayor was asked his position on abortion: Riordan said he agreed "very strongly" with the Catholic Church in opposing the procedure, because, "I think it's murder." When Riordan ran for mayor two years later, though, he claimed to support abortion rights. In a city in which Republicans are in the minority, the pro-choice position view helped make him acceptable to many Democrats, especially women.[9] Woo's campaign aired a portion of the tape, but it did little to help his losing effort.

South, however, kept the tape; he tucked it away for years in a climate-controlled storage room. The veteran political consultant then dredged up the tape when Riordan became a threat to Governor Davis nearly a decade later. After focus groups indicated the mayor's former anti-abortion views could hurt him, the Davis campaign spent millions of dollars to point out to voters the contradiction in Riordan's stands on abortion over the years.

The thrust of the attack came in two separate 30-second television ads. The first, titled "Right," pointed out Riordan's contributions to anti-abortion candidates and organizations. His foundation had donated $250 to the Right to Life League of Southern California in 1987, while in 1991 it gave $10,000 to Americans United for Life.[10] He had also helped raise money for advertising to support Robert Bork's nomination to the U.S. Supreme Court in 1987. In 2002, Riordan's GOP primary campaign was centered on his being a "different kind of Republican" sympathetic to abortion rights (he argued no anti-abortion Republican could beat Davis in November).

The former mayor tried to counterattack Davis. He argued the $10,000 contribution went for advertising encouraging girls to put children up for adoption. And he said the Democrat's focus on abortion was a planned political attack designed to divert attention from issues with the potential to wound Davis, such as the energy crisis.

But then the governor's campaign then released a second spot, "Listen," which featured Riordan's own words from his 1991 cable appearance, when he called abortion "murder." During that interview, Riordan had said, "Being fairly liberal-minded, I surprise myself at my emotions on the abortion issue. 'Cause I feel very—I think it's murder." The commercial's narrator then concluded, "For years, Riordan helped finance the anti-abortion movement and said abortion was murder. Now he says he's pro-choice. Riordan—is this a record we can trust?"[11] South recalled that in focus groups, the effect was devastating. Pro-lifers—who tend to dominate Republican primaries in California—thought he was a disingenuous turncoat who actually did oppose abortion but had changed his stance to run for office. Pro-choicers, on the other hand, just thought he was a liar. Further, the ad pointed out, in Riordan's own words, how "liberal-minded" he was on other issues, a characteristic not likely to go down well in a Republican primary.

Had the Riordan campaign spent a few thousand dollars on opposition research to investigate the background of its own candidate, standard operating procedure in a big-budget, statewide campaign, they could have ferreted out the tape and prepared a response. But he appeared to be caught blindsided by the attacks. He assumed the Republican primary would be an easy win, and he looked forward to the November campaign against Davis. As soon as the ads aired, Riordan's positive ratings in the polls began to plummet. South recalled that once the attacks began, internal survey data showed Riordan "was sliding faster than a greased pig down a pole." Riordan had led in the polls by as much as forty points, but ended up losing the Republican primary to Simon, a strongly anti-abortion candidate, by eighteen points.

After the election, Riordan strategist Kevin Spillane said the ad featuring the long-ago Riordan interview had "a dramatic impact," costing the candidate substantial support. "We would have won the primary if they had not put on the abortion ad." He added, "It was a character ad, and it became more than just about abortion."[12]

Unfortunately for Simon, the upset primary victory proved to be the high point of his campaign. In the general election Governor Davis went highly negative on the novice candidate, running a series of television ads pointing out that Simon opposed abortion and gun control. Davis also attacked Simon as a "a true blue think tank conservative," noting that he had been on the board of the Heritage Foundation.[13] Davis ultimately spent $65 million for the entire campaign and beat Simon by the relatively narrow margin of 47 percent to 42 percent. This was hardly a strong statement of support for an incumbent governor; survey data at the time showed that even as Davis won, six in ten of those casting ballots disliked the incumbent, and more than half said the state was heading down the wrong track.[14]

Though in 2002 Davis eked out a second term, the governor was not long for the political world. In October 2003 voters booted him from office in a historic recall election and replaced him with Republican Arnold Schwarzenegger, the movie actor and former bodybuilder. Commentators at the time suggested voters' willingness to oust Davis from office was his revenge for his political hardball tactics nearly two years before, when he meddled in the Republican gubernatorial primary to pick his preferred opponent. But South dismisses such notions. The Davis campaign tested that idea in focus groups during the general election campaign in 2002, asking participants if they remembered the incident and what they thought about it. "People just shrugged and said, 'That's just what politicians do, it's not unusual. They always attack their opponents.'"[15]

THE POLITICS OF INSINUATION

Los Angeles is not a political city like New York, Boston, Philadelphia, or Chicago, where the inner workings and machinations of municipal government are a major focus of residents' lives. Because of L.A.'s sprawl, its focus on the entertainment industry, reasonably consistent warm weather that invites recreational activities, and other factors, campaigns and elections are just not that enthralling to many Angelinos. Nonetheless, the 2001 mayor's race aroused relatively intense interest. With Mayor Richard Riordan forced from office by term limits, the race to succeed him as the leader of the nation's second largest city spawned a heated scramble for the post. Much was at stake in the election. In addition to perennial Southland problems like traffic congestion, a police corruption scandal brewed, and the suburban San Fernando Valley sought to secede from Los Angeles.

Six major candidates jumped into the field, some with vast personal fortunes, and others well funded by special interests. Because no candidate scored more than 50 percent of the vote during the April 10 primary, the top two vote-getters squared off for the general election, on June 5. Coming in first was former state Assembly Speaker Antonio Villaraigosa from East Los Angeles, a charismatic campaigner who sought to become the city's first Latino mayor since 1872, when the future metropolis was little more than a dusty outpost. Finishing second was a white candidate, City Attorney James K. Hahn. Though lacking a flashy personality, he sported a golden local political name. His father was longtime Los Angeles County Supervisor Kenneth

Hahn, renowned for his effectiveness in civic improvements, such as filling potholes, and for helping to lure the Brooklyn Dodgers baseball club to Los Angeles in 1958.

Polls showed the pair relatively neck and neck throughout the runoff portion of the campaign. Villaraigosa held sway with voters in Hispanic communities and was popular among liberals on Los Angeles's Westside. Hahn, meanwhile, drew considerable support from African-American communities, where his father's memory ran strong, and more conservative suburban areas in the San Fernando Valley. These demographics provided the backdrop to a television commercial aired late in the runoff campaign that proved singularly effective in souring Villaraigosa's political fortunes. The ad brought to light Villaraigosa's actions regarding Carlos Vignali, a convicted drug trafficker. The mayoral candidate had once sought White House intervention to free Vignali, whose father just happened to have contributed money to Villaraigosa's campaign.[16] The effort apparently paid off. On his last day in office President Bill Clinton granted Vignali clemency, though not a pardon. The Hahn ad mentioned these facts, but most notably it included an image of a crack cocaine pipe being held to a flame, which then cut to grainy photos of Villaraigosa. The ad ended with the tagline, "Los Angeles can't trust Antonio Villaraigosa."[17]

The commercial drew immediate criticism from Latino groups and others who felt it implied a linkage between drug dealers and a Hispanic candidate. Villaraigosa himself said the ad "begins with someone cutting cocaine, smoking out of a pipe, trying to imply cynically and wildly that I'm somehow for those things. I'm not and he knows it, and to imply that with ad like this is way beyond the pale." The former Assembly speaker at first also quibbled with the facts of the commercial. He denied writing to the White House, saying he had sent a letter to the judge overseeing Vignali's appeal. Later, when presented with a copy of the letter to the president, he said that writing it had been a mistake but that he had written from the heart, as a father would for a son.[18]

Hahn's campaign defended the commercial, saying he disagreed with the concept of pardoning drug dealers for campaign donors. The fact that Villaraigosa and the drug dealer in question were Hispanic was irrelevant, Hahn added. On Election Day his viewpoint won out. Voters elected him with 53.5 percent of the vote to Villaraigosa's 46.5 percent. Fair or not, the ad was effective. Hahn and Villaraigosa were both liberal Democrats, and for the general election each needed to move to the center, at least somewhat, to gain votes in the moderate and more conservative portions of the sprawling city. The ad clearly helped cement the image of Villaraigosa as a soft-on-crime liberal. Compared with Villaraigosa, Hahn looked almost like a conservative Republican.

Poll numbers showed that GOP swing voters seemed to have been most moved by Hahn's negative portrayal of Villaraigosa. It is impossible to say if the "crack pipe" commercial was the linchpin in Hahn's victory, as the numbers were already moving his way, according to a *Los Angeles Times* poll. At the very least, it helped cement in voters' minds unflattering images they had of his opponent, the crucial ingredient of a successful negative campaign ad.[19]

THE KNOCKOUT PUNCH

Rarely can a single television commercial be credited with forcing a candidate to withdraw from a political campaign. But one ad did exactly that to state senator Mike Taylor of Montana, the Republican nominee for U.S. Senate there in 2002. Taylor blamed the ad, which showed him working as a hairdresser years before, for destroying his reputation by suggesting he was gay.

Not that Taylor was likely to beat incumbent Democratic Senator Max Baucus, anyway. The Republican's own poll numbers showed him 19 points behind the veteran lawmaker, then the chairman of the powerful Senate Finance Committee. Still, Taylor, a millionaire from his days in the hair-care business, took great issue with the ad, whose purpose was ostensibly to criticize him for business practices employed when he ran the Michael Taylor Institute of Hair Design for ten years, through 1988.

The advertisement, aired by the Democratic Senatorial Campaign Committee (DSCC), not the Baucus campaign, accused Taylor of defrauding students and cheating the state out of tax revenues—of "abusing the student loan program and diverting money to himself." Regarding that charge, Taylor acknowledged he had once been investigated. Ultimately he had signed settlements with the U.S. Department of Education and the Colorado Student Loan Program and paid $27,250 to cover audit allegations. Both sides agreed that the settlement was not an admission of wrongdoing by either party.[20]

But charges of financial improprieties were not what stoked Taylor's anger. Instead, he pointed to the most incendiary part of the Democratic ad, which opened to the sound of disco music. At the same time, the viewer saw Taylor, bearded and looking noticeably thinner, at work in a hair salon. The scene was a clip from a long-ago series of television shows, "Beauty Corner," which Taylor had once produced in Denver, promoting fashion, beauty tips, and hair care products. Wearing a three-piece suit with his shirt half open, exposing his chest and gold chains, Taylor was twice shown applying lotion to a man's temples. On the screen appeared the words "Facial Demonstration."[21] Taylor, who had been married for 22 years and had two sons, angrily said the ad suggested he was gay. In response, DSCC officials noted the ad never said the candidate was gay or even hinted at it in words. It was the visual of Taylor—touching a man's face, rubbing lotion on him—that spurred the controversy. DSCC officials said they had no control over the visuals and were only reporting facts about Taylor that were on the public record.

Whether or not that explanation rang true, the ad was undoubtedly effective. A Taylor spokesman at the time said that when the commercial ran, internal polls showed him trailing Baucus by nineteen points; then the Republican fell thirty-five points behind four days after it started playing. Taylor suspended his campaign, saying he simply could not continue under the cloud that the ad had caused. "It was character assassination and personal destruction," Taylor told the *New York Times.* "Even if I wasn't going to win, I can't run for something else now. This goes against the American dream."[22]

Taylor said he had anticipated that the campaign against Baucus would be hard-hitting on both sides. But the challenger added he did not expect "personal slanders of the vilest kind" and the "sea of sleaze" that he believed Baucus sanctioned through the Democrats' television ad (the Baucus campaign denied any involvement). In announcing his departure from the race, Taylor suggested going negative in response was the only option for continuing the campaign—one that he was not willing to pursue. "Perhaps I may be able to repair the damage my opponent has inflicted upon my good name and that of my family, but at what price? . . . I would have to blanket the airwaves with slime. I will not."[23]

By the time Taylor decided to withdraw, it was too late in the election cycle for his name to be removed from the ballot. In late October he resumed his campaign, saying that on principle an inaccurate, mean-spirited negative ad should not force a candidate out. His resumption of the campaign made little difference, though. In a strong Republican year nationally, Baucus won 63 percent to 32 percent, carrying all but two small counties.

"KING ROY"

The most influential advertisement of the 2002 Georgia governor's race never ran on television or radio. Instead the ad, by Republican candidate Sonny Perdue, won popularity at Republican house parties, on the Internet, and through massive news coverage. The film featured a rat romping through the Peach State, representing Democratic Governor Roy Barnes's alleged arrogance and imperiousness. Release of the commercial flaying the incumbent governor became a breakout moment for Perdue, a little-known former state senator. Though Barnes outspent Perdue six to one, the "King Roy" ad proved to be the great equalizer in the challenger's long-shot and ultimately successful bid to oust the heavily favored incumbent and become Georgia's first Republican governor in 130 years.

That Barnes could lose seemed almost unthinkable to political observers through most of the 2002 election cycle. After being elected governor in 1998 he had steered a middle course in the conservative-leaning state, by pushing transportation improvements, a property tax cut, and HMO regulation. As a Southern moderate, he was mentioned by political pundits as a presidential candidate in the near future.

Below the surface, however, discontent with Barnes burned strong. In 2000, he had guided into law an education overhaul plan that required annual testing for students, and held teachers accountable for results. That included bonuses for some teachers and adverse consequences for those who were less successful in spurring their students to achieve; the plan also ended tenure for newly hired teachers. The new law drew the enmity of many educators whose livelihoods were threatened.

Then Barnes took on an issue still radioactive in Southern politics, the Confederate flag. The Georgia flag had prominently featured the Confederate stars and bars since 1956, when state lawmakers sought to demonstrate their resistance to federal desegregation efforts. This had long been a sore point for many in the state among not only blacks and progressive-minded Georgians of other races but also businessman who felt it drove commerce away by undercutting its message of being part of the New South, where ugly racial-tinged actions were in the past. Various attempts at changing the flag over the years had drawn resistance. Then in early 2001 Barnes unveiled a new design, in which the state seal would occupy most of the flag; it would also include at the bottom small depictions of five flags that have flown over the state, including that of the Confederacy. Barnes amassed majorities in both legislative chambers, then controlled by Democrats, and pushed through the change in six days. In the process, however, he antagonized many voters, particularly in rural areas, who still paid homage to the Confederate-emblem flag of old. Squads of protesters ("flaggers") dogged the governor's public appearances waving the former state flag. As the 2002 election approached, "Boot Barnes" signs that featured the banished banner began to sprout along rural roads.

Because of these efforts on education and the state flag, and skirmishes over other issues like transportation funding, and redrawing of district lines for state and federal lawmakers, Republican critics and some in the Georgia press had begun calling Barnes "King Roy" for his seemingly imperious style. To capitalize on this negative perception of the governor, Perdue's media consultant, Fred Davis, came up with the idea of depicting Governor Barnes in a video as a giant rat named "King Roy," which would terrorize the state of Georgia, gnawing everything in sight. Thinking it over in his Atlanta hotel room during the middle of the night, Davis, a highly-regarded Hollywood-based producer of political commercials, recalled. "The first image I got was a rat hugging the gold dome of the capitol and kissing it. That was his own fiefdom, as opposed to being an elected servant of the people." [24]

The idea became the basis for a 10-minute film, *A New Day Dawning*. The final product that emerged weeks later opened with aerial shots of Georgia's beautiful coastal plains and lush rolling hills. It then cut to images of crowded highways, a dispirited-looking teacher, and slum neighborhoods. "Who let our beloved state collapse to keep himself and his party in office?" asked the narrator. The giant royal rodent then appeared, and viewers saw the creature claw its way over Stone Mountain, storm down Peachtree Street in Atlanta, and scale the state capitol dome. All the while, the narrator continued to tap into the hot-button issues of Georgia politics. "This wily ol' trial lawyer just thought he knew better than us . . . He blamed our hardworking, underpaid teachers for the problems in public education, instead of the real problem—his desire to rule from Atlanta how every school should operate . . . He even decreed what our new flag should be. And suddenly it was flying without us getting to voice a word."[25] While the rat part obviously portrayed the governor negatively, the rest of the 10-minute video painted Perdue in a warm and fuzzy light, tracing his upbringing in rural Bonaire, his career as a veterinarian, successful agribusiness man, and state legislator, along with his reputation for being a devoted family man.

Creation of the ad itself was a major production, and because of its expense, a risky strategy. Its $150,000 cost would eat up more than half the Perdue's available campaign cash, all for a 10-minute promotion that would be available only through direct contact with people who wanted to watch it. It used sets constructed in Nashville, myriad special effects, helicopters and a Lear jet mounted with cameras strafing Georgia cities and the countryside, and a $40,000 custom-made rat suit, complete with its own air-conditioning system (Davis got the cost cut in half to $20,000 by returning it at the end of the year to the Hollywood costume shop that made it.)[26] Production took 45 days, recalled Davis, whose work is in high demand among Republican campaigns (he played a key role in producing ads for the Bush-Cheney 2004 reelection effort).

The gubernatorial candidate's campaign distributed the video to Republican activists and the news media, who were invited to its public release at an Atlanta fundraiser for Perdue. It would also be available for downloading on the campaign's website. The Perdue campaign released the ad in May, while he was still trying to win the Republican primary, which would take place in August. While costly, if successful, the ad would not only soften up Governor Barnes for the general election but would also distinguish Perdue from his Republican primary opponents, Linda Schrenko, the state superintendent of education, and longtime Cobb County Commission Chair Bill Byrne. "What I was looking for was something to kick-start our campaign," Davis said.[27]

Many considered the ad shocking. The image of a rat crawling over the state capitol was something more strident than had usually been seen in campaign commercials. But the ad became an almost immediate political cult classic, tapping into a vein of anger about Barnes's governorship. Television played it repeatedly, producing an avalanche of free media. Perdue's campaign headquarters were inundated with calls from CNN, Fox News Channel and local television stations. Online, the ad received so much attention that its host website shut down temporarily until it could be reconfigured to handle more traffic.

Perdue's Republican primary opponents criticized him for what they called an undignified pouncing on the Democratic governor. While they sniped at the ad, the Perdue campaign addressed the issues that had made Barnes so unpopular. He advocated more flexibility for schools that performed well, and made other overtures to teachers. He also promised to fight for a referendum on the old flag.

With his primary rivals still complaining about the "Rat" ad, Perdue became a focal point for anti-Barnes sentiment. At that point, Perdue pulled ahead of his Republican rivals in fundraising and in the polls and emerged as the likely nominee. He won the primary with 50.8 percent of the vote, avoiding a runoff.

The "King Roy" ad had given Perdue the financial support and media exposure to launch a full-frontal assault against the sitting governor. The Perdue team knew they had a winner, as the ad had effectively tapped into voters' views of Barnes as arrogant and aloof. Not surprisingly, Barnes was none too happy with the video. The governor declared himself "sad and disappointed" and promised to focus on issues.[28] His campaign manager, Tim Phillips, was blunter. "It's insulting to the governor and insulting to the people of Georgia," he said. "Whatever a candidate's partisan differences, I think most Georgians feel that someone running for the office of governor ought to have respect for that office."[29] But these remarks only drew more attention to the campaign film.

In the general election, Perdue continued his criticisms of Governor Barnes, both in person on the campaign trail and through the media. Barnes's counterattacks, however, were largely limited to television commercials. Partly because of the persistent "flaggers" who came out to protest his public appearances, Barnes did not keep up as busy a campaign-trail schedule as he might have. Perdue, meanwhile, hit every Friday night football game and fish fry possible. On election night he upset Barnes 51 percent to 46 percent.

The "King Roy" video was certainly not the only factor in Perdue's win. Barnes's defeat was part of a disastrous election night for Georgia Democrats. Republican Congressman Saxby Chambliss upset Democratic Senator Max Cleland's reelection bid. Two new U.S. House seats drawn expressly for Democrats in a partisan gerrymander instead fell to Republicans. And the state Senate majority leader and longtime state House speaker also lost. Perdue certainly benefited from this Republican wave, a partial result of President Bush's heavy presence in Georgia. Making repeated campaign trips to neighboring Florida to bolster the reelection bid of his brother, Governor Jeb Bush, the president often stopped off in Georgia. While the rallies were held mainly to benefit Chambliss's Senate bid, Perdue was often on stage at the campaign events, giving the gubernatorial candidate a boost.

The 10-minute video undoubtedly made Perdue a serious contender, despite being massively outspent, and allowed him to define the issues of the campaign for voters in a humorous and memorable way. Because the film cost so much and contained visuals that were open to criticism (comparing the governor to a rat), it was, in a sense, a last, desperate attempt that paid off handsomely, similar to a Hail Mary pass in football. Some of Perdue's campaign staff members initially doubted the wisdom of the strategy, but the candidate gave the green light. "The one who had the guts to pull the trigger on this was Sonny Perdue," Davis said. "If it hadn't worked, Sonny probably would not be governor."[30]

A LESSON FOR THE AGES: FIGHT BACK!

The 1988 presidential race is the most analyzed, scrutinized, and thoroughly plumbed political contest in modern history. Virtually every angle of this campaign to succeed President Ronald Reagan has been examined and exhausted. Yet Vice President George H. W. Bush's victory over Massachusetts Governor Michael Dukakis deserves at least a brief review here because of its role in influencing future political contests—a reminder to candidates that negative attacks from opponents cannot be ignored. "You've got to be ready for it," Dukakis said years later. "You've got to anticipate it" and be prepared to fight back.[31]

Many of the wounds Dukakis suffered were self-inflicted, such as his willingness to be filmed and photographed at a Michigan plant that made Army tanks. With his head barely sticking out of the turret wearing a helmet, the Massachusetts governor looked rather like a turtle peeking out of its shell.[32] And one of the most serious blows was his unwillingness to seriously answer charges that his gubernatorial administration had temporarily furloughed William Horton, a convicted murderer, who fled and raped a woman in Maryland. Attack ads from the Bush campaign focused on the failed prison-furlough program, but omitted a specific mention of Horton, who was black (the furlough issue was first raised in spring 1988 by a Democratic primary rival of Dukakis, Senator Al Gore of Tennessee). Stronger ads from an independent group, the National Security Political Action Committee, showed a picture of the criminal and mentioned his name—now shortened to the more menacing-sounding Willie Horton. The ads drew only legalistic responses from Dukakis, when he chose to answer them at all. Dukakis figured voters would see through what he viewed as false and unfair charges. He was wrong.

Other criticism against the Democrat, left largely unanswered, focused on his veto of a state law requiring public school teachers to lead students in the Pledge of Allegiance to the flag and pollution growth in Boston Harbor under his watch, countering his claim of having presided over a "Massachusetts miracle" of the local environment. The Bush campaign was even effective at turning bad news about itself into negatives for Dukakis. For example, in late August, after a still-struggling Bush selected Senator Dan Quayle of Indiana as his running mate, the decision came under scrutiny due to Quayle's level of experience and questions about his service in the National Guard during the Vietnam War. Bush took the offensive and said in a speech that Quayle "did not go to Canada, he did not burn his draft card, and he damn sure didn't burn the American flag."[33] The next day, Republican Senator Steve Symms of Idaho claimed knowledge of a photograph of Kitty Dukakis, the Democrat's wife, burning an American flag in 1970. The Quayle issue had been spun into the issue of whether a potential first lady had burnt the flag, and it took a few precious campaign days of denials and reporting to debunk Symms's claim.

Hammered as a liberal throughout the general election, Dukakis's loss proved once and for all that negative campaigning works if not responded to. Indeed, the 1988 campaign introduced a series of phrases into the political lexicon, which became synonymous with political ineptness, such as "Dukakis in a tank" and "Willie Horton." (Coincidentally, it was Dukakis who was the first to be tagged with the negative-campaigner charge. In 1987, two of Dukakis's top advisers were forced to resign from his campaign when it was revealed that they had put together what the press regularly referred to as an "attack video," which juxtaposed clips from British Labour Party Leader Neil Kinnock and Senator Joseph Biden, in order to show that the Democrat from Delaware had been plagiarizing speeches from Kinnock.)[34]

The effectiveness of the negative campaign against Dukakis showed in Bush's Electoral College victory, which was broad but shallow. The vice president won 426 Electoral College votes to 112 for Dukakis, but Bush's margins of victory in many states were relatively slim (California, 51–48 percent; Connecticut, 52–47 percent; Illinois, 51–49 percent; Maryland, 51–48 percent; Missouri, 52–48 percent; New Mexico, 52–47 percent; Pennsylvania, 51–48 percent; Vermont, 51–48 percent). The vote differentials in other Electoral College–rich states were not considerably larger. With a campaign more responsive to attacks thrust upon them and being more aggressive in setting the issues agenda, Democrats might very well have been able to win—whether with Dukakis or another nominee, such as former Senator Gary Hart of Colorado, the self-proclaimed "candidate of new ideas" whose White House aims imploded in May 1987 amid evidence of marital infidelity.

The 1988 presidential campaign taught a generation of candidates about the perils of ignoring attacks from opponents. One who went to school on that campaign was the governor of Arkansas, Bill Clinton. The rising political star had seriously considered running for the 1988 Democratic nomination himself, but demurred. Throughout that campaign he consistently provided advice to the Massachusetts governor, urging him to fight back against the Bush campaign and set the agenda in issues he wanted to run on, recalled Susan Estrich, Dukakis's campaign manager in 1988.[35] By the time Clinton ran successfully in 1992 against President George H. W. Bush, he had in place the "war room" mentality, in which the campaign pushed back immediately against any charges from Republicans, and leveled fresh ones of their own.

Another lasting legacy from the 1988 presidential campaign was the changes it spawned in how the news media cover negative advertising. As a result of what many news folk considered misleading charges by the Bush campaign, "ad watches" emerged to check up on the veracity of campaign commercials, particularly negative ones. The ad reviews forced candidates to cite sources to document their claims.

Bush's campaign was managed by Lee Atwater, a conservative political consultant who had joined the fledgling campaign team in 1985. He would become famous—and feared—for his readiness to attack opponents and his skill in carrying out those attacks. Atwater had won notoriety in 1980 as the consultant for South Carolina Republican Congressman Floyd Spence, who defeated Democratic state senator Tom Turnipseed with a combination of personal attacks and legally shady tactics. "Atwater's antics included phony polls by 'independent pollsters' to 'inform' white suburbanites that I was a member of the NAACP, because my congressman opponent was afraid to publicly say so, and last-minute letters from Senator Strom Thurmond (R-S.C.) warning voters that I would disarm America and turn it over to the liberals and Communists," Turnipseed later wrote.[36]

In 1988, Atwater, convinced that conservative voters in New Hampshire and the South could win the nomination for Bush over more colorful Republican candidates, shepherded a successful primary campaign with ferocious attacks on Republican rivals Bob Dole and Jack Kemp. According to veteran political scribes Jack Germond and Jules Witcover, when the general election got under way, Atwater handed research director Jim Pinkerton an index card and told him to fill it with negative information on Dukakis. "You get me the stuff to beat this little bastard and put it on this three-by-five card. I'm giving you one thing. You can use both sides of the three-by-five card."[37]

This tiny file contained the most negative issues that Atwater saw he could use against Dukakis—prison furloughs, the Pledge of Allegiance, and national security—and its points were tested on focus groups to see which issues could turn the most voters against the unknown Dukakis. Atwater figured that a barrage of negative attacks after the Democratic convention could weaken Dukakis and get Bush in striking distance in the polls—enough to bolster Republican morale and set up the successful fall campaign. To those who complained that the campaign was empty and unpleasant, Atwater replied, "We had only one goal in the campaign: to help elect George Bush. That's the purpose of any political campaign. What other function should a campaign have?" He also disputed that the campaign issues had been trivial, saying they effectively played into the belief among many Americans that Dukakis was an out-of-touch elitist who lacked common sense.[38]

After Bush's victory, Atwater went on to serve as chairman of the Republican National Committee. He died in 1991 at age 40 after a yearlong fight against a brain tumor. Shortly before his death, Atwater is reported to have recanted many of his most negative campaign feats, apologies largely, though not uniformly, accepted by those on the receiving end of the attacks. One believer in the sincerity of Atwater's recantings was Turnipseed, the former Democratic House candidate in South Carolina, who attended the funeral.

THE ROVE METHOD

An Atwater colleague, Karl Rove, rose to national prominence by planning the 2000 White House run of Texas Governor George W. Bush—the son of the 1988 presidential victor. As will be described shortly, Bush's win in South Carolina's crucial presidential primary in 2000 illustrated the handiwork of Rove, George W. Bush's chief political strategist.

First, a bit of background. Rove began his political career heading the College Republicans in Washington, D.C., from 1973 to 1974 (though he had bounced around several universities and had not obtained an undergraduate degree). In this role he met George W. Bush. Rove worked in various Republican circles for the next several years and on the elder Bush's unsuccessful bid for the GOP presidential nomination in 1980. Rove came into his own after founding a direct mail consulting firm, Karl Rove & Co., in Austin, Texas, in 1981. Over 20 years, he played a key role in turning Democratic-dominated Texas into a Republican state. Among his clients were Bill Clements, the first Republican in a century who was elected governor of Texas, and Phil Gramm, elected to the House as a nominal Democrat and who switched parties in Congress and won election to the U.S. Senate as a Republican.

Rove's lucrative direct mail practice swelled, and in 1993 he began advising the gubernatorial campaign of George W. Bush, then part owner of the Texas Rangers baseball team. Bush won the governorship the following year against incumbent Democratic Governor Ann Richards in a race that featured a rumor that she was a lesbian (Rove denied any involvement). Rove's consulting business continued until 1999, when he sold it to focus full time on Bush's (ultimately successful) bid for the presidency.

During his early years working on campaigns, Rove developed a reputation for unconventional political tactics. According to one biography, in the early 1970s Rove sneaked into the campaign office of Illinois Democrat Alan Dixon and stole some letterhead. He printed fliers on the letterhead promising "free beer, free food, girls and a good time for nothing" and distributed the fliers at rock concerts and homeless shelters. Rove later called the incident a youthful indiscretion and political prank.[39] Rove also gained attention in 1986 when, just before a crucial debate in the election for governor of Texas, he announced that Clements's office had been bugged by the Democrats. There was no proof, and it was later alleged he had bugged his own phone for the media coverage that the incident generated so it could be blamed on Democrats. No proof of that existed, either, and no charges were ever filed. What did emerge was a pattern of alleged win-at-all-costs tactics.

Against this backdrop came the 2000 Republican presidential primary in South Carolina. Rove, the manager of Bush's successful Texas gubernatorial campaigns in 1994 and 1998, set in place a front-loaded strategy for the presidential run. He tied up money and endorsements early—within a month of Bush's June 1999 announcement, the campaign raised $36.4 million.[40] But after spending the summer and fall assuming the GOP nomination was locked up, Bush lost to Arizona Senator John McCain by 48 to 30 percent in the New Hampshire primary.

The next major primary would occur eighteen days later in South Carolina, where GOP voters were considerably more conservative than their northeastern counterparts and likely to be more favorable to Bush. After the New Hampshire loss, Bush's double-digit poll lead in South Carolina fell to something between a tie and a five-point deficit.[41] Rove and the Bush team crafted a two-pronged strategy to pull their candidate out of the fire. First, Bush would be sold to voters as a "reformer with results," to defuse McCain's appeal as an insurgent without big money support. Second, McCain would be assaulted in every way without making Bush look like a negative campaigner.

The negative strategy played out in the open as well as under the radar, with allegations of dirty campaigning that became infamous. The above-ground negative strategy was marked by rapid response and quick pivoting of issues. At one campaign event, Bush watched J. Thomas Burch Jr., chairman of the National Vietnam and Gulf War Veterans Committee, claim that McCain, a decorated Vietnam veteran and prisoner of war, "came home [and] forgot us" after returning to the United States. McCain counterattacked, and five senators (including John Kerry, Democrat of Massachusetts) sent the Bush campaign a letter demanding an apology for the Texas governor's appearance with Burch. But the Bush campaign held fast. Scott McClellan, later White House press secretary, said the letter showed "that the McCain campaign is worried about the strong support Governor Bush has from veterans."[42] Indeed, by letting the attack float in the news, Bush seemed to benefit. In the end, Bush (who served in the National Guard during Vietnam) tied McCain for the votes of veterans.

The Bush team was also effective in turning one line in a negative McCain ad into a perceived slander against Bush. On February 8, McCain launched an ad in which he told the camera that a Bush ad airing in the state "twist[ed] the truth like Clinton."[43] There was no direct comparison of the Texas governor to the Democratic president, whose personal approval among South Carolina Republicans was abysmal. But the Bush team put an ad on the air 72 hours later, featuring their candidate looking straight at the camera and saying "When John McCain compared me to Bill Clinton and said I was untrustworthy, that was over the line."[44] Bush reiterated the comeback at campaign stops and at a February 15 debate, where he confronted McCain and said, "Do not question my trustworthiness and do not compare me to Bill Clinton.

That's about as low a blow as you can give in a Republican primary."[45] McCain's point was lost amid the impression that he had attacked Bush's character.

Beyond this typical political maneuvering, the race was marked by under-the-radar anti-McCain tactics that got the attention of national media outlets. An e-mail sent by Bush supporter Richard Hand, a professor at fundamentalist Bob Jones University, alleged that "McCain chose to sire children without marriage." Republican state representative Jim Merrill caught a couple of kids placing fliers on cars outside a seniors' center that alleged that McCain had a black daughter and showed a picture of him with his adopted Bangladeshi daughter, Bridget. Lois Eargle, the head of one of South Carolina's branches of the Christian Coalition, later said that the group had helped stoke a whispering campaign about the mental health of McCain's wife.[46] The candidate faced the classic dilemma about whether to denounce some of the sleazier allegations and risk spotlighting them for people who hadn't heard them in the first place, said Rick Davis, McCain's campaign manager. "It was beyond anything any of us had ever imagined, and we'd all run negative campaigns," Davis recalled.[47]

The most widely discussed dirty campaigning allegation was "push-polling," which aimed to plant negative ideas about McCain, masquerading as a legitimate voter survey.[48] Dick Bennett of the American Research Group pollsters told *Vanity Fair* that his callers constantly encountered people who had just been push-polled: "It wasn't a question of a few calls. It was blanket coverage."[49] The *New York Times* reported on people showing up to McCain rallies complaining of anonymous negative calls, which one voter called "a 'diatribe' against Mr. McCain that suggested he was a hypocrite and a liberal" before a plea to vote for Bush.[50] At one McCain rally, supporter Donna Duren claimed she had received a call attacking McCain as a "liar and a cheat and a fraud," and reporters sought out details from the Bush camp. Bush spokesman Ari Fleischer (who became Bush's first White House press secretary) admitted that the campaign had been making "advocacy" calls to voters about McCain's negative advertising. But Fleischer denied the substance of the calls discussed at McCain rallies, leading McCain political director John Weaver to say "any staff that would be low enough to make calls like that is low enough to have a phony script and lie about it." For his part, McCain made a plea for Bush's camp to halt negative campaigning, as McCain would "pull down every negative ad that I have."[51] Bush denied that anyone in his campaign would make the kind of negative calls that McCain was talking about.

The negative campaign, coupled with Bush's new "reformer with results" positive offensive, took a toll on McCain. Over the course of the 18-day campaign, the Arizona senator's lead disappeared, and his approval ratings among Republican voters declined. In ten days, McCain's unfavorable rating rose from 4 percent to 18 percent. But at the same time, Bush's unfavorable rating dropped from 26 percent to 20 percent.[52] Despite the high profile of the negative attacks on both sides, public opinion showed voters believed Bush had run the more positive campaign.[53] A major reason for this was Bush's reaction to the Clinton mention in McCain's early negative ad and how the campaign turned this into an unacceptable character smear. Bush also managed to ride negative attacks on McCain's character, like the insult from J. Thomas Burch, by quickly distancing himself from them. The negative impression didn't go away, but Bush was no longer associated with it. He won the South Carolina primary comfortably, 53 percent to 42 percent, setting him on the road to the Republican nomination, and ultimately, the presidency.

The episode demonstrated once again that negative campaigning is a most effective tool when employed with precision and skill. It can raise question marks in voters' minds about candidates, and when timed and executed correctly, can prove difficult to overcome.

NOTES

1. Steve Bosquet, "Endorsement Stirs Up Stem Cell Controversy: An Antiabortion Group Backs U.S. Senate Candidates Mel Martinez and Johnnie Byrd," *The St. Petersburg Times*, July 20, 2004.

2. Charles Babington, "For Fla. GOP, Morning after the Night before," *The Washington Post*, Sept. 5, 2004.

3. David B. Magleby, J. Quin Monson, and Kelly D. Patterson, eds., *Dancing without Partners: How Candidates, Parties and Interest Groups Interact in the New Campaign Finance Environment* (Provo, Utah: Center for the Study of Elections and Democracy, Brigham Young University, 2005), 197.

4. "McCollum for GOP: The Mel Martinez Campaign's Unprincipled Attacks on Bill McCollum Show Martinez to Be Unworthy of Support in Tuesday's Republican Senate Primary," a *St. Petersburg Times* editorial, Aug. 30, 2004.

5. *St. Petersburg Times*, Aug. 30, 2004.

6. Steve Bosquet, "Bitterness Boils Over at GOP Debate: The Rivalry between U.S. Senate Candidates Bill McCollum and Mel Martinez Takes a Nastier Turn during a Live TV Debate," *The St. Petersburg Times*, Aug. 28, 2004.

7. Ellen Gedalius, "Martinez Leads McCollum in Poll," *The Tampa Tribune*, Aug. 27, 2004.

8. Interview with author, by telephone, Jan. 24, 2005.

9. George Skelton, "$10,000 Spent by Strategist in '93 Served '02 Davis Campaign Well," *The Los Angeles Times*, Jan. 13, 2003.

10. Michael Finnegan, "Davis Ads Have Riordan on Defensive over Abortion Issue: Latest Spot Shows GOP Candidate Saying, 'I Think It's Murder,' in '91 Interview," *The Los Angeles Times*, Feb. 5, 2002.

11. Ads courtesy of Garry South, Santa Monica, Calif.

12. Gerald C. Lubenow, ed., *California Votes: The 2002 Governor's Race and the Recall That Made History* (Berkeley, Calif.: Berkeley Public Policy Press, 2003), 121.

13. Davis also profited from a series of self-inflicted wounds by Simon. The Republican flip-flopped on whether his tax returns would be released. In October Simon revealed an ad with a photograph that he said showed Davis accepting a contribution in the lieutenant governor's office. But the photo was actually taken in a private Los Angeles home.

14. Mark Z. Barabak, "California Governor: Don't Vote, It Will Only Encourage Them," in *Midterm Madness: The Elections of 2002*, ed. Larry J. Sabato (Lanham, Md.: Rowman & Littlefield Publishers, Inc., 2003), 188.

15. E-mail to author, Jan. 26, 2005.

16. Michael Finnegan, "Parks Calls Mayor's '01 Actions 'Racist': Councilman Criticizes TV Attack Ad Linking a Rival to a Drug Felon. A Spokesman for Hahn Denies the Campaign Sent a Negative Message," *The Los Angeles Times*, Feb. 12, 2005.

17. Beth Shuster, "Villaraigosa Backers Decry Hahn Ad as Unfair," *The Los Angeles Times*, May 29, 2001.

18. Shuster, *Los Angeles Times*, May 29, 2001.

19. Villaraigosa extracted political revenge four years later, when in a rematch he beat Hahn decisively. During his mayoral tenure Hahn had made a series of

unpopular decisions. He had ousted the black police chief, Bernard C. Parks, and had angered many San Fernando Valley residents by campaigning against the area's proposed secession from L.A. Villaraigosa, meanwhile, kept his political ambitions alive by winning a Los Angeles City Council seat. In the 2005 mayoral race he again came in first in the primary, and in the runoff campaign that followed faced attacks by Hahn for his intervention in the Vignali drug case nearly a decade earlier. The Hahn campaign even used the same slogan, "Los Angeles can't trust Antonio Villaraigosa," accusing the former president of the local chapter of the American Civil Liberties Union of being soft on crime.

The second time around, Villaraigosa fought back harder, accusing the mayor of trying to create "a climate of fear." Villaraigosa downplayed singular support from Hispanics and pledged repeatedly to "be mayor for everyone." He also aggressively criticized Hahn's management of city government, which at the time was facing several ethics and law enforcement inquiries about the propriety of some city contracts it had awarded. On Election Day Hahn suffered from the erosion of his winning coalition of four years previously: whites in the San Fernando Valley and blacks in South Los Angeles. On his was to a 59 percent to 41 percent victory, Villaraigosa also broadened the base of Latinos and white liberals that he had established in 2001.

20. Jim Gransberry, "Taylor Quits Senate Race in Montana," *The Billings Gazette*, Oct. 10, 2002.

21. Michael Janofsky, "Montana Candidate, Citing Smear Campaign, Ends Senate Bid," *New York Times*, Oct. 11, 2002.

22. Janofsky, *New York Times*, Oct. 11, 2002.

23. Gransberry, *The Billings Gazette*, Oct. 10, 2002.

24. Interview with author, by telephone, March 16, 2005.

25. Video courtesy of Strategic Perception, Inc., Hollywood, Calif.

26. David Beiler, "Southern Trilogy: How Republicans Captured Governorships in Georgia, South Carolina and Alabama," *Campaigns & Elections*, June 2003.

27. Interview with author, by telephone, March 16, 2005.

28. Jim Galloway, "Critics Call Rat Video Tasteless," *The Atlanta Journal-Constitution*, May 23, 2002.

29. Jim Galloway, "Perdue Video Likens Barnes to a Rat," *The Atlanta Journal-Constitution*, May 22, 2002.

30. Interview with author, by telephone, March 16, 2005.

31. Interview with author, by telephone, Feb. 1, 2005

32. Jules Witcover, *Party of the People: A History of the Democrats*, (New York: Random House, 2003), 640.

33. "Enough on the Guard, More on Quayle," a *New York Times* editorial, Aug. 24, 1988.

34. William G. Mayer, "In Defense of Negative Campaigning," *Political Science Quarterly*, Fall 1996.

35. Interview with author, Los Angeles, Dec. 1, 2004.

36. Tom Turnipseed, "What Lee Atwater Learned and the Lesson for His Protégés," *The Washington Post*, April 16, 1991.

37. Jack Germond and Jules Witcover, *Whose Broad Stripes and Bright Stars? The Trivial Pursuit of the Presidency 1988* (New York: Warner Books, 1989), 157.

38. Michael Oreskes, "Lee Atwater, Master of Tactics for Bush and G.O.P., Dies at 40," *The New York Times*, March 30, 1991.

39. Lou Dubose, Jan Reid, and Carl Cannon, *Boy Genius: Karl Rove, the Brains behind the Remarkable Political Triumph of George W. Bush* (New York: PublicAffairs, 2003), 10.

40. Dubose, Reid, and Cannon, *Boy Genius*, 133.

41. Judy Keen and Jill Lawrence, "South Carolina Cottons to McCain," *USA Today*, Feb. 4, 2000.

42. Marc Lacey, "Five Senators Rebuke Bush for Criticism of McCain," *The New York Times*, Feb. 5, 2000.

43. Peter Marks, "McCain Launches a New Salvo," *The New York Times*, Feb. 9, 2000.

44. Howard Kurtz, "He Hit Me First! Did Not! Did Too! Bush and McCain Trade Shots in Escalating Negative Spots," *The Washington Post*, Feb. 12, 2000.

45. Judy Keen and Jill Lawrence, "Fingers Point As Bush, McCain Clash in S.C.," *USA Today*, Feb. 16, 2000.

46. Richard Gooding, "The Trashing of John McCain," *Vanity Fair*, November 2004.

47. Interview with author, Alexandria, Va., Feb. 10, 2005.

48. As noted in this book's opening chapter, critics of McCain used push polling to suggest that McCain's Bangladeshi born daughter was his own illegitimate black child.

In February 2000, Kathy Frankovic, director of polls for CBS News, noted one widely reported survey question by the Bush campaign that asked, "John McCain calls the campaign finance system corrupt, but as chairman of the Senate Commerce Committee, he raises money and travels on the private jets of corporations with legislative proposals before his committee. In view of this, are you more likely to vote for him, somewhat more likely to vote for him, somewhat more likely to vote against him, or much more likely to vote against him?"

Whether or not this counted as a push poll is a matter of dispute. The call had the telltale signs of a push poll—the callers represented themselves as nonpartisan members of a polling organization, then provided negative information about the opposing candidate. But the question was part of what was about a 20-minute questionnaire, a conventional length for a voter survey and much longer than a typical push poll. It was also couched between a number of other questions regarding public-policy issues that would be part of a legitimate poll. (www.cbsnews.com/stories/2000/02/14/politics/main160398.shtml)

49. Gooding, *Vanity Fair*, Nov. 2004.

50. Alison Mitchell, "More Complaints about Negative Phone Calls," *The New York Times*, Feb. 13, 2000.

51. Dan Balz and Dana Milbank, "GOP Rivals Escalate Fight; McCain Attacks Bush over Phone Calls to Voters," *The Washington Post*, Feb. 11, 2000.

52. Dubose, Reid, and Cannon, *Boy Genius*, 143.

53. Gooding, *Vanity Fair*, Nov. 2004.

It's in the Mail: Negative Campaigning Comes Home

In October 2004, residents in the 8th congressional district of Illinois opened their mailboxes to find smiling pictures of their longtime congressman, dressed in Bermuda shorts, standing in front of beautiful white sand and glimmering aqua-blue ocean. "Phil Crane sends greetings from Costa Rica!" read the message on the mass mailing. Similar items had their representative in Congress saying hello from Scotland (dressed in a kilt), Antigua, and Rome. Still another, featuring more glossy travel pictures, arrived in voters' mailboxes in the form of a foldout paper crown.

These were not vacation postcards but political direct mail pieces hostile to the veteran Republican lawmaker. Crane's constituents quickly learned why he was so well traveled: Large text inside the crown mailing declared, "All hail Phil Crane King of Junkets!" and informed voters that "Seeking to curry his favor, Washington special interests paid for all of King Phil's junkets and journeys—$109,000 worth."[1] The ads, sent out by the Democratic Congressional Campaign Committee, hammered home the message that after thirty-five years in Congress Crane was more interested in foreign trips paid for by well-heeled favor-seekers than in representing his suburban Chicago constituents. The direct mail pieces reflected a major theme of the insurgent campaign by his Democratic opponent, technology consultant Melissa Bean. The tactic worked. In November 2004 Crane was one of only two incumbent House Republicans defeated and one of just seven members overall to lose their seats.

The anti-Crane pieces, created by the Washington, D.C., firm MSHC Partners, Inc., are success stories from the world of political direct mail, one of the most consistently effective and underestimated tactics in negative campaigning. While hard-hitting television ads often receive the lion's share of attention and notoriety during the rough and tumble of campaign season, direct mail offers candidates the opportunity to target specific households with specially tailored messages. This long-standing, "dead tree" medium and newer, increasingly used formats of negative campaigning like Web video, blogs, along with cultural phenomena like politically oriented books and movies, will be examined in this chapter.

POWER OF SPECIFIC MESSAGE

The merits of campaigning through direct mail are clear. Senders choose exactly whom to reach, unlike television and radio campaigners. And the sponsor of the direct mail piece controls the message; news reports cannot take selective quotes out of context. "It's rifle-shot advertising," said Richard A. Viguerie, a pioneer of conservative direct mail. "It's the most personal form of advertising." Crucially, the direct mail method is also less traceable by the competing camp than television and radio ads or websites. "One advantage that direct mail has is that the opposition does not know if you've mailed ten letters or ten million," Viguerie said.[2]

Nor are direct mail pieces usually subject to significant press coverage. When it comes to television commercials, "ad watches" in newspapers and on the Internet each campaign cycle scrutinize the veracity and accuracy of facts presented. Because direct mail is such an under-the-radar operation, it is often difficult for reporters to discover the extent of a mail drop and get their hands on some of the juicier items. That leaves room for significantly harder-hitting messages. And there is often very little time for the opposition to counterattack a stinging direct mail program, as many pieces arrive late in the campaign cycle. Unlike television commercials, which can generate a response within hours, there is still lag time in getting direct mail pieces into voters' hands.

The power of direct mail as a negative campaign technique goes back to Upton Sinclair's 1934 gubernatorial campaign in California. The socialist had unexpectedly won the Democratic nomination; at the height of the Great Depression, when much of the country was in desperate straits and seemingly open to ideas of revolutionary change, big business and other interests feared that a Sinclair governorship would lead to a command economy, and business fortunes would decline precipitously. Business interests organized a well-funded movement to derail Sinclair's campaign and boost the candidacy of Republican Frank Merriam, the former lieutenant governor who held the job due to the death the previous year of Governor James Rolph.

Merriam generally kept a low profile during the effort, as negative tactics were employed by business and allied groups in the first modern media political campaign. The onslaught included a flood of anti-Sinclair tracts sent out by Merriam supporters, the first broad uses of direct mail to tailor messages to target audiences. Virtually every group or special interest in the state received a mailing of its own, from Catholics to doctors to Stanford University alumni. Each mailing declared in its own way that Sinclair was a threat to institutions like church and private property. Most had the same format: four oblong-shaped pages (nine inches high by four inches wide) with simple but attractive type printed in black on coated white paper. A typical banner blared, "The Proof That Upton Sinclair Preaches Revolution and Communism." Most of the brochures closed with the question, "Will You Turn California Over to the Mercies of Upton Sinclair?"[3] These and other coordinated negative campaign tactics proved highly effective. Merriam won his own term as governor over Sinclair, 48 percent to 37 percent, with another 13 percent going to third-party progressive candidate.

Sophistication and usage of direct mail grew and evolved through the following decades, largely in conservative circles, from members' feelings of alienation from the mainstream culture. Viguerie noted that from the 1950s through the 1970s both major parties were under the control of their liberal or moderate wings, except for a few months in 1964 when conservatives managed to seize the Republican nomination for Arizona's Barry Goldwater. At the same time, conservatives also felt shut out from getting their viewpoints expressed in the mainstream media, as NBC, CBS, and ABC, along with the *New York Times*, the *Washington Post*, and a few other key media outlets basically decided what news was. According to conservative activists, each was infused with a liberal outlook. After the Goldwater washout in 1964, conservatives began using political direct mail to communicate with each other and build a sustained movement. Democrats, in control of the White House and Congress, didn't take seriously a vehicle they denigrated as "junk mail."[4]

Direct mail became a factor in campaigns during the early 1970s. In 1972 Democratic presidential nominee George McGovern, the South Dakota senator, was a heavy target for conservative direct mail. Various pieces focused on his support for amnesty for draft resisters, deep cuts in military programs, and his vow to dramatically overhaul a tax system that he said favored the rich. A stream of critics portrayed McGovern as a weakling whose stances would open the door to economic decline, national dishonor, and Communist expansion.[5] The mass mailings undoubtedly contributed to his 49-state landslide defeat at the hands of President Richard Nixon.

Around this time emerging computer technology also began to make possible narrow targeting of specific groups, rather than sending out general mailings. Viguerie, often called "the funding father of the conservative movement," recognized the potential of computerized mailing lists and helped his candidates gain an edge over their Democratic rivals through a variety of cutting-edge marketing techniques.

For one thing, the GOP built an advantage in collecting contributions generated by angry direct mail letters, a tactic born of necessity. From 1930 to 1994, Democrats controlled Congress, except for brief interruptions in both the House and Senate in the late 1940s and early 1950s, and in the Senate for six years in the 1980s. Being in the minority in Congress most of that time, Republicans had a tendency to send out the fundraising queries year-round, in bids to stay competitive. These letters often invoked the names of political enemies such as Senator Edward M. Kennedy, Democrat of Massachusetts, and, later, Hillary Rodham Clinton. The idea was to scare potential donors by claiming that these enemies of conservatives, and similar liberal-minded legislators, would be running the country, if Republicans did not receive the financial support to stop them. "The negative is what raises money, not the positive," Viguerie told C-SPAN in 2004. "If everything is going fine and everything is good, there's no problems out there, people are not going to respond."[6]

Democrats eventually adopted the tactic as well, with similar effectiveness. House Speaker Newt Gingrich, House Majority Leader Tom DeLay, political strategist Karl Rove, and Vice President Dick Cheney became favorite targets for direct mail pieces.

The angry appeals had many benefits. In addition to raising money and getting conservatives out to vote on Election Day, the mailings discussed in detail important issues of the day. The missives also asked the recipients to pass the letters on to others, thereby spreading the message. And the letters asked the recipients to take action, including mailing letters to members of Congress.[7] These techniques would all be adapted to e-mail in later years, with increased speed and efficiency.

As recounted earlier, during the 1970s, the Congressional Club, led by associates of Senator Jesse Helms, Republican of North Carolina, perfected the art of the angry appeal. The issues would include calls to cut taxes and bolster traditional family values. The medium also became a major factor in national campaigns during the 1980 election cycle, when the National Conservative Political Action Committee (NCPAC) used a coordinated direct mail program to defeat four Democratic senators it targeted: McGovern in South Dakota, the former presidential nominee; Frank Church of Idaho and Birch Bayh of Indiana, both presidential candidates in 1976; and John Culver in Iowa, a former Harvard fullback and graduate of Harvard Law School, who was first elected to the House at age 32, and to the Senate a decade later. These were independent expenditure campaigns, which aimed to circumvent new contribution limits enacted in the 1974 Federal Election Campaign Act. NCPAC had tasted its first political success in helping defeat one-term Senator Dick Clark, Democrat of Iowa, in 1978. In 1980, NCPAC's targeting of Democratic incumbents helped Republicans win control of the Senate for the first time in twenty-six years; the organization spent more than $1.2 million in the states where incumbents were targeted, much of it on direct mail.

NCPAC's influence reached its high-water mark in the 1980 election cycle. In 1982, NCPAC targeted six prominent liberal senators and spent $3 million, but all of its candidates lost.[8] Though NCPAC's electoral success was fleeting, its precedents would be long-lasting. Even as technology improved, with television ads becoming more pervasive and the later Internet and other interactive technologies taking hold as important tools in the art of negative campaigning, direct mail remained a tried and true method of attacking opponents.

The old-fashioned yet reliable method played an important role in the 2004 presidential campaign, when some of the toughest tactics were applied through direct mail. Take a piece sent by the Republican National Committee, which attacked Senator John Kerry's record on fighting terrorism. The advertisement contained several images of the World Trade Center towers smoking and burning. The caption read, "How can John Kerry lead America in a time of war?" On the other side of the political spectrum, a mailing by the liberal advocacy group late in the campaign accused Republicans of suppressing black voters in Missouri. It showed a 1960s-era photograph of a firefighter blasting a black man with a hose. "This is what they used to do to keep us from voting," the caption said. "Don't let them do it again."[9]

For the Swift Vets and POWs for Truth, the high-profile group that questioned Senator Kerry's military heroics in Vietnam, direct mail was just as important as its television commercials, which received the bulk of attention. Raising questions about Kerry's medals and criticizing his 1971 testimony before Congress about Vietnam, one direct mail piece accused the senator of dishonoring the men he served with. The olive green-and-white mailing, resembling the colors of military fatigues, splashed the banner "Betrayal" across its center. One section read, "John Kerry has mocked our symbols of honor and our revered national institutions. He threw away his Purple Hearts and other medals so gallantly earned and treasured by our veterans. He despises our heritage." It concluded by calling Kerry "A man who so grossly distorts his military record, who betrays his fellow soldiers, who endangers our soldiers and sailors held captive, who secretly conspired with the enemy. . . ."[10] This and other mailings went to millions of voters in battleground states like Ohio, Florida, Iowa, and New Mexico. The mailings all helped reinforce the Swift Vets' message that Kerry was not somebody who could be trusted to lead the military. Again, these pieces were sent to highly selected audiences already inclined to vote against Kerry. The mailings served as an extra motivation to get those folks to the polls on Election Day.

Congressional races in 2004 were also fertile ground for hundreds of emotion-laden direct mail pieces. In South Dakota, where Senate Minority Leader Tom Daschle lost a close race to Republican John Thune, the National Rifle Association sent mail depicting the incumbent as a puppet, with Democratic Senators Kennedy of Massachusetts and Hillary Rodham Clinton of New York pulling the strings.

In an open-seat Senate race in Florida, direct mail became a major vehicle for alleging the Democratic nominee, former state Education Commissioner Betty Castor, was soft on terrorism. Republican Mel Martinez repeatedly criticized how, as president of the University of South Florida (USF), she handled the case of Sami al-Arian, a computer science professor who was suspected of raising money through campus groups for Palestinian Islamic Jihad (PIJ), linked to the murder of Israeli civilians. In the late 1990s Castor suspended al-Arian with pay but reinstated him after two years, based on a lack of evidence against him. She also condemned Islamic Jihad and terrorism, but not al-Arian himself. Then, in 2003, al-Arian and another former USF teacher, Ramadan Abdullah Shallah, were among eight people indicted on racketeering and conspiracy to murder, maim, or injure persons outside the United States.[11] The indictment charged that al-Arian, Shallah and others were able to "utilize the structure, facilities and academic environment of the University of South Florida to conceal the activities of the PIJ," which included "paying compensation to the families of PIJ 'martyrs' (suicide bombers) and 'detainees.'" Castor's successor as USF president, Judy Genshaft, fired al-Arian in 2003, after he was indicted.

Martinez made the episode a major campaign issue, to hammer home the point that his opponent was less than resolute in combating terror. On his behalf, the National Republican Senatorial Committee sent out a series of splashy mailers showing Castor's picture side by side with al-Arian. The inside fold of one mailer blared, "While president of the University of South Florida, Betty Castor let a suspected terrorist teach our children." Another mailing declared, "Betty Castor: Easy on Terrorists, Putting Florida's Families at Risk."[12] The direct mail piece went out in the closing days of the neck-and-neck Senate campaign; they were mailed to Republicans and Independents in the northern and central regions of Florida, the most conservative parts of the state. The pieces undoubtedly contributed to Martinez's narrow victory over Castor, 50 percent to 48 percent.[13]

WEB VIDEO

When Senator John Kerry clinched the Democratic presidential nomination in February 2004, the deep-pocketed Bush–Cheney '04 campaign wasted no time spending its campaign cash to attack his record. The Republicans' earliest ads included a spot that raised many of the themes used to hammer Kerry throughout the campaign; it caricatured the Massachusetts senator as an indecisive, weak, and hypocritical politician who had taken both sides of many major public policy issues. The 60-second commercial, "Unprincipled," claimed Kerry was beholden to special interests, which he regularly denounced on the campaign trail. But the ad was nowhere to be found on television stations—in battleground states, or anywhere else. Rather, the ad was a full-fledged campaign commercial online, an original video production. On February 12, the Bush-Cheney campaign sent the ad by e-mail to six million supporters, with the intent of generating early excitement among core Republican partisans. The spot then received substantial media coverage, on television, and through coordinated e-mail campaigns. It picked up so much traction that the Kerry campaign felt compelled to respond with an Internet counterattack. Original Internet ads, particularly those featuring Web video, had arrived as a new and cutting-edge form of negative campaigning.[14]

Low in cost to create, Internet ads generally do not have the same function as political commercials seen on television. They are not meant to persuade undecided voters. Instead, capitalizing on the anything-goes ethos of the Internet, such spots are often used to gin up the party base and ensure activists are still excited as Election Day approaches. In addition, most states allow some sort of early voting, either at a traditional polling place or by mail, and Internet ads have the potential to be particularly effective vehicles to get supporters to cast ballots at the earliest possible opportunity.

And while political television ads usually last 30 seconds, Web video commercials can go on as long the sponsors like. Because those viewing the ad are already likely interested in the political race at hand, they are more apt to sit through and watch the entire show. Usually television viewers with limited or no interest in politics will not stay tuned to their candidate's advertisement. "Some of the most extreme ads are meant to pump up the base vote," noted David Schwartz, of the American Museum of the Moving Image, in Queens, N.Y. "It's the nature of the Internet."[15]

Notably, Web video political commercials also do not carry the "stand by your ad" requirement. So candidates are free from the stricture of having to endorse their own Internet spots, which is mandated for radio and television political commercials. As a result, ads run exclusively on the Internet are often longer and more hard-hitting than those featured on television. That trend became clear from a couple of spots aired during the 2004 election cycle that clearly played to the sentiments of those already deeply passionate about the emerging presidential race, rather than undecided voters who would likely have been turned off by the content.

In January 2004, MoveOn.org, the leftist political advocacy organization, held a contest inviting the public to design the best anti-Bush commercials. The results would be shown on the group's website. Commercials submitted came mainly from amateurs who created the spots largely on home computers. Not surprisingly, most were pretty hard-hitting, slamming the president for the Iraq war, job losses, and myriad other problems. While critical, the ads were generally within bounds of conventional political discourse.

But two went far past the edge, as they showed images of Adolph Hitler, with implicit comparisons to President Bush. One amateur commercial showed a picture of the president with text saying, "God told me to strike at al Qaeda," before turning to images of Adolph Hitler with the words, "And then He instructed me to strike at Saddam." The submission ended with the words, "Sound familiar?" on a black-and-white screen. Another Web commercial used a tape recording of the Nazi leader speaking, while it showed images of the dictator and German military troops marching in formation. At the end of the ad, a photo of Bush raising his hand to take the oath of office appeared. "A nation warped by lies. Lies fuel fear. Fear fuels aggression. Invasion. Occupation. What were war crimes in 1945 is foreign policy in 2003," the ad said.

An immediate outcry followed. Republican National Committee Chairman Ed Gillespie called the spot "the worst and most vile form of political hate speech," while an Anti-Defamation League leader flayed the liberal group for running an ad using the genocidal dictator as a political prop. MoveOn.org took down the ad, saying it was one of 1,512 submissions from the general public. "We agree that the two ads in question were in poor taste and deeply regret that they slipped through our screening process," the group said in statement.[16]

The controversy did not end there, however. One of the ads featuring a Hitler picture reemerged in an Internet campaign spot in June 2004. The Bush-Cheney campaign ran an original commercial on its website showing a picture from one of the MoveOn.org ads that had been taken down, to dramatize the lengths Bush's critics would go in demonstrating disdain for the president. The Bush Internet video spliced together clips of the Nazi ruler, Kerry, 2000 Democratic nominee Al Gore, and 2004 Democratic presidential candidate Howard Dean. The 77-second video showed the images of these Democratic candidates and left-wing film director Michael Moore, calling them Kerry's "Coalition of the Wild-eyed." Gore was shown giving a heated speech criticizing the Bush administration. The screen then cut to the words, "This is not a time for pessimism and rage."[17]

The campaign distributed the Web video ad electronically to six million supporters. Democrats decried the use of Hitler in a political ad under any circumstances, but the Bush-Cheney campaign held its ground, saying the video from MoveOn.org demonstrated the type of vitriolic rhetoric being used by the president's opponents.

THE BLOGOSPHERE AND THE CAMPAIGN TRAIL

In 2004 former Republican Congressman John Thune of South Dakota fought a bitter campaign to unseat Senate Minority Leader Tom Daschle. Thune had lost an achingly close Senate race two years before to incumbent Democratic Senator Tim Johnson by a mere 524 votes. In his second bid Thune had the advantage of facing one of the top Republican targets in the country. As Democratic leader, Daschle had fought the agenda of President George W. Bush on taxes, drilling for oil in the Artic National Wildlife Refuge in Alaska, and scores of other issues.

Republicans were most galled by what they called Daschle's tendency to talk one way in conservative South Dakota and act differently in Washington, D.C., where as leader he had to please some of his party's most liberal interests. Among their grievances was Daschle's assurance to South Dakota voters that he supported a state law defining marriage as between a man and a woman, while in July 2004 he voted against a similar proposed constitutional amendment. They also cited statements at home that he favored gun rights, while receiving low grades from the NRA for his votes on firearms issues.[18]

Republicans had a 51–49 Senate majority going into the 2004 elections, and with control of the chamber at stake, the South Dakota race became one of the most closely watched and well-funded races in the nation. A flood of independent groups seeking to aid or defeat one of the candidates spent heavily. The pro-Thune forces included bloggers, the website operators who offered staccato-form postings dozens of times each day. Bloggers had increasingly helped drive news events in recent years. They had helped expose fake news documents backing up Dan Rather's September 2004 *60 Minutes II* story on President Bush and the Air National Guard, which eventually led to a scathing report and the news anchor's early departure from his post as anchor of the *CBS Evening News*. Two years before, liberal blogs had relentlessly publicized comments by incoming Senate Majority Leader Trent Lott (R-Miss.) praising retiring Senator Strom Thurmond (R-S.C.) in a manner that seemed nostalgic for the days of segregation. Lott was subsequently forced to relinquish his leadership post.

While most bloggers were clearly partisan and opinionated, it was widely assumed they acted independently. Not so with Thune's campaign. According to reports later filed with the Federal Election Commission, the campaign paid two bloggers who ran anti-Daschle websites a total of $35,000. The blogs were founded independently of the Thune team and existed for months before their proprietors were paid by the Republican's campaign. But the fact that they received compensation was not revealed before Election Day.

The sites in question pointed out seeming inconsistencies between Daschle's campaign rhetoric and his actual Senate votes. They also critiqued coverage of the campaign by the state's largest newspaper, the *Argus Leader* of Sioux Falls, which they considered highly biased toward Daschle (the chief political reporter had attended college with the senator). The blogs repeatedly pounded the newspaper for allegedly ignoring stories unfavorable to Daschle and for not giving Thune a fair shake.

Thune narrowly defeated Daschle, making him the first Senate party leader to lose in more than a half century and helping Republicans boost their majority in the chamber to fifty-five seats, to forty-five for the Democrats. The episode pointed to the growing influence of blogs and other websites as tools in the arsenal negative campaign tactics. Blogs have the potential to increasingly become proxies for campaigns through the Internet, a medium in which little regulation exists. Unlike television commercials, where candidates must appear, on radio, where their voices must be heard, or in direct mail, where the sponsor's name must at least appear in print, blogs and other Internet sites have no disclosure requirements. Online ethics standards are not the same as for traditional news outlets, if they exist at all.

Many blogs are fueled by unsubstantiated rumors, which quickly travel around the Internet and are then often trumpeted by mainstream news organizations. Separating fact from speculation can be a daunting task. Many bloggers make little effort to check their information and think nothing of posting a personal attack without calling the targets first, or contacting them at all. Accordingly, ostensibly independent blogs will likely serve increasingly as fronts for campaigns, to create the illusion of grassroots support while mounting attacks on opponents and disseminating information to which candidates do no want their names attached.[19]

BOOKS

Popular culture has also moved to the forefront of creative tactics in the negative campaigning wars, through books and movies. In 2004, attack books became an important element in a campaign environment filled with searing rhetoric, heated charges, and tough accusations. *Unfit for Command,* by John E. O'Neill and Jerome R. Corsi, an unrelenting assault on Senator John Kerry's Vietnam combat record, spent weeks on best-seller lists and sold hundreds of thousands of copies. The book helped generate anger and opposition among Kerry's critics that, even if it did little to convince undecided voters, helped solidify hostility toward the Democratic nominee among Republican-oriented voters. The work was one of many books, spanning the political spectrum, which portrayed the president and his challenger in scathing terms as liars, hypocrites, and corrupt, noted Peter Osnos, then the publisher and CEO of PublicAffairs, an influential New York–based book publishing house.[20]

Partisan books aimed at influencing the outcome of elections were nothing new. During the 1964 presidential campaign, a series of "dirty books" emerged against President Lyndon B. Johnson, whose climb up the greasy pole of politics to attain high office made him an inviting target. There was J. Evetts Haley's *A Texan Looks at Lyndon,* which depicted the president as completely without scruples. It promoted conspiratorial connections to paint LBJ in the worst possible light. For instance, it suggested sinister implications in the fact that Lee Harvey Oswald had once stayed overnight in Jim Wells County, Texas, where Johnson is alleged to have stolen his initial Senate election victory, in the 1948 Democratic primary runoff.[21] In a different volume, with a broader focus, John Stormer's *None Dare Call It Treason* argued that left-wingers of both parties were in pursuit of a "new world order."

Shortly after Johnson's landslide win in November 1964, *Publisher's Weekly* estimated that 50 paperbacks had been released during the campaign that referred substantially to the presidential election.[22] As with modern books by ideological authors, it is doubtful that many minds were changed, but the works served an important purpose in rallying bases of support.

In the early twenty-first century conservative books timed around elections have become a particularly lucrative venture for publishers. Ann Coulter's books, *Treason*, *Slander*, and *How to Talk to a Liberal (If You Must)*, have become such moneymakers for traditional trade publishers that several of the larger houses have launched conservative imprints, such as Crown Forum and Sentinel/Penguin.

The release of books seemingly designed to take down candidates is getting increasingly early, often years before an election. Edward Klein's *The Truth About Hillary: What She Knew, When She Knew It, and How Far She'll Go to Become President*, was hyped to contain a series of explosive revelations about the senator from New York and former first lady, which would sink her 2008 presidential candidacy. The more lurid allegations included claims that "the culture of lesbianism at Wellesley College shaped Hillary's politics" and that much later "she set up an elaborate system to monitor her husband's girlfriends."

But Klein's book, released in June 2005, had little effect on Clinton's potential candidacy. Critics savaged the work for relying heavily on rumor, innuendo, and warmed-over stories from the 1990s that were poorly sourced or considered old news. Instead of hurting her potential candidacy, the book had an opposite effect, inoculating the ambitious politician from better-sourced lines of criticism that might have been brought up by political opponents.

TALK RADIO AND NEGATIVE CAMPAIGNING

The recall of California Govenor Gray Davis in 2003 might never have happened without talk radio. Conservative radio show hosts kept up a drumbeat of criticism against the Democratic governor in the months following his hard-fought 2002 reelection victory.

The recall effort was originally the brainchild of conservative activists who pushed signature drives to gain ballot access for the recall measure. That required signatures of 12 percent of the total number of voters in the previous election—in the case of Davis, about 897,000. That was a difficult hurdle to overcome—there had previously been thirty-one petition drives to recall a California governor, and each had failed to make the ballot.

Recall sponsors, led by antitax crusader Ted Costa, appeared on conservative talk radio shows in early 2003 and quickly built momentum for their ultimately successful crusade. An appearance by outgoing California Republican Party Chair Shawn Steel on a San Francisco radio talk show, in which he suggested a recall, also sparked interest.[23] More than enough signatures were submitted.

Once the recall measure was certified and the special election scheduled, momentum against Davis grew quickly; the October 2003 balloting resulted in his ouster and Republican Arnold Schwarzenegger winning the top job.

The episode illustrated the power of talk radio in the arsenal of negative campaigning, a medium capable of delivering large blocs of true believers to become active in politics. The influence of talk radio on elections, particularly from the conservative end of the spectrum, has long been building. It began in a serious way in 1987, when the Federal Communications Commission repealed the Fairness Doctrine, which dictated that if someone attacked a political position on air the opposition had to be given equal time for a rebuttal. The rule long limited the ability of broadcasters to advocate against candidates, as sanctions could be as stiff as revocation of a radio station's broadcasting license.

Within a few years of the Fairness Doctrine's repeal, market demand led to more than a thousand radio stations switching to a talk-radio format.[24] Talk radio as a campaign tool took on new importance in the run-up to the 1994 midterm elections, when on-air hosts helped foment anger against President Bill Clinton and his policies. Leading the pack was Rush Limbaugh; his mix of entertaining delivery and strongly conservative message grew so influential that in 1994 he was named an honorary member of the new Republican-majority Congress. In the years since, talk radio has become embedded in the fabric of political campaigns and has become an indispensable tool in knocking opposition candidates off-stride.

TELEVISION AND MOVIES

Television programming has become another medium for offering negative critiques of candidates. In fall 2004, weeks before the presidential election, controversy ensued over the planned airing of the documentary *Stolen Honor: Wounds That Never Heal*, a 45-minute film that featured POWs who believed Kerry's antiwar statements had made their captivity more brutal. Sinclair Broadcast Group, whose avowedly conservative owners controlled about 25 percent of network affiliates in U.S. television markets, planned to show the film on all their stations. Heated protests from Democrats and the threat of shareholder lawsuits caused Sinclair to retreat and instead air a 60-minute panel discussion on the controversy that documentaries could stir up in presidential campaigns (it included a total of five minutes from *Stolen Honor*).[25]

In 2004, the big screen also emerged as a forum for attacking political candidates, no matter how skewed the facts or presentation. The most overtly political film, released with the express purpose of influencing an election (defeating President George W. Bush), was Michael Moore's *Fahrenheit 9/11.* The conspiracy-laden tract provided the filmmaker an outlet for venting virtually every frustration the conspiratorial hard-left felt toward Bush. It suggested, among other things, that the president was hesitant to confront the Saudis because of his family's business ties to the royal family. More broadly it argued that Bush got elected under fraudulent circumstances and proceeded to blunder through his duties. According to Moore, when the September 11, 2001, terrorist attacks happened, Bush failed to take immediate action to defend the nation, and imperiled its citizens. Most outrageously, the film even suggested that the United States had gone to war in Afghanistan not to destroy al-Qaeda but to benefit the Unocal Corporation, which wanted to build a natural gas pipeline across that country.[26]

The movie rallied Bush-haters and liberals on the fringe of the respectable political spectrum, but also won tacit endorsements from many mainstream Democrats. Its capital premiere at a large theatre in an upscale Washington, D.C., neighborhood was attended by the glitterati of the Democratic Party, including Democratic National Committee Chairman Terry McAuliffe and several U.S. senators and House members. "I think anyone who goes to see this movie will come out en masse and vote for John Kerry," McAuliffe said outside the movie's premiere.[27]

The film played well in deep "blue" state areas of the country, including New York City, San Francisco, and Seattle. But the film also had the reverse effect of motivating conservative voters, who saw in Moore's work only unbridled hatred for a wartime president who had defined the stakes of a tough national security policy and was willing to aggressively prosecute the war on terror. "*Fahrenheit 9/11* represents an unabashedly partisan piece of propaganda whose primary purpose (proudly and repeatedly announced by its irrepressible creator) involved the attempt to discredit and, ultimately, defeat the Bush administration," wrote Michael Medved, a conservative radio talk show host and film critic.[28] Despite Moore's claims that the film was changing minds across the country, the movie severely underperformed in "red state" areas of the nation, particularly in crucial battleground states, such as Tampa/St. Petersburg, Florida, Columbus, Ohio, and Detroit, Michigan.[29]

Ultimately, the election did not go the way Moore intended to guide it. President Bush won a second term. But the filmmaker introduced a new political form, the documentary as negative campaign tool. Should partisan nonfiction films emerge as a major force in politics in the years following Moore's 2004 anti-Bush movie, the success will be traced to *Fahrenheit 9/11*, which helped turn popular culture into part of the negative campaign cycle.[30] The film may one day be seen as a landmark event in negative campaigning, the way the televised presidential debates in 1960 between Senator John F. Kennedy and Vice President Richard M. Nixon showed for the first time the potential of television in influencing political contests.

NOTES

1. Direct mail pieces courtesy of MSHC Partners, Washington, D.C. The Crane "crown" piece evolved from an idea thought up originally by Democratic direct mail specialist Jeff Gumbiner.

2. Interview with author, Manassas, Va., Sept. 14, 2004.

3. Greg Mitchell, *The Campaign of the Century: Upton Sinclair's Race for Governor of California and the Birth of Media Politics* (New York: Random House, 1992), 362.

4. Richard A. Viguerie and David Franke, "The Big Winners," *The Washington Post,* Oct. 24, 2004.

5. Michael Leahy, "What Might Have Been: George McGovern, the Senior Member of a Rare and Burdened Tribe, Reveals Just How Long It Takes to Get Over Losing the Presidency," *The Washington Post Magazine,* Feb. 20, 2005.

6. Transcript, *Booknotes* interview with Richard A. Viguerie for his book, *America's Right Turn: How Conservatives Used New and Alternative Media to Take Power,* C-SPAN, Sept. 5, 2004.

7. Transcript, *Booknotes* interview with Richard A. Viguerie.

8. Stephen Ansolabehere and Shanto Iyengar, *Going Negative: How Political Advertisements Shrink and Polarize the Electorate* (New York: The Free Press, 1995), 130.

9. Glen Justice, "In Final Days, Attacks Are in the Mail and Below the Radar," *The New York Times,* Oct. 31, 2004.

10. Direct mail piece courtesy of Chris LaCivita, chief strategist for Swift Vets and POWs for Truth.

11. Tom Curry, "Terrorism Charges Dominate Florida Senate Race: Republican Martinez Jabs at Democrat Castor over Islamic Jihad Leader at Her Former University," MSNBC.com, Oct. 4, 2004.

12. Direct mail piece courtesy of Chris LaCivita, Richmond, Va.

13. In December 2005, a federal jury acquitted Sami al-Arian of conspiring to aid a Palestinian group in killing Israelis through suicide bombings. The Tampa, Fla., jury found al-Arian not guilty on eight of 17 counts, including conspiracy to maim or murder. Jurors deadlocked on the rest of the charges.

14. Daniel Manatt, "Web Video: The Biggest ePolitics Innovation of 2004," *Campaigns & Elections*, June 2004.

15. Interview with author, Queens, N.Y., Aug. 30, 2004.

16. FOXNews.com, "Ad Comparing Bush to Hitler Gets Heat," Jan. 6, 2004.

17. Jennifer C. Kerr, "Hitler Image Used in Bush Campaign Web Ad," *Associated Press*, June 27, 2004.

18. Kimberley A. Strassel, "All about Tom: South Dakota's Senate Race Is a Referendum on Filibuster Politics," *The Wall Street Journal* editorial page, Oct. 15, 2004.

19. Brian Faler, "On Bloggers and Money: Some Seek Disclosure Rules for Web Sites Paid by Candidates," *The Washington Post*, May 3, 2005.

20. Peter Osnos, "Mud Flies, Books Fly off Shelves," *The Los Angeles Times*, Sept. 20, 2004.

21. Bruce L. Felknor, *Dirty Politics* (Lincoln, Neb.: iUniverse.com, Inc. [originally published by W. W. Norton], 1966, 2000), 71.

22. Felknor, *Dirty Politics*, 224.

23. John Fund, "Radio Free California: The Davis Recall Is a Triumph for the New Media, *The Wall Street Journal*, Oct. 2, 2003.

24. Richard A. Viguerie and David Franke, *America's Right Turn: How Conservatives Used New and Alternative Media to Take Power* (Chicago: Bonus Book, 2004), 178.

25. John Fund, "'The Last Mission: The Swift Boat Veterans Gather to Assess Their Impact on the Campaign," *Opinionjournal.com*, Nov. 15, 2004.

26. Byron York, *The Vast Left Wing Conspiracy: The Untold Story of How Democratic Operatives, Eccentric Billionaires, Liberal Activists, and Assorted Celebrities Tried to Bring Down a President—and Whey They'll Try Even Harder Next Time* (New York: Crown Forum, 2005), 107.

27. York, *The Vast Left Wing Conspiracy*, 107.

28. Michael Medved, "A Movie with Legs: 'Fahrenheit 9/11' Is Already Dated, but 'The Passion' Will Endure," *The Wall Street Journal*, Jan. 27, 2005.

29. York, *The Vast Left Wing Conspiracy*, 118–119.

30. "Box Office Shepherds," *TIME*, Dec. 27–Jan. 3, 2005.

Conclusion: The Future of Negative Campaigning

For decades political strategists often wasted their campaigns' precious resources, because insufficient research data led them to target wrong people with ineffective messages. Soft targeting strategies, often little more than a guessing game, have now evolved into very specific "microtargeting" efforts aimed at appealing to individual voters. To do this, consultants comb public and private documents to create political profiles. They use voter registration files to get party affiliation and to determine whether the voter cast ballots in recent elections. Real estate documents—typically filed in city or county courthouses—show how much a person paid for a home and how much its property taxes may have risen. And private market research information, available for a fee from list brokers and other sources, detail what magazines a person gets and what kind of car he or she drives.

This massive evolution in targeting voters has the potential to boost the level of negative campaigning in the future and streamline the ways attacks are delivered. Text-messaging through Blackberries, Palm Pilots, and cell phones is going to be used more often to individualize negative attacks to fit the specific viewpoints and concerns of small voting blocs. If a voter has signed a petition to place on the ballot a local bond measure to fund schools or hospitals, it's not a huge leap of faith to guess that he or she is open to the idea of paying more in taxes for public works. So, a politician would send that voter a message, through a variety of high-tech means, explaining that the pol's opponent was anti-education and against public health issues.

Negative political television commercials in the future will reach smaller and smaller groups of people. This ad-buying model became a staple of the 2004 presidential election, when the campaigns spent a lot of money placing candidate commercials around shows that were likely to appeal to certain voting groups. Strategists for Senator John Kerry knew that he needed women voters, to offset President George W. Bush's advantage among men. The Massachusetts senator's campaign ran thousands of ads on daytime programs popular with women, such as *Oprah*, *The Ellen DeGeneres Show*, *Dr. Phil*, and *Live with Regis and Kelly*. Conversely, in closely contested battleground states, ads for the president aired around *America's Most Wanted*, *Cops*, *JAG*, *Law and Order*, and *NYPD Blue*, along with programming on the Golf Channel and during NASCAR races.

As microtargeting in advertising develops, many different versions of negative spots may very well be aired around programs. The different versions of one ad would aim to appeal to small clusters of people whom consultants think are open to a certain message, be they senior citizens, middle-class white men, young single women, or Hispanic voters under age 45 with college degrees.

Get-out-the-vote efforts, including old-fashioned house calls and handing out leaflets on street corners, are going to evolve with microtargeting. Think about the grassroots strategies that Bush-Cheney's 72 Hour Task Force mobilization plan used in 2004. In the three days leading up to Election Day, the campaign delivered customized messages to voters based on issues deemed most important to them. In Ohio, Florida, and other battleground states pro-Bush and anti-Kerry information was delivered by friends, through the mail, via e-mail, over the phone, and on cable television, to contact potential supporters about exactly the things they cared about most.

Banner ads on the Internet may prove to be the fastest growing forum for launching microtargeted campaign attacks because so much information can be gathered on individual Web viewers based on the sites they have visited and data they must often submit to gain access. Banner ads—boxy, billboard-like graphics that appear on the periphery of a site—combine the targeting power of both television ads and direct mail. Ads can be tailored to geographic locations based on ZIP codes or other pieces of information gathered on a website. On news sites, banner ads can be made to show up only above stories about specific topics, such as health care or tax cuts.[1]

There are limits to such a segmented approach, however, particularly on television. It costs considerable money to redo ads several ways (one for each segment of the voting population a candidate wants to reach). Similarly, microtargeting requires lots of expensive research, to splice and dice the electorate to such a minute point that each separate ad is reaching the proper individuals. Such resources are unaffordable luxuries for many campaigns.

Moreover, campaigns face increasing challenges to even getting voters to see the ads at all. Thanks to ever-improving technology, television viewers have gained more power to control what ads they see. Digital video recorders (DVRs), such as TiVo, let viewers skip commercials. Considering that the vast majority of television viewers are not political junkies and follow electoral horse races and policy disputes with only a passing interest at most, they're most likely to hit the button at the first sign of a grainy black-and-white picture of a candidate—a clear indication of a campaign attack ad.

While viewers will have more control in tuning out political television commercials, they may instead receive more political solicitations over the phone. The federal Do Not Call Registry legislation enacted in 2003 contains a loophole that allows political solicitations. And purveyors of negative campaigning lost little time in capitalizing on it. So much so that Congresswoman Virginia Foxx (R-N.C.) introduced legislation in April 2005 to let people place themselves on a "do not call" for recorded political telephone messages, or what are known in the political industry as "robo calls." Her "ROBO C.O.P" bill (Robo Calls off Phones), would have directed the Federal Trade Commission to revise its regulations for the registry by adding politically oriented recorded messages to the list. Foxx, on the receiving end of a barrage of negative campaign tactics in her bitterly contested primary-runoff victory in 2004 (see chapter 10), said the idea for the measure came from constituents, who had received dozens of annoying robo calls in the weeks before the election.

NEGATIVE CAMPAIGNING CONSTANTLY BEING REINVENTED

The history of American politics shows some negative campaign tactics are enduring, while others disappear after a few years. During the late 1980s and

early 1990s, for instance, it was popular to include in ads "third-party valida-
tors," independent sources of information such as newspaper stories and editorials, to support attacks on opponents. In the Internet age, that technique
has diminished because of the proliferation of the information sources. "People's antennas are up, and they feel like you can find something in print anywhere to support your point, or is maybe taken out of context," noted Jim
Margolis, the Democratic media specialist.[2]

One element of the campaign cycle that won't fade away is the haste with
which negative attacks are delivered. And advances in digital editing technology can only speed up the television political-attack-ad cycle. Campaigns now
have scriptwriters, video editors, and voiceover artists on standby to create almost instantaneous comebacks. In late September 2004, the Bush campaign
released an ad that showed Senator Kerry windsurfing in opposing directions,
charging that his positions changed "whichever way the wind blows." It took
little more than an hour for Kerry campaign media specialists to put together
a counterattack, in the form of a television ad that decried U.S. casualties, kid-
nappings, and beheadings in Iraq. The Kerry spot sought to turn the tables on
the president, declaring, "George Bush's answer is to run a juvenile and tasteless attack ad."[3] Of course, the Bush campaign then quickly sent out e-mail to
counter Kerry's attacks.

The negative campaigning now continues long *after* Election Day. In his 1980
book, *The Permanent Campaign: Inside the World of Elite Political Operatives*,
Sidney Blumenthal, a journalist and later a senior advisor to the Clinton White
House, said that campaigning and governing had become almost completely in-
terlinked. Campaign consultants moved without pause from the campaign trail
to work for the victorious elected officials, helping them shape their policy messages and frame issues for advantage in the next election cycle. The legislative
arena itself became a political battleground, where speeches and amendments
were offered for the sole purpose of putting other politicians on record. The
heat of the permanent campaign got turned up several notches during the mid-
1980s when House Republicans, chafing in the minority, began winning national media attention under the banner of the Conservative Opportunity
Society (COS). Georgia congressman and COS leader Newt Gingrich, the future
House speaker, Congressman Vin Weber of Minnesota, and other colleagues
helped a small band of Republicans turn the House floor into a theater for partisan warfare, through television, live on C-SPAN.

The permanent campaign's successor is what CNN political analyst Bill Schneider has dubbed the permanent negative campaign: American politics, at least in the near future, is likely to see all attacks, all the time, even when no election is looming immediately.[4] The process includes members of Congress returning to their districts on weekends to find their local newspapers stuffed with ads warning them about the electoral consequences of voting a certain way on legislation. Menacing television and radio commercials are becoming a mainstay on the airwaves year-round, not to mention the websites that continually attack elected officials.

The permanent negative campaign, the never-ending cycle of fundraising, polling, and candidate positioning, is most visible in an age of relative partisan parity. George W. Bush's 2000 victory was earned with a bare majority in the Electoral College, and he won reelection four years later with a slightly more comfortable margin. In 2000 the popular vote for the House was 49 percent Republican to 48 percent Democratic, a repeat of two years earlier. Two years later, Republicans picked up some support—51 percent to the Democrats' 46 percent, still a hardly overwhelming margin.[5] So, as long as neither party has a commanding majority, the battle for public opinion before the heat of election cycles will be increasingly hard-fought.

The permanent negative campaign has certainly taken hold on Capitol Hill. Senate Democrats in early 2005 set up a "war room" to ensure their Republican-bashing message got through clearly enough to the public. The Senate Democratic Communications Center aimed to combine television and radio appearances by lawmakers with political websites and blogs, to get their message out and hammer the opposition. "The intent is to leave no attack unchallenged," veteran Democratic communications strategist Jim Manley told the *Los Angeles Times* shortly after the war room's inception. "You need to respond not only to the day's news, but get ahead of the day's news. It's become very similar to what we've seen in presidential campaigns, with the give and take, the cut and thrust."[6]

The Democratic war room was the brainchild of the new minority leader at the time, Senator Harry Reid of Nevada, who had observed the fate of his predecessor, Senator Tom Daschle of South Dakota. As previously noted, throughout the Bush presidency Republicans had made Daschle the target of attacks in the halls of Congress, on conservative talk radio, the Internet, and other forums. The criticism eventually sunk in among voters in South Dakota, to the point that they voted Daschle out of office in 2004.

Not surprisingly, Reid's war room attracted derision from Republicans, who wasted no time in offering their own version of the permanent negative campaign. Shortly after Reid assumed his leadership post, the Republican National Committee e-mailed a 13-page document to a million people, asking, "Who is Harry Reid?" The answer: "Chief Democrat Obstructionist."[7] (Reid, in turn, stepped up the thrust and parry of the permanent negative campaign. He promptly went to the Senate floor to denounce the document as a "hit piece" and called on President George W. Bush to repudiate it.)[8]

The ultimate winners in the permanent negative campaign will be those who take the most effective control of the language and vernacular of politics. How an opponent is described or an issue framed goes a long way toward influencing voter perceptions. In 1990, GOP strategists in Washington urged state legislative Republican candidates to step up rhetorical bombasts against Democratic opponents. GOPAC, a committee for the training of Republican candidates, offered a list of terms that included *sick, pathetic, liberal, incompetent, tax-spending,* and *traitor.* Other derogatory words in the glossary included *decay, unionized bureaucracy, greed, radical, permissive,* and *bizarre.* To describe themselves, the candidates were told to use *humane, visionary, confident, candid, hardworking,* and *reformer.*

GOPAC was run by Newt Gingrich, the Georgia congressman and minority whip. The directive on terminology, "Language: A Key Mechanism of Control," reflected the bombastic style he had brought to the Democratic-controlled House since his first election in 1978. Though GOPAC officials and House Republicans at the time backed off some of the harsher terms, the document illustrated the importance of using language carefully in the art of negative campaigning. "The words and phrases are powerful," the memo noted. "Read them. Memorize as many as possible. And remember that like any tool, these words will not help if they are not used."[9]

Republicans have often held the upper hand in the rhetorical/framing wars since capturing control of Congress in 1994. They have integrated into the national political vocabulary phrases such as "the death tax" (estate tax), "energy exploration" (oil drilling in the Arctic National Wildlife Preserve), "opportunity scholarships" (school vouchers), and "personalizing" Social Security (private accounts).

And then there's the evolution of the word *liberal,* which Democrats used to wear with pride. To old-school Democrats, a liberal was one who accepted the idea of progressive change and looked forward in a rapidly evolving world. In his 1959 inaugural address, California Governor Pat Brown used the word liberal or liberalism seven times in the first eight paragraphs. The catchphrase of his Democratic administration became "responsible liberalism."[10]

Over time the word turned into a pejorative, a synonym in some quarters for a Communist sympathizer who was soft on crime and favored redistributing income. Republican pollster Arthur J. Finkelstein specialized in labeling his clients' opponents liberals. In 1988, his client Connie Mack of Florida beat Democrat Buddy MacKay with an ad that shouted, "Hey, Buddy, you're liberal!" In 1992, another Finkelstein client, Senator Alfonse D'Amato of New York, won reelection with spots calling the Democratic state attorney general, Robert Abrams, "hopelessly liberal" and "too liberal for New York." Then in the 1994 Republican landslide year, a D'Amato protégé, little-known state senator George E. Pataki, ousted Democratic New York Governor Mario Cuomo by tagging him "too liberal, too long."[11] By that time, Democrats had stopped calling themselves liberal, preferring instead the term "progressive."

Still, the effectiveness of using "liberal" as a pejorative has begun to weaken. When the late Senator Paul Wellstone of Minnesota, perhaps the chamber's most left-wing member, ran for reelection in 1996, his Republican opponent taunted him as "unbelievably liberal," "ultra-liberal," and "embarrassingly liberal." The verbal onslaught made little difference in a state traditionally dominated by labor. Wellstone won reelection handily. And he was the rare member of the Democratic Party who embraced the term with gusto, later writing *The Conscience of a Liberal* (a play on the title of Republican stalwart Barry Goldwater's ideological manifesto, *The Conscience of a Conservative*).

Democrats, too, have used language effectively as a means of negative campaigning. For years they have labeled Republicans as "mean-spirited" and "extremist" for their efforts to curtail federal spending, balance the budget, and return tax dollars to citizens. The Democrats started using this approach with fervor against the Gingrich-led Republican majority Congress, first elected in the 1994 political tidal wave. The demonizing had begun to pick up steam back in 1980, when many Democrats seemed to relish the Republicans' nomination for president of Ronald Reagan, Senator Goldwater's old stalwart supporter. Incumbent President Jimmy Carter and speakers at the party's convention in New York City tried to make an issue of Reagan's perceived "extreme" positions on military power and social issues, but national attitudes on such matters were already tacking rightward. The former California governor's positions were obviously not seen as extreme by a majority of voters, but rather as bold digressions from the norms of the unpopular Carter years, and Reagan won a landslide. The "extreme" label largely lacked salience for Democratic candidates in the following years, a period, from the early 1980s through mid-1990s when Republicans got the most mileage from labeling their opponents "liberal."

Democrats got the most traction from the "extreme" label in 1996, when President Bill Clinton cruised to reelection over former Senator Bob Dole of Kansas, one of the leaders of the increasingly unpopular Republican majority in Congress. The president's mantra became variations of "Dole-Gingrich is extreme, and I'm trying to protect you." That line of attack worked in many close races that year. Iowa Democratic Senator Tom Harkin used it to keep his seat away from Republican Congressman Jim Ross Lightfoot by 52 percent to 47 percent. In a debate, Harkin blamed ugly Washington politics on Republicans like Lightfoot, saying, "We need to get rid of the extremists and stop the gridlock."[12] In an open U.S. Senate seat from New Jersey that same year, Democratic Congressman Robert Torricelli trounced moderate Republican colleague Dick Zimmer 53 percent to 43 percent by tying him to an "extreme" GOP congressional majority.[13]

Meanwhile, during the Clinton years, Democrats began using a series of optimistic terms to describe their agenda. Rarely did a Democrat say, "We need to increase spending on federal domestic programs." Rather, it was "critical investments in education and training." The language flip put the burden of proof on anyone who would balk at "investing" in workers and children.[14] Democrats again took up this effort at framing political issues after massive defeats in the 2004 elections. George Lakoff, a linguistics professor at the University of California at Berkeley became a popular speaker to Democratic members of Congress and activists, for his advice that liberals have too often accepted conservative terminology in political discourse, rather than setting the verbal agenda themselves.

NEGATIVE CAMPAIGNING: KEEP IT COMING

The issues and themes of negative campaigning will vary by decade and era, but the use of those tactics by ambitious politicians is not going away. Nor should it. Voters should be given as many facts about potential officeholders as possible, so they can make up their own minds about what is and is not important and relevant. Positive ads can be more misleading because candidates omit key pieces of information about themselves. What a candidate chooses *not* to discuss is usually as important as what he or she prefers to emphasize. If a candidate has a deep character flaw, voters should know that before casting their votes.

Further, despite claims that negative campaigning turns voters off, it's the most partisan races that often bring more people to the polls. The 2004 presidential campaign, one of the most heated in recent memory, produced a voter turnout of roughly 60 percent, the highest in 36 years.[15] Senator John Kerry's vote total was up 16 percent from Vice President Al Gore's; President George W. Bush's vote total was up 23 percent from what it had been four years before. That fits a historical pattern, as turnout rose during the years following the Civil War, when campaigns were very biting; Republicans were accused of "waving the bloody shirt" and Democrats labeled "disloyal." "Enthusiasm in politics usually contains a large element of hatred," noted political commentator Michael Barone, coauthor of the biannual *The Almanac of American Politics.*[16]

Finally, the way candidates respond to negative campaign tactics can be indicative of how they would perform in office. In a democratic society, public officials must be willing to accept a tremendous amount of criticism about their public actions and personal lives—much of it unfair. If they wilt under attacks or fail to respond to negative charges, it may be a sign they would not perform particularly well in the rough and tumble of elected office. "Part of what people look for is how he answers it. Does he stand up to it? Does he hide from it?" said Carter Wrenn, the veteran North Carolina Republican political consultant and former captain of Senator Jesse Helms's old political machine, the Congressional Club.[17]

Ultimately, much of the responsibility for the tone of American political campaigns rests with voters themselves. In the Internet age, with news sources legion, voters have no excuse for not finding sufficient information to make decisions on whether to support or oppose political candidates. Yes, votes in a legislative body can be twisted to make it seem something they are not. But there's plenty of information available to overcome such distortions, if voters only make minimal efforts to educate themselves.

As seen throughout this book, whether or not voters reward negative campaigning depends on the circumstances of each individual race. The modern history and evolution of negative campaigning provide another lesson: When candidates present clear, stark, and open differences between themselves and opponents, it is the voters who ultimately benefit.

NOTES

1. Steve Friess, "With Banner Ads, Candidates Tailor Their Messages: Online Marketing Opens New Arena for Reaching Voters," *The Boston Globe*, July 27, 2004.

2. Interview with author, Washington, D.C., Feb. 18, 2005.

3. Howard Kurtz, "Some Kerry Spots Never Make the Air," *The Washington Post*, Oct. 20, 2004.

4. William Schneider, "The Permanent Negative Campaign," *National Journal*, March 5, 2005.

5. Michael Barone, "American Politics in the Networking Era," *National Journal*, Feb. 25, 2005.

6. Mark Z. Barabak, "No Rest for the Elected: They and Any Serious Rivals Have to Stay in Campaign Mode Every Year, Every Day. Money and the Media Keep Them Running Full Time," *The Los Angeles Times*, April 4, 2005.

7. Schneider, *National Journal*, March 5, 2005.

8. Sheryl Gay Stolberg, "Called an Obstructionist, a Senator Is Fighting Back," *The New York Times*, Feb. 9, 2005.

9. Michael Oreskes, "For G.O.P. Arsenal, 133 Words to Fire," *The New York Times*, Sept. 9, 1990.

10. Ethan Rarick, *California Rising: The Life and Times of Pat Brown* (Berkeley: University of California Press, 2005), 115.

11. Howard Kurtz, "GOP Consultant's Strategy: Label Opponents Liberally; D'Amato Ally Setting Theme in Senate Races," *The Washington Post*, Oct. 22, 1996.

12. Jason Gertzen, "Many Issues Split Harkin and Lightfoot U.S. Senate Hopefuls Meet In TV Debate," *Omaha World-Herald*, Oct. 18, 1996.

13. Alan Finder, "Strategy of Torricelli Painted Foe as Extreme," *The New York Times*, Nov. 6, 1996. (Torricelli served only one term in the Senate, after fourteen years in the House. He abruptly ended his reelection bid in September 2002, in the midst of

an increasingly competitive race against Republican Doug Forrester. Torricelli decided not to run for reelection after being implicated in a bribery scandal with a businessman connected to China named David Chang.)

14. John J. Pitney, "Tongue of Newt: The Political Power of Language—Republican Leader Newt Gingrich," *Reason*, February 1999.

15. Barabak, *The Los Angeles Times*, April 4, 2005.

16. Michael Barone, Real Clear Politics (www.realclearpolitics.com), April 18, 2005.

17. Interview with author, Raleigh, N.C., Feb. 22, 2005.

Selected Bibliography

Ambrose, Stephen E. *Nixon: The Education of a Politician* (New York: Simon & Schuster, 1987).

Ansolabehere, Stephen, and Shanto Iyengar. *Going Negative: How Political Advertisements Shrink and Polarize the Electorate* (New York: The Free Press, 1995).

Barone, Michael, and Richard E. Cohen. *The Almanac of American Politics 2002* (Washington, D.C.: National Journal Group, Inc., 2001).

———. *The Almanac of American Politics 2004* (Washington, D.C.: National Journal Group, Inc., 2003).

Bell, Jonathan. *The Liberal State on Trial: The Cold War and American Politics in the Truman Years* (New York: Columbia University Press, 2004).

Black, Earl, and Merle Black. *The Rise of Southern Republicans* (Cambridge, Mass.: The Belknap Press of Harvard University, 2002).

Boller, Paul F. Jr. *Presidential Campaigns: From George Washington to George W. Bush* (New York: Oxford University Press, 2004).

Burton, Michael John, and Daniel M. Shea. *Campaign Mode: Strategic Vision in Congressional Elections* (Lanham, Md.: Rowman & Little Publishers, Inc., 2003).

Cannon, Lou. *Ronnie and Jesse: A Political Odyssey* (Garden City, N.Y.: Doubleday & Company, Inc., 1969).

———. *Governor Reagan: His Rise to Power* (New York: PublicAffairs, 2003)

Caro, Robert A. *The Path to Power: The Years of Lyndon Johnson* (New York: Vintage, 1982).

———. *Means of Ascent: The Years of Lyndon Johnson* (New York: Vintage, 1990).

———. *Master of the Senate: The Years of Lyndon Johnson* (New York: Alfred A. Knopf, 2002).

Cohen, Celia. *Only in Delaware: Politics and Politicians in the First State* (Newark, Delaware: Grapevine Publishing LLC, 2002).

Dallek, Matthew. *The Right Moment: Ronald Reagan's First Victory and the Decisive Turning Point in American Politics* (New York: Free Press, 2000).

Dallek, Robert. *Lyndon B. Johnson, Portrait of a President* (New York: Oxford University Press, 2004).

Dubose, Lou, Jan Reid, and Carl Cannon. *Boy Genius: Karl Rove, the Brains behind the Remarkable Political Triumph of George W. Bush* (New York: PublicAffairs, 2003).

Duncan, Philip D., and Christine C. Lawrence. *Politics in America 1996: The 104th Congress* (Washington, D.C.: Congressional Quarterly, Inc., 1995).

Felknor, Bruce L. *Dirty Politics* (Lincoln, Neb.: iUniverse.com, Inc. [originally published by Norton], 1966, 2000).

Freeman, Joanne B. *Affairs of Honor: National Politics in the New Republic* (New Haven, Conn.: Yale University Press, 2001).

Furgurson, Ernst B. *Hard Right: The Rise of Jesse Helms* (New York: W.W. Norton & Company, 1986).

Garfield, Bob. *And Now, A Few Words From Me: Advertising's Leading Critic Lays Down the Law, Once and For All* (New York: McGraw-Hill, 2003).

Garrett, Major. *The Enduring Revolution: How the Contract with America Continues to Shape the Nation* (New York: Crown Forum, 2005).

Gellman, Irwin F. *The Contender: Richard Nixon The Congress Years, 1946–1952* (New York: The Free Press, 1999).

Germond, Jack W. *Fat Man in a Middle Seat: Forty Years of Covering Politics* (New York: Random House, 1999).

Germond, Jack, and Jules Witcover. *Whose Broad Stripes and Bright Stars? The Trivial Pursuit of the Presidency 1988* (New York: Warner Books, 1989).

Goldberg, Robert Alan. *Barry Goldwater* (New Haven, Conn.: Yale University Press, 1995).

Gould, Lewis L. *Grand Old Party: A History of the Republicans* (New York: Random House, 2003).

Hall Jamieson, Kathleen. *Packaging the Presidency: A History and Criticism of Presidential Campaign Advertising* (New York: Oxford University Press, 1984).

———. *Dirty Politics: Deception, Distraction and Democracy* (New York: Oxford University Press, 1992)

Harris, John F. *The Survivor: Bill Clinton in the White House* (New York: Random House, 2005).

Helms, Senator Jesse. *Here's Where I Stand: A Memoir* (New York: Random House, 2005).

Hollihan, Thomas A. *Uncivil Wars: Political Campaigns in a Media Age* (Boston: Bedford, 2001).

Kamber, Victor. *Poison Politics: Are Negative Campaigns Destroying Democracy?* (New York: Insight Books, 1997).

Kazin, Michael. *The Populist Persuasion: An American History* (Ithaca, N.Y.: Cornell University Press, 1995).

Kelley, Stanley Jr. *Professional Public Relations and Political Power* (Baltimore: Johns Hopkins University Press, 1956).

Kern, Montague. *30-Second Politics: Political Advertising in the Eighties* (New York: Praeger, 1989).

Lau, Richard R., and Gerald M. Pomper. *Negative Campaigning: An Analysis of U.S. Senate Elections* (Lanham, Md.: Rowman & Littlefield, 2004).

Longley, Kyle. *Senator Albert Gore, Sr.: Tennessee Maverick* (Baton Rouge, La.: Louisiana State University Press, 2004).

Lubell, Samuel. *The Future of American Politics* (Garden City, N.Y.: Doubleday & Co., Inc., 1956).

Lubenow, Gerald C., ed. *California Votes: The 2002 Governor's Race and the Recall That Made History* (Berkeley, Calif.: Berkeley Public Policy Press, 2003).

Magleby, David B., J. Quin Monson, and Kelly D. Patterson, eds. *Dancing without Partners: How Candidates, Parties and Interest Groups Interact in the New Campaign Finance Environment* (Provo, Utah: Center for the Study of Elections and Democracy, Brigham Young University, 2005).

Maisel, L. Sandy. *Parties and Elections in America: The Electoral Process,* fourth edition (Lanham, Md.: Rowman & Littlefield Publishers, Inc., 2005).

Maraniss, David, and Ellen Nakashima. *The Prince of Tennessee: The Rise of Al Gore* (New York: Simon & Schuster, 2000).

Mitchell, Greg. *The Campaign of the Century: Upton Sinclair's Race for Governor of California and the Birth of Media Politics* (New York: Random House, 1992).

Moore, James C., and Wayne Slater. *Bush's Brain: How Karl Rove Made George W. Bush Presidential* (New York: John Wiley & Sons, Incorporated, 2004).

Morris, Dick. *Power Plays: Win or Lose—How History's Great Political Leaders Play the Game* (New York: ReganBooks, 2002).

Newman, Bruce I., ed. *Handbook of Political Marketing* (Thousand Oaks, Calif.: Sage Publications, Inc., 1999).

Perlstein, Rick. *Before the Storm: Barry Goldwater and the Unmaking of the American Consensus* (New York: Hill and Wang, 2001).

Polsby, Nelson W., and Aaron Wildavsky. *Presidential Elections: Strategies and Structures of American Politics,* 11th ed. (Lanham, Md.: Rowman & Littlefield Publishers, Inc., 2004).

Price, David E. *The Congressional Experience,* 3rd ed. (Cambridge, Mass.: Westview Press, 2004).

Rarick, Ethan. *California Rising: The Life and Times of Pat Brown* (Berkeley: University of California Press, 2005).

Rollins, Ed, with Tom DeFrank. *Bare Knuckles and Back Rooms: My Life in American Politics* (New York: Broadway Books, 1996).

Sabato, Larry J., ed. *Midterm Madness: The Elections of 2002* (Lanham, Md.: Rowman & Littlefield Publishers, Inc., 2003).

Schiesl, Martin, ed. *Responsible Liberalism: Edmund G. "Pat" Brown and Reform Government in California, 1958–1967* (Los Angeles: Edmund G. "Pat" Brown Institute of Public Affairs, 2003).

Schultz, David A., ed. *Lights, Camera, Campaign!* (New York: Peter Lang, 2004).

Schwartz, Tony. *The Responsive Chord* (Garden City, N.Y.: Anchor Books, 1973).

Shields-West, Eileen. *The World Almanac of Presidential Campaigns* (New York: World Almanac, 1992).

Shirley, Craig. *Reagan's Revolution: The Untold Story of the Campaign That Started It All* (Nashville: Nelson Current, 2005).

Snider, William D. *Helms & Hunt: The North Carolina Senate Race, 1984* (Chapel Hill: The University of North Carolina Press, 1985).

Summers, Mark Wahlgren. *Party Games: Getting, Keeping, and Using Power in Gilded Age Politics* (Chapel Hill: The University of North Carolina Press, 2004).

Taranto, James, and Leonard Leo, eds. *Presidential Leadership: Rating the Best and the Worst in the White House* (New York: Free Press, 2004).

Taylor, Paul. *See How They Run: Electing the President in an Age of Mediaocracy* (New York: Alfred A. Knopf, 1990).

Thomas, Evan, and the Staff of *Newsweek. Election 2004: How Bush Won and What You Can Expect in the Future* (New York: PublicAffairs, 2004).

Thurber, James A., and Candice J. Nelson, eds. *Campaigns and Elections American Style*, 2nd ed. (Boulder, Colo.: Westview Press, 2004).

Turque, Bill. *Inventing Al Gore: A Biography* (New York: Houghton Mifflin Company, 2000).

Viguerie, Richard A., and David Franke. *America's Right Turn: How Conservatives Used New and Alternative Media to Take Power* (Chicago: Bonus Book, 2004).

West, Darrell M. *Air Wars: Television Advertising in Election Campaigns, 1952–1996* (Washington, D.C.: Congressional Quarterly, Inc., 1997).

West, Darrell M., and John Orman. *Celebrity Politics* (Upper Saddle River, N.J.: Prentice Hall, 2003).

White, Theodore H. *The Making of the President 1964* (New York: Atheneum, 1965).

Whitfield, Stephen J. *The Culture of the Cold War*, 2nd ed. (Baltimore: The Johns Hopkins University Press, 1996).

Wicker, Tom. *One of Us: Richard Nixon and the American Dream* (New York: Random House, 1991).

Witcover, Jules. *Party of the People: A History of the Democrats* (New York: Random House, 2003).

York, Byron. *The Vast Left Wing Conspiracy: The Untold Story of How Democratic Operatives, Eccentric Billionaires, Liberal Activists, and Assorted Celebrities Tried to Bring Down a President—and Whey They'll Try Even Harder Next Time* (New York: Crown Forum, 2005).

Zelizer, Julian E., ed. *The American Congress: The Building of Democracy* (New York: Houghton Mifflin Company, 2004).

Index

Costa, Jim: negative ads run against
    backfire, 167–68
Costa, Ted, 225–26
Coulter, Ann, *Treason, Slander,* and *How
    to Talk to a Liberal (If You Must),*
    224–25
"Courage" ad, 2002 George U.S. Senate
    race, 133–39. *See also* Chambliss,
    Saxby and Cleland, Max
Crane, Phil, 213–14
Creel, George, 26
CREEP. *See also* Committee to Reelect
    the President
Crockett, Hudley, 76, 82, 83
Crown Forum, 225
Culver, John, 217
Cuomo, Mario, 237

The Daily Worker, 32
"Daisy Girl" ad, 6, 41, 46–47, 174; legacy
    of in political advertising, 47–48
D'Amato, Alfonse, 237
Daschle, Tom, 129, 137, 218, 222–24, 235
D'Aubuisson, Roberto, 95, 99
Davis, Fred, 161; "King Roy," ad, 2002
    Georgia governor's race, 197–98, 200
Davis, Gray, 21, 225–26; involvement in
    2002 California Republican
    gubernatorial primary, 69, 188–92
Davis, Rick, 114, 116, 121, 206
Dean, Howard, 124, 157, 160, 180–81, 221
Declaration of Independence, as
    negative document against the
    British crown, 19
DeFazio, Peter, 127
DeLay, Tom, 216; Democrats try to link
    Republican opponents to, 120–21,
    125n20

Delaware politics: civility of, 177–80
Democratic Congressional Campaign
    Committee, 13
Democratic Leadership Council, 121
Democratic National Committee, 12,
    113, 144, 152; coordination with
    1996 Clinton reelection campaign,
    115–16; soft money donations to
    banned under BCRA, 154–56
Democratic National Convention: 1984,
    94; 1992, 121
Democratic Senatorial Campaign
    Committee (DSCC): runs
    controversial "hair dresser" ad against
    2002 Montana U.S. Senate candidate,
    194–95
Dent, Harry, 80
Department of Veterans Affairs, 131
Dewey, Thomas, 29
Diedrich, Larry, 161
digital video recorders (DVRs), effects
    on negative campaigning, 233
DiPinto, Joseph, 177–78
direct mail as negative campaign tool, 4,
    26–27, 106, 213–22
dirty tricks in campaigns, definitions of
    2–3; phone jamming in New
    Hampshire on Election Day 2002,
    12n2
Dixon, Alan, 204
Do Not Call Registry, 233
Dole, Bob, 7, 138, 155, 203, 238;
    approach to 1995–1996 government
    shutdown, 113–14; Electoral College
    margin of loss, 111; history of
    engaging in negative campaigning,
    117–18; presidential campaign adopts
    "Daisy Girl" ad theme, 50;

228; ads run against in 1956 reelection campaign as vice president,
and 1960, 43–44; gubernatorial race
defeat, 1962, 58, 63, 145; interest
and involvement in 1970 U.S. Senate
race in Tennessee, 80–82;
presidential bid, 1968, 145–46;
presidential campaign, 1960, 60;
presidential campaign and victory,
1968, 75, 76, 77; resignation from
presidency, 85; "Southern Strategy,"
1968 presidential bid, 73; U.S.
Senate campaign, 1950, 30, 65, 112
Nofziger, Lyn, 60–61, 64
North America Free Trade Agreement,
121
North Carolina, history of tough
political campaigns, 92–93
North Carolina School of Science and
Mathematics, 95
NYPD Blue, 232

Obama, Barack, 178
O'Connor, Sandra Day, 154
Oklahoma City bombing, 50, 112
O'Malley, Martin, 146–47
O'Neill, John E. *See Unfit for Command:
Swiftboat Veterans Speak Out against
John Kerry*
O'Neill, Tip, 69, 115
"On the Media," 10
Operation Townhouse, 86
Oprah, 232
Osnos, Peter, 224
Oswald, Lee Harvey, 224

Pacific Mutual, 26
Palance, Jack, 64

Palestinian Islamic Jihad, 219
Panama Canal turnover, as campaign
issue, 93, 106, 107
Parker, William 59
Parks, Bernard C., 208–9n19
Parr, George, 40
Pataki, George E., 237
Patriot Act, 128
Pearce, Gary, 100
Pearson, Drew, 61
Pepper, Claude, 31–32
Percy, Charles, 173–75
Perdue, Sonny: and "King Roy" ad, 2002
Georgia Governor's Race, 196–200
Perdue, Tom: "Courage" ad, 2002
Georgia U.S. Senate race, 129,
134–35, 136–37, 138
permanent negative campaign, 234–36.
See also war room
Perry, Rick, 123, 168–69
Pew Charitable Trusts, 12–13n3
Pew Research Center for People and the
Press, 13n3
Phillips, Tim, 199
Pickens, T. Boone, 155
Pika, Joseph A., 179
Pinkerton, Jim, 203
Pinochet, Augusto, 95
Pledge of Allegiance, 201
politics of fear, as emerging tool in post
9/11 negative campaigning arsenal,
129
polling, increasingly sophisticated
methods of, used to guide negative
campaign tactics, 80–81
Pomper, Gerald M. *See Negative
Campaigning: An Analysis of U.S.
Senate Elections*

About the Author

David Mark is editor-in-chief of *Campaigns & Elections* magazine in Washington, D.C. A seasoned political journalist, he is a frequent political analyst on television and radio and in print publications. He has lectured in the United States and overseas about campaigns and elections to diplomatic, business, academic, and journalism groups. Further information is available at www.davidmark.org.